Reflection on Islamic Beliefs and Resurrection

Reflection on Islamic Beliefs and Resurrection

Sharif Ahmed

CYBER TECH PUBLICATIONS
4264/3, Ansari Road, Daryaganj, New Delhi-110002 (India)
Ph.: 011-23244078, 011-43559448 Fax: 011-23280028
E-Mail: cyberpublicationsdelhi@yahoo.com
Website: www.cybertechpublications.com

REFLECTION ON ISLAMIC BELIEFS AND RESURRECTION

Sharif Ahmed

First Edition 2010

Published by : Asian Offset Printers

G.S. Rawat for **Cyber Tech Publications**

4264/3, Ansari Road, Daryaganj, New Delhi-110002 (India)

Ph.: 011-23244078, 011-43559448 Fax: 011-23280028

E-Mail: cyberpublicationsdelhi@yahoo.com

Website: www.cybertechpublications.com

Preface

Verily, all praise is due to Allaah, we praise Him and we seek His Aid and we ask His Forgiveness and we seek refuge with Allaah from the wickedness of ourselves and the evil of our deeds. Whomsoever Allaah guides, there is none can misguide him and whomsoever Allaah sends astray, there is none can guide him. And I testify that none is worthy of worship except Allaah, Alone, without partners and I testify that Muhammad is His slave and His Messenger.

Allah has sent His messenger Muhammad, peace be upon him, with the real guidance and the true religion as a mercy to mankind, as a model for those who do good, and as His argument against mankind. Through Muhammad and what was revealed to him (the Qur'an and the Prophetic sayings), Allah showed mankind all means of reforming itself and straightening its religious and mundane affairs in sound beliefs, right conduct, fine morals, and laudable manners. The Prophet, peace be upon him, "left his followers on a clear straight path, only the doomed will deviate from it"(Ibn Majah and Ahmad). His followers, the Companions, their followers, and those who followed them faithfully are the best of mankind. They established his law, upheld his way, and held fast to it as a belief and practice, a moral and manner. Thus "they are considered the party who are victorious, on the straight path, unharmed by those who are against them till the end of the world" (Bukhari and Muslim).

Thanks to Allah, we are following their footsteps and are being guided by their examples, which are supported by the Qur'an and the prophetic traditions. We are saying this only as an announcement of Allah's blessings and as a clarification of what every Muslim should believe. We pray to Allah that He may keep us and our brothers on the straight path in this life and in the hereafter. May He give us mercy, for He is the Giver.

— *Author*

CONTENTS

1

Introduction

The sources of Islam are two: the Quran and the HadIs (Sayings or Traditions), usually called the Sunnah (customs), both having their center in Muhammad. The Quran contains the Prophets revelations (wahy); the HadIs, all that he did or said, or enjoined, forbade or did not forbid, approved or disapproved. The word HadIs, singular in form, is also used collectively for all the traditions taken together, for the whole sacred tradition.

Muslim theologians make no distinction between the Quran and the HadIs. To them both are works of revelation or inspiration. The quality and degree of the revelation in both works is the same; only the mode of expression is different. To them, the HadIs is the Quran in action, revelation made concrete in the life of the Prophet. In the Quran, Allah speaks through Muhammad; in the Sunnah, He acts through him. Thus Muhammads life is a visible expression of Allahs utterances in the Quran. God provides the divine principle, Muhammad the living pattern. No wonder, then, that Muslim theologians regard the Quran and the HadIs as being supplementary or even interchangeable. To them, the HadIs is wahy ghair matlU (unread revelation, that is, not read from the Heavenly Book like the Quran but inspired all the same); and the Quran is hadIs mutwAtir, that is, the Tradition considered authentic and genuine by all Muslims from the beginning.

Thus the Quran and the HadIs provide equal guidance. Allah with the help of His Prophet has provided for every situation. Whether a believer is going to a mosque or to his bedroom or to the toilet, whether he is making love or war, there is a command and a pattern to follow. And according to the Quran, when Allah and His Apostle have decided a matter, the believer does not have his or her own choice in the matter.

And yet situations do arise when the guidance is lacking. It is said of ImAm ibn Hanbal that he never ate watermelons, even though he knew that the Prophet had done so, because he did not know his manner of eating them. The same story is related even of BAyazid BistAn, a great Sufi, whose mystical teachings went against orthodox Quranic theology.

Though the non-Muslim world is not as familiar with the Sunnah, or HadIs, as with the Quran, the former even more than the latter is the most important single source of Islamic laws, precepts, and practices. Ever since the lifetime of the Prophet, millions of Muslims have tried to imitate him in their dress, diet, hair-style, sartorial fashions, toilet mores, and sexual and marital habits. Whether one visits Arabia or Central Asia, India or Malaysia, one meets certain conformities, such as the veil, polygamy, ablution, and istinjA (abstersion of the private parts). These derive from the Sunnah, reinforced by the Quran. All are accepted not as changing social usages but as divinely ordained forms, as categorical moral imperatives.

The subjects that the HadIs treats are multiple and diverse. It gives the Prophets views of Allah, of the here and the hereafter, of hell and heaven, of the Last Day of Judgment, of ImAn (faith), salAt (prayer), zakAt (poor tax), sawm (fast), and hajj (pilgrimage), popularly known as religious subjects; but it also includes his pronouncements on jihAd (holy war), al-anfAl (war booty), and khums (the holy fifth); as well as on crime and punishment, on food, drink, clothing, and personal decoration, on hunting and sacrifices, on poets and soothsayers, on women and slaves, on gifts, inheritances, and dowries, on toilet, ablution, and bathing; on dreams, christianing, and medicine, on vows and oaths and testaments, on images and pictures, on dogs, lizards, and ants.

The HadIs constitutes a voluminous literature. It gives even insignificant details of the Prophets life. Every word from his lips, every nod or shake of his head, every one of his gestures and mannerisms was important to his followers. These are remembered by them as best as they could and passed on from generation to generation. Naturally those who came into greater contact with the Prophet had the most to tell about him. Aisha, his wife, Abu Bakr and Umar, his aristocratic followers, Anas b. MAlik, his servant for ten years, who died at the ripe age of in A.H., and Abdullah b. AbbAs, his cousin, were fertile sources of many ahAdIs. But another most prolific source was Abu Huraira, who is the authority for, traditions. He was no relation of the Prophet, but he had no particular work to do except that he specialized in collecting traditions from other Companions. Similarly,, traditions derive from the authority of JAbir, who was not even a Quraish but belonged to the Khazraj tribe of Medina, which was allied to Muhammad.

Every hadIs has a text (matn) and a chain of transmission (isnAd). The same text may have several chains, but every text must be traced back to a Companion (as-hAb), a man who came into personal contact with the Prophet. The Companions related their stories to their successors (tAbiUn), who passed them on to the next generation.

At first the traditions were orally transmitted, though some of the earliest narrators must have also kept written notes of some kind. But as the Companions and the Successors and their descendants died, a need was felt to commit them to writing. There were two other reasons. The Quranic injunctions were probably sufficient for the uncomplicated life of the early Arabs, but as the power of the Muslims grew and they became the masters of an extended empire, they had to seek a supplementary source of authority to take into account new situations and new customs. This was found in the Sunnah, in the practice of the Prophet, already very high in the estimation of the early Muslims.

There was an even more pressing reason. Spurious traditions were coming into being, drowning the genuine ones. There were many motives at play behind this development. Some of these new traditions were merely pious frauds, worked up in order to promote what the fabricators thought were elements of a pious life, or what they thought were the right theological views. There were also more personal motives at work. The traditions were no longer mere edifying stories. They were sources of prestige and profit. To have ones ancestors counted among the Emigrants or Helpers, to have them present at the Pledge of al-Aqabah or included among the combatants at the Battles of Badr and Uhud-in short, to have them mentioned in any context of loyalty and usefulness to the Prophet-was a great thing. So Traditionists who could get up right traditions were very much in demand. Traditionists like ShurahbIl b. Sad utilized their power effectively; they favored and blackmailed as it suited them. Spurious traditions also arose in order to promote factional interests. Soon after Muhammads death, there were cutthroat struggles for power between several factions, particularly the Alids, the Ummayads, and later on the Abbasides. In this struggle, great passions were generated, and under their influence new traditions were concocted and old ones usefully edited.

The pious and the hero-worshipping mind also added many miracles around the life of Muhammad, so that the man tended to be lost in the myth.

Under these circumstances, a serious effort was made to collect and sift all the current traditions, rejecting the spurious ones and committing the correct ones to writing. A hundred years after Muhammad, under KhalIfa Umar II, orders were issued for the collection of all extant traditions under the supervision of Bakr ibn Muhammad. But the Muslim world had to wait another hundred years before the work of sifting was undertaken by a galaxy of traditionists like Muhammad IsmAIl al-BukhArI, Muslim ibnul-HajjAj, Abu IsA Muhammad at-TirmizI, Abu DAUd as-Sajistani and others.

BukhArI laid down elaborate canons of authenticity and applied them with a ruthless hand. It is said that he collected, traditions but accepted only, of them as authentic. Abu DAUd entertained only, traditions out of a total of,. It is also said that, names were mentioned in different chains of transmission but that BukhArI accepted only, as genuine. As a result of the labor of these Traditionists, the chaotic mass was cut down and some order and proportion were restored. Over a thousand collections, which were in vogue died away in due course, and only six collections, the SihAh Sitta as they are called, became authentic SahIs, or collections. Of these, the ones by ImAm BukhArI and ImAm Muslim are at the top-the two authentics, they are called. There is still a good deal of the miraculous and the improbable in them, but they contain much that is factual and historical. Within three hundred years of the death of Muhammad, the HadIs acquired substantially the form in which it is known today. To the infidel with his critical faculty still intact, the HadIs is a collection of stories, rather unedifying, about a man, rather all too human. But the Muslim mind has been taught to look at them in a different frame of mind. The believers have handled, narrated, and read them with a feeling of awe and worship. It is said of Abdullah ibn MasUd (died at the age of seventy in A.H.), a Companion and a great Traditionist (authority for traditions), that he trembled as he narrated a hadIs, sweat often breaking out all over his forehead. Muslim believers are expected to read the traditions in the same spirit and with the same mind. The lapse of time helps the process. As the distance grows, the hero looms larger.

We have also chosen the SahIh Muslim as the main text for our present volume. It provides the base, though in our discussion we have often quoted from the Quran. The Quran and the HadIs are interdependent and mutually illuminating. The Quran provides the text, the HadIs the context. In fact, the Quran cannot be understood without the aid of the HadIs, for every Quranic verse has a context, which only the HadIs provides. The HadIs gives flesh and blood to the Quranic revelations, reveals their more earthly motives, and provides them with the necessary locale.

To clarify certain points, we have also quoted here and there from the Prophets traditional biographies, which are no more than ordered traditions arranged chronologically around events in the life of the Prophet. Apart from several maghAzI books (books about the Prophets campaigns) which went before, almost the very first definitive biography was that of Ibn IshAq, who was born in Medina and died in Baghdad. Other biographers of note who succeeded him and who amply made use of his labors were Al-WAqidI, Ibn HishAm, and At-TabarI. An English translation of IshAqs SIrat RasUl Allah by A. Guillaume is available under the title The Life of Muhammad. Until now only partial English translations of some HadIs collections were available. Therefore, we must thank Dr. Abdul HamId SiddIqI for filling up this gap and giving us a full-scale translation of the SahIh Muslim. The translation of an Eastern text by an Eastern mind has one advantage: it retains the flavor of the original. It may not be in the Queens English and may seem rather exotic to those whose mother tongue is English, but it is faithful and reproduces the atmosphere of the original.

Dr. SiddIqI has done more than translate the original work. He has provided copious explanatory notes. In a SahIh containing, ahAdIs, he provides, footnotes. In addition to clarifying obscure points and references, the notes give us an authentic taste of traditional Muslim scholarship. In fact, because the notes are set in a well-established scholarly lore, they could be an important subject of treatment in their own right. They show that the role of scholarship in Islam is secondary-that it is the handmaid of the Quran and the HadIs, unmotivated by any seeking of its own, but capable of cleverness and even brilliance within its self-chosen role of justifying and defending. Here and there, we have also quoted from the notes-about forty-five times-to give the reader a sampling of Islamic scholarship.

Now a word about how the present volume came to be written. When we read Dr. SiddIqIs translation, we felt that it contained important material about Islam which should be more widely known. Islam, having been dormant for several centuries, is again on the march. Even before the Europeans came on the scene, the Muslims had their own variation of the white mans burden of civilizing the world. If anything, their mission was even more pretentious for it was commanded by Allah Himself. Muslims wielded their swords to root out polytheism, dethrone the gods of their neighbors, and install in their place their own godling, Allah. That they received plunder and established an empire in the process is another matter. These were accidental terrestrial rewards for disinterested celestial labors. Thanks to the new oil wealth of the Arabs, the old mission is being revived. A kind of Muslim Cominform is taking shape in Jidda. The oil-rich Arabs are assuming responsibility for Muslims everywhere, looking after their spiritual needs as well as their more temporal interests. Their money is active throughout the Muslim world, in Pakistan and Bangladesh, in Malaysia, Indonesia, and even India, with a large Muslim population.

The Arabs are still militarily weak and dependent on the West, but the full fury of their interference is to be seen in countries of Asia and Africa which are economically poor and ideologically weak. Here they work from the bottom as well as from the top. They buy local politicians. They have bought the conversion of the presidents of Gabon and the Central African Empire. They have adopted the Muslim minorities of Darul Harb, i.e., infidel countries which have not yet been fully subdued by Muslims. They are using these minorities to convert these countries into Darul Islam, or countries of peace, i.e., countries where Islam dominates. Even in the best of circumstances, it is difficult to assimilate Muslim minorities into the national mainstream of a country. Arab support has made the task still more difficult. It was this support which was behind the rebellion of the Moro Muslims in the Philippines. In India, there is a continuing Muslim problem that refuses solution despite the division of the country. Arab interference has complicated matters still further. A new fundamentalism is sweeping over the Muslim world, throwing up leaders like Khomeini and Muammar Qaddafi. Wherever it triumphs, dictatorship comes in its wake. Fundamentalism and authoritarianism are twins.

According to some thinkers, this fundamentalism is nothing but a search by Muslims for self-identity and self-assertion. It is a weapon of self-defense, derived from the available symbols of their culture, against the materialist and bourgeois values of the West. But on calm reflection, it is also something more; it is also their dream of recapturing the grandeur of their old imperial days. Islam is by nature fundamentalist; and this fundamentalism in turn is aggressive in character. Islam claims to have defined human thought and behavior for all time to come; it resists any change, and it feels justified in imposing its beliefs and behavior patterns on others. Whether this fundamentalism is considered resurgence or reversal and the threat of the reappearance of an old imperialism will depend on ones point of view. But anything that throws light on any aspect of the problem will be a great contribution. This we find the HadIs literature most fitted to do. It gives a living picture of Islam at its source and of Islam in the making, providing an intimate view of the elements that constitute orthodox Islam in their pristine purity. Indeed, it is these very elements of Islam that Muslims find most fascinating, and thus, motivated by a compulsive atavism, they repeatedly appeal to them and revert to them. For this purpose, we have chosen as our guide the SahIh Muslim, which has the advantage of being available in an English translation. Since most HadIs collections contain the same core material, this self-limitation is no great disadvantage. On the other hand, it fruitfully defines the field of our study and inquiry. It has one drawback, though, both of commission and omission. While we have in this way touched on many points, we have discussed none in full. And, similarly, since we have followed the lead of the SahIh Muslim, some matters quite important in themselves remain undeveloped and even untouched because they are not treated in the SahIh. This problem was unavoidable, but we have tried to overcome it here and there by going beyond the confines of this particular SahIh. In spite of the limitations of the procedure we have adopted, the SahIh Muslim remains a very comprehensive and informative source on Islamic beliefs and behavior, and we have quoted extensively and faithfully from it. It gives us, traditions divided into, chapters. In many instances the same text is reported in several chapters with only minor variations but with different chains of transmission. Therefore, in many cases, one hadIs stands for a number of ahAdIs, and to quote one hadIs is really to quote a whole chapter.

In this volume, we have quoted about individual hadIs having this representative character. Another of the ahAdIs we have quoted are group ahAdIs or their summaries. Portions that deal with mere rituals and ceremonies and have no particular importance to non-Muslims we omitted altogether, but we readily included anything that had a deeper ring, although such instances are rather rare. For example, in the long Book of Pilgrimage (KitAb al-Hajj), containing traditions, there is not a single one that remotely suggests the idea of the inner pilgrimage about which mystics speak so much. Similarly, in the Book of JihAd and Campaigns, comprising traditions, there is hardly anything that would suggest the sentiment of jihAdl-akbar, the greater warfare directed against ones own lower nature (nafs). Most of the discussion lacks inwardness.

The SahIh Muslim, like other HadIs collections, also gives very intimate glimpses of the life of the Prophet, an impressionistic view that makes him seem more a living, breathing person than the portrayals given in his more formal biographies. Here one comes to know him, not through his pompous deeds and thoughts, but through his more workaday ideas and actions. There is no makeup, no cosmetics, no posturing for posterity. The Prophet is caught as it were in the ordinary acts of his life-sleeping, eating, mating, praying, hating, dispensing justice, planning expeditions and revenge against his enemies. The picture that emerges is hardly flattering, and one is left wondering why in the first instance it was reported at all and whether it was done by his admirers or enemies. One is also left to wonder how the believers, generation after generation, could have found this story so inspiring.

The answer is that the believers are conditioned to look at the whole thing through the eyes of faith. An infidel in his fundamental misguidance may find the Prophet rather sensual and cruel-and certainly many of the things he did do not conform to ordinary ideas of morality-but the believers look at the whole thing differently. To them morality derives from the Prophets actions; the moral is whatever he did. Morality does not determine the Prophets actions, but his actions determine and define morality. Muhammads acts were not ordinary acts; they were Allahs own acts. It was in this way and by this logic that Muhammads opinions became the dogmas of Islam and his personal habits and idiosyncrasies became moral imperatives: Allahs commands for all believers in all ages and climes to follow.

2

Islamic Faith

The very first book of the SahIh Muslim is the Book of Faith (KitAb al-ImAn). It contains traditions (ahAdIs) divided into ninety-two chapters. It discusses questions regarding faith. Someone comes to Muhammad from a great distance, yet without any sign of fatigue, and says: Muhammad, inform me about al-Islam. The Messenger of Allah replies: Al-Islam implies that you testify that there is no god but Allah and that Muhammad is the Messenger of Allah, and you establish prayer, pay ZakAt, observe the fast of RamzAn [Ramadan] and perform pilgrimage. Later on, when the inquirer is gone, Muhammad tells Umar: He was Gabriel. He came to you in order to instruct you in matters of religion. This is the very first hadIs narrated by Umar, the future KhalIfa, through several chains of narrators.

This theme runs through hundreds of ahAdIs. Al-Islam is faith in Allah, faith in Muhammad as His Messenger, faith in His Book, in His angels, in the resurrection, in the hereafter, and in the payment of the poor tax (zakAt) and the observance of fast (RamzAn) and pilgrimage.

ALLAH IS NOT ENOUGH

Belief in Allah alone in not sufficient. It must be accompanied by belief in the apostleship of Muhammad. A delegation of the tribe of RabIa visits Muhammad. He tells the delegates: I direct you to affirm belief in Allah alone, and then asks them: Do you know what belief in Allah really implies Then he himself answers: It implies testimony to the fact that there is no god but Allah, and that Muhammad is the Messenger of Allah. Other things mentioned are prayer, zakAt, RamzAn, and that you pay one-fifth of the booty. We shall hear more about war booty in its proper place.

In the same vein, Muhammad tells MuAz, whom he sends out as governor of Yemen: First call them to testify that there is no god but Allah, that I [Muhammad] am the Messenger of Allah; and if they accept this, then tell them that Allah has made ZakAt obligatory for them.

There is a still clearer statement of Muhammads mission. I have been commanded to fight against people till they testify that there is no god but Allah, that Muhammad is the Messenger of Allah, and they establish prayer, and pay ZakAt and if they do it, their blood and property are guaranteed protection on my behalf.

Muhammad retails the word Allah profusely, but there are times when even Allah occupies a backseat. None of you is a believer till I am dearer to him than his child, his father and the whole mankind, Muhammad tells the believers.

Allah and his Messenger-rather, Muhammad and his God-prayer, zakAt, RamzAn, and pilgrimage are sometimes called the five pillars of Islam, but there are other beliefs and institutions no less important which recur again and again in the HadIs. These are, to name the more important ones, Paradise, Hell, Doomsday, jihAd (holy war against polytheists,) jizyA (the poll tax paid by polytheists), war booty (ghanImah), and khums (the holy one-fifth). These are the staples of the religion preached by Muhammad. Allah becomes concrete in His threats and punishments of Hell, and in His promises and rewards of Paradise. Similarly, in the history of Islam, jihAd and war booty have played a more important role than even pilgrimage or zakAt. All of these concepts will come up for review in this study in their proper places.

GOOD AND EVIL DEEDS

What are good deeds and what are bad deeds These questions have been the concern of many religions, many philosophies, and many teachers. Islam too has provided its characteristic answers. It tells us that good deeds are not a matter of indifference but must be coupled with the choice of the right religion. Abdul HamId SiddIqI, the translator of the SahIh Muslim, gives the Islamic view in the following words: The good deeds performed in the state of ignorance (outside the fold of Islam) are indicative of the fact that a man is inclined towards piety. But to be truly pious and virtuous it is quite essential to have the correct understanding of the Will of God. This can be confidently known only through the Prophets and is embodied in Islam. Thus without having faith in Islam we cannot serve our Master and Lord according to His Will.... The acts of virtue may be good in their own way but it is by coming within the fold of Islam that these become significant and meaningful in the eyes of the Lord.

In the eyes of Muhammad, a wrong theology is worse than wicked deeds. When asked, Which sin is the gravest in the eyes of Allah he replies: That you associate a partner with Allah. To kill your child and to commit adultery with the wife of your neighbor are second and third in gravity according to Muhammad.

In fact, only a wrong theology can keep a Muslim out of Paradise. But no morally wicked act-not even adultery and theft-can prevent his entry. Muhammad tells us: Gabriel came to me and gave me tidings: Verily he who died amongst your Ummah [sect, nation, group] without associating anything with Allah would enter paradise. In clarification, Abu Zarr, the narrator of the hadIs, asks Muhammad whether this is true even if the man committed adultery and theft. Muhammad replies: Yes, even if he committed adultery and theft. The translator clarifies the point further: He says that adultery and theft are both serious offences in Islam... but these do not doom the offender to the eternal hell, but polytheism or associating any god with the Lord is an unpardonable crime and the man who commits it is doomed to Hell.

If polytheism is the worst of crimes, monotheism, by the same token, is the best of virtues. Muhammad is asked about the best of deeds. He replies: Belief in Allah. What next he is asked. JihAd, he replies. In Muslim theology the formula belief in Allah of course means belief in Allah and His Messenger. Once one accepts the theological belief in Allah and His Messenger, ones past crimes are obliterated, and future ones hold no great terror. Muhammad gave this asSurance to some polytheists who had committed a large number of murders and had excessively indulged in fornication, but who were ready to join him. To another person who felt a sense of guilt about his past, Muhammad said: Are you not aware of the fact that Islam wipes out all the previous misdeeds.

MORAL VALUES

Muhammads religion is predominantly theological, but moral values are not altogether neglected. The pre-Muslim Arabs believed in many moral values common to all mankind. Muhammad retained these values but gave them a sectarian twist. A Muslim owes everything to the ummah, very little to others. He has no obligations, moral or spiritual, toward non-Muslims as part of the human race, except to convert them by sword, spoils, and jizyA. For example, sincerity is a universal human value, and we should exercise it in our relations with one another irrespective of creed and nationality. But in Islam, it is limited to Muslims. Muhammad at one place defines al-din (the religion, i.e., Islam) as sincerity and well-wishing, which should be a good definition for any religion. But on being asked, Sincerity and well-wishing for whom he replies: For Allah, His Book, His Messenger and for the leaders and general Muslims. JarIr b. Abdullah reports that he pledged allegiance to the Apostle of Allah on sincerity and well-wishing for every Muslim.

Again, other moral values are given the same twist, and the universal is turned into the sectarian. Muhammad tells his followers: Abusing a Muslim is an outrage and fighting against him is unbelief.

THEOLOGY DISTORTS MORALS

No wonder that such a sectarian and preponderantly theological approach should now and then teach us topsy-turvy morals. Thanks to this approach, despoiling a whole people is meritorious if they are polytheists, but stealing booty once it is in the possession of Muslims is a mortal sin. A slave of Muhammad died in a holy war, thus automatically earning a place in Paradise as a martyr.

But Muhammad saw him in the Fire for the garment or cloak that he had stolen from the booty. On hearing this, some people were greatly perturbed. One of them who had presumably committed a similar act of pilfering, came to Muhammad with a lace or two laces and said: Messenger of Allah, I found them on the day of Khaibar [name of a battle]. The Holy Prophet remarked: This is a lace of fire or two laces of fire. This means, as another text puts it, that like the two pieces of lace the man had stolen, there will be two columns of fire like unto these waiting for him in the hereafter.

To rob a whole people is piety, but to remove a paltry something from a looted treasure is moral depravity of a magnitude that deserves eternal fire. Men driven by ordinary temptations indulge only in petty crimes and small lapses, but committing real enormities needs the aid of an ideology, a revelation, a God-ordained mission.

THE PRE-MUSLIM ARABS

Muslim theologians and writers are in the habit of painting a very dark picture of pre-Islamic Arabia. They describe it as morally depraved and utterly lacking in any sense of chivalry and generosity, referring to this period of history as the state of ignorance or barbarism (jahilIyya). Everything good began with Muhammad. But there are many ahAdIs which prove the contrary. We are told that one HakIm b. HIzam did many deeds of religious purification... in the state of ignorance. Another hadIs tells us that he freed one hundred slaves and donated one hundred camels in this state.

Ordinarily such good acts do not avail a polytheist; but if he embraces Islam, it is a different story, and the whole complexion of his acts is changed. They are no longer wasted; they become fruitful and are credited to his account. Muhammad assures HakIm: you have accepted Islam with all the previous virtues that you had practised.

EVIL THOUGHTS AND EVIL DEEDS

A Muslim is Allahs prodigal son as well as His spoiled child. His past is forgotten unless it is good, his future is assured, and many things are permissible for him that are not permissible for a polytheist or even for a Jew or a Christian, the Peoples of the Book. Jesus spoke of lusting with the eyes regarding it as bad as lust in its more visible form. But Muhammad gave greater latitude to his followers: Verily Allah forgave my people the evil promptings which arise within their hearts as long as they did not speak about them or did not act upon them. This idea is expressed with less partiality and in more universal terms in the Indian spiritual tradition. God knows that man is weak and forgives his lapses and failure but supports his strength and multiplies his good. The less theistic but not less exalted yogic systems would put this idea somewhat differently and in more psychological terms-we should not harp too obsessively on our lapses, but should dwell more lovingly on the Divine within us.

MUHAMMAD HAS THE LARGEST FOLLOWING ON THE DAY OF JUDGMENT

Muhammad tells us that he will have the greatest following on the Day of Resurrection. And understandably so, for the hellfire is on his side. The hellfire will be busy consuming the opponents of Muhammad, and there will be no one left for Paradise to receive except the Muslims.

Muhammad tells us: He who amongst the community of Jews and Christians hears about me, but does not affirm his belief in that with which I have been sent and dies in this state of disbelief, he shall be but one of the denizens of Hell-Fire. The Jews and Christians will suffer in hell not only for their own unbelief in Muhammad, they will also act as proxies for any Muslims who happen to be sent there. There would come people amongst the Muslim on the Day of Resurrection with as heavy sins as a mountain, and Allah would forgive them and he would place in their stead the Jews and the Christians, Muhammad tells us. This would also, incidentally, solve the problem of space in heaven: Space in paradise would be provided by Christians and Jews being thrown into Hell-Fire, the translator tells us.

Another important segment of the infernal population is made up of women. Muhammad says, O womenfolk... I saw you in bulk amongst the dwellers of Hell. When a woman asks him why it should be so, Muhammad tells her: You curse too much and are ungrateful to your spouses. I have seen none [like them] lacking in common sense and failing in religion but robbing the wisdom of the wise. The proof of the lack of common sense in them is the fact that in Allahs law promulgated by Muhammad himself, the evidence of two women is equal to one man; and the proof of their failing in religion, as he tells them, is that you spend some nights and days in which you do not offer prayer and in the month of RamzAn you do not observe fast. Women sometimes abstained from voluntary fasts because the Prophet had commanded that it was more meritorious for them to do their duty by their husbands than to fast. Aisha, the Prophets wife, did not observe some fasts due to the regards for the Apostle of Allah. But, it seems, the very merit of women turns into its opposite: predestined damnation.

THE DAY OF JUDGMENT

The Day of Judgment (qiyAmat), the Last Day (yaumul-Akhir), is an indispensable prop of Muslim theology. In the Quran, the word qiyAmat appears seventy times and in addition has seventy-five synonyms, as shown by Mirza Hairat in his Mukaddma TafsIrul Furqan. Along with its attendant concepts, Paradise and Hell, it pops up from practically every page of the HadIs too. The dreaded day (yaum), colorfully described as the day of reckoning (hisAb), or of separation (fasl), or of standing up (qiyAmah), is mentioned over three hundred times in the Quran.

The arrival of the Last Day will be announced by many signs. When you see a slave woman giving birth to her master-that is one sign; when you see barefooted, naked, deaf and dumb as the rulers of the earth-that is one of the signs of Doom. And when you see the shepherds of the black camels exult in buildings-that is one of the signs of Doom. In short, when the poor and the deprived inherit the earth, that is the end of it according to Muhammad.

There is a vivid account of the Day of Resurrection in eighty-two ahAdIs at the end of the Book of Faith. Muhammad tells us that on this day, Allah will gather people, a bridge would be set over the hell, and I [Muhammad] and my Ummah would be the first to pass over it.

Unbelievers, of course, will be thoroughly miserable on this day but even the Jews and the Christians-the Peoples of the Book-will fare no better. For example, Christians will be summoned and asked, What did you worship When they reply, Jesus, the son of Allah, Allah will tell them, You tell a lie; Allah did not take for Himself either a spouse or a son. Then they will be asked what they want. They will say: Thirsty we are, O our Lord! Quench our thirst. They will be given a certain direction, and Allah will ask: Why dont you go there to drink water When they go there, they will find that they have been misguided; the water is no more than a mirage, and it is really hell. Then they will fall into the Fire and perish.

On this day, no other prophet or savior will avail except Muhammad. People will come to Adam and say: Intercede for your progeny. He will reply: I am not fit to do this, but go to IbrAhIm, for he is the friend of Allah. They will go to IbrAhIm, but he will reply: I am not fit to do this, but go to Moses, for he is Allahs Interlocutor. They will go to Moses, but he will reply: I am not fit to do this, but you go to Jesus, for he is the Spirit of Allah and His Word. They will go to Jesus, and he will reply: I am not fit to do this; you better go to Muhammad. Then they will come to Muhammad, and he will say: I am in a position to do that. He will appeal to Allah, and his intercession will be granted.

In many ahAdIs, Muhammad tells us that among the apostles he has a special intercessory power, for no Apostle amongst the Apostles has been testified as I have been testified. If this is true, it gives substance to his claim that among the apostles he would have the largest following on the Day of Resurrection. Thanks to his special role, seventy thousand persons of [my] Ummah would enter Paradise without rendering an account, and Muslims would constitute half the inhabitants of Paradise. Considering that unbelievers, infidels, and polytheists are strictly kept out, and that the entry of Jews and Christians also is prohibited, one wonders who will be the other half of the population of Paradise.

How did Muhammad acquire this special intercessory power Muhammad himself answers this question: There is for every Apostle a prayer which is granted, but every prophet showed haste in his prayer. I have, however, reserved my prayer for the intercession of my Ummah on the Day of Resurrection. The translator makes this statement clearer for us. He says: The Apostles are dear to Allah and their prayers are often granted. But with every Apostle there is one request which may be called decisive with regard to his Ummah, and with it is decided their fate; for example, Noah in a state of distress uttered: My Lord! leave not any one of the disbelievers in the land (al-Quran.). Muhammad reserved his prayer for the Day of Resurrection and he would use it for the salvation of the believers.

We have no means of knowing about the curse of Noah, but this kind of cursing is quite in Muhammads line. For example, look at his curse against several tribes: O Allah! trample severely Muzar and cause them a famine... O Allah! curse LihyAn, Ril ZakwAn, Usayya, for they disobeyed Allah and His Messenger.

In any case, when the disbelievers are being hurled into the Fire, Muhammad will not intercede even when he knows that no other intercession would avail: Thou shalt not damn thy enemies, but needst not go out of your way to save them.

THE PROPHETS FATHER AND UNCLES

We must admit, however, that Muhammad was consistent. He reserved his power for saving his ummah, those who believed in Allah to the exclusion of AllAt and UzzA, and in his own apostleship. He did not use it to save even his dearest and nearest ones like his father and uncle. Regarding his father, he told a questioner: Verily, my father and your father are in the Fire. But he was somewhat more kind to his uncle, Abu

TAlib, who brought him up and protected him but who did not accept his religion. About him, Muhammad tells us: I found him in the lowest part of the Fire and I brought him to the shallow part. But even this shallowest part must have been roasting the poor uncle. Muhammad assures us that among the inhabitants of the Fire Abu TAlib would have the least suffering, and he would be wearing two shoes of Fire which would boil his brain. Would you call that much of a relief.

Though Muhammad took pride in establishing ties of relationship, he himself repudiated all ties with the generations of his forefathers and their posterity. Behold! the posterity of my fathers... are not my friends, declares Muhammad. On the Day of Resurrection, their good works will not avail them. Aisha, the Prophets young wife, reports: I said: Messenger of Allah, the son of JudAn [a relation of hers and one of the leaders of the Quraish] established ties of relationship, fed the poor. Would that be of any avail to him He said: it would be of no avail to him.

Gods mind is made up with regard to the polytheists; therefore, a true believer should not even seek blessing on their behalf. As the Quran says: It is not meet for the Prophet and for those who believe, that they should beg pardon for the polytheists, even though they were their kith and kin, after it had been known to them that they were the denizens of Hell.

MUHAMMADS NIGHT JOURNEY TO HEAVEN

Various other matters, such as Muhammads night journey to Jerusalem, and the coming of DajjAl and Jesus before the Day of Resurrection, are also discussed in the Book of Faith. These are quite important in Islamic lore.

One night, riding on al-BarAq, an animal white and long, larger than a donkey but smaller than a mule, Muhammad was taken to the Temple in Jerusalem and from there to the different regions, or circles (as Dante called them), of heaven, on the way meeting different apostles. Adam he met in the first heaven, Jesus in the second, Moses in the sixth, and Abraham in the seventh. Then he met Allah, who enjoined on the Muslims fifty prayers a day. But on the advice of Moses, Muhammad made a representation to Allah and the number was reduced to five. Five and at the same time fifty-one prayer will now count for ten-for what has been said will not be changed. So nothing was really lost in efficacy, and five will do the work of fifty.

The more mystic-minded explain this journey spiritually, but Muhammads Companions and later on most Muslim scholars believe that the journey or ascension (mirAj) was physical. Many in his day scoffed at Muhammad and called his journey a dream. But our translator argues that precisely because it was not believed, it was not a dream! For had it been only a dream, there would have been no occasion for such a reaction about it. Visions like this can flit across the imagination of any man at any time.

JESUS

Muhammad had a belief of a sort in Jesus. In fact, this belief, along with his belief in the apostleship of Moses and Abraham, is often cited as a proof of Muhammads liberal and catholic outlook. But if we look at the matter closely, we find it was more a motivated belief, meant partly to prove his own apostolic pedigree, and partly to win converts from among the Jews and the Christians. In any case, his opinion of Jesus does not amount to much. He turned Jesus into a mujAhid (crusader) of his entourage. When Jesus returns in the Second Coming, no more than a pale copy of Muhammad, he will be waging war against the Christians as well as others: The son of Mary will soon descend among you as a just judge. He will break crosses, kill swine, and abolish Jizya, Muhammad proclaims. How The translator explains: Cross is a symbol of Christianity. Jesus will break this symbol after the advent of Muhammad. Islam is the dIn (religion) of Allah and no other religion is acceptable to him. Similarly, the flesh of the swine is a favorite dish of the Christians. Jesus will sweep out of existence this dirty and loathsome animal. The whole of the human race would accept Islam and there would be no zimmIs left, and thus Jizya would be automatically abolished. Jesus is regarded as a just Judge, but this only means that he will judge according to the sharIah of Muhammad. For, as the translator explains, the SharIah of all the earlier prophets stands abrogated with the advent of Muhammads Apostleship. Jesus will, therefore, judge according to the law of Islam.

PURIFICATION

The next book is the Book of Purification. It deals with such matters as ablution, defecation, and abstersion. It relates not to inner purity but to certain acts of cleanliness, physical and ritualistic, that must be performed before reciting the statutory daily prayers. The main topics discussed in Muslim fiqh (canon law) under this heading are: wuzU, minor ablution of the limbs of the body, prescribed before each of the five daily prayers and omitted only if the worshipper is sure that he has not been polluted in any way since the last ablution; ghusl, the major, total ablution of the whole body after the following acts which make a person junub, or impure: coitus (jimA), nocturnal pollution (ihtilAm), menses (hayz), and childbirth (nifAs); tayammum, the minor purification with dust in the place of water; fitra, literally nature, but interpreted as customs of the previous prophets, including acts like the use of the toothpick (miswAk), cleansing the nose and mouth with water (istinshAq), and abstersion (istinjA) with water or dry earth or a piece of stone after evacuation and urination; tathIr, the purification of objects which have become ritualistically unclean.

Some broad injunctions on the subject of purification are given in the Quran (e.g., verses), but they acquire fullness from the practice of the Prophet.

ABLUTION (WUZU)

Muhammad emphasizes the need for bodily cleanliness. He tells his followers that cleanliness is half of faith and that their prayer will not be accepted in a state of impurity till they perform ablution. But impurity here has a strictly ritualistic meaning.

Muhammad was a Unitarian in his theology but a Trinitarian in his ablution. He performed his ablution like this: He washed his hands thrice. He then rinsed his mouth and cleaned his nose three times. He then washed his face three times, then washed his right arm up to the elbow three times, then washed his left arm like that, then wiped his head, then washed his right foot up to the ankle three times, then washed his left foot, and so on.

Muhammad said that he who performs ablution like this ablution of mine... and offered two rakahs [sections] of prayer... all his previous sins are expiated. This became the standard ablution. According to Muslim canon scholars, this is the most complete of the ablutions performed for prayer. There are twenty-one ahAdIs repeating Muhammads practice and thought on the subject as given above.

CLEANSING THE NOSE

The nose should be properly cleansed. Muhammad says: When any one of you awakes from sleep... he must clean his nose three times, for the devil spends the night in the interior of ones nose.

Cleaning the Teeth (Miswak)

Muhammad loved toothpicks and used them often. Were it not that I might overburden the believers-I would have ordered them to use the toothpick at every time of prayer, he said.

The Five Acts (Fitra)

There are nine ahAdIs on five acts natural to man and proper to Islam: circumcision, shaving the pubes, cutting the nails, plucking the hair under the armpits, and clipping the moustache.

About the moustache and the beard, the Prophet said: Act against the polytheists, trim closely the moustache and grow beard. The next hadIs substitutes the word fire-worshippers for polytheists. The translator provides the rationale for this injunction: Islam created a new brotherhood on the basis of belief and good conduct.... For the identification of faces, the Muslims have been ordered to trim the moustache and wear the beard, so that they may be distinguished from the non-Muslims who grow a moustache and shave beard.

Bodily Functions

Now Muhammad takes us to the toilet. He forbids his followers to face the qibla [i.e., toward the mosque at Mecca] at the time of excretion or urination, or cleansing with right hand or with less than three pebbles.

Cleansing after excretion must be done an odd number of times, and one must not use dung or bone for this purpose. There is a story explaining why the use of bones and dung is forbidden. Muhammad once spent a night with jinns (genii) reciting the Quran to them. When they asked him about their provision of food, he told them: Every bone on which the name of Allah is recited is your provision. The time it will fall in your hand it would be covered with flesh, and the dung of the camels is fodder for your animals. He therefore told his followers: Dont perform istinjA with these things for these are the food of your brothers.

He also tells his followers: When anyone amongst you enters the privy, he must not touch the penis with his right hand.

Aisha tells us that the Messenger of Allah loved to start from the right-hand side in his every act, i.e., in wearing shoes, in combing, and in performing ablution.

Tathir

Muhammad enjoins that when the dog licks the utensil, wash it seven times, and rub it with earth the eighth time.

DONT EXPOSE YOUR PRIVATE PARTS

Muhammad says that a man should not see the private part of another man, nor should men lie together under one covering. In this connection, he also tells us that the Jews used to take their baths naked and looked at each others private parts, but Moses took his bath alone. Instead of feeling ashamed for not following their leaders example the Jews taunted him. They said he refrained from exposing his private parts because he suffered from scrotal hernia. But God vindicated him. Once, while taking his bath, Moses put his clothes on a rock, but the rock moved away. Moses ran after it crying: O stone, my clothes; O stone, my clothes. The Jews then had a chance to see Moses private parts, and said: By Allah, Moses does not suffer from any ailment.

SOILED CLOTHES

Aisha tells us that the Messenger of Allah washed the semen, and then went out for prayer in that very garment and I saw the mark of washing on it. There is another hadIs´of similar import, but it also narrates some material of Freudian significance. A guest who was staying at Aishas house had a nocturnal seminal emission. Next day he dipped his clothes in water for washing. A maidservant observed this and informed Aisha. She asked the guest: What prompted you to act like this with your clothes He replied, I saw in a dream what a sleeper sees. Then Aisha asked him: Did you find any mark of fluid on your clothes He said: No. She said: Had you found anything you should have washed it. In case I found that semen on the garment of the Messenger of Allah dried up, I scratched it off with my nails.

BATHING AFTER A SEMINAL EMISSION

There are a dozen ahAdIs on the subject of bathing after a seminal emission. Once Muhammad called out an ansAr who was in the midst of sexual intercourse. He came out and water was trickling down from his head. Muhammad said: perhaps we put you to haste. The man said yes. The prophet said: When you made haste and semen is not emitted, bathing is not obligatory for you, but ablution is binding. In another hadIs, Muhammad says that when a man leaves his wife in the midst of an intercourse without having experienced orgasm, he should wash the secretion of his wife, and then perform ablution and offer prayer. But when there is a seminal emission bath becomes obligatory.

Once there was a controversy on this point between some muhAjirs (Emigrants or Refugees) and some ansArs (Helpers). One of them came to Aisha for clarification, asking: What makes a bath obligatory for a person She answered: You have come across one well-informed. Then she reported what Muhammad had said on the subject: When anyone sits amidst fore parts of the woman, and the circumcised parts touch each other a bath becomes obligatory. And on yet another occasion, a man asked Muhammad whether a bath is obligatory for one who parts from intercourse with his wife without having had an orgasm. The Prophet, pointing to Aisha, who was sitting by him, replied: I and she do it and then take a bath.

Tayammum

If water is not available, you can take to tayammum, i.e., wiping your hands and feet and forehead with earth, and that should be as good as ablution with water. The translator explains why. He says that the main purpose behind ablution and bathing is a religious one and the hygienic one is a matter of secondary importance.... Allah has directed us to perform tayammum in case water is not available... to retain the spiritual value of ablution as a means of directing us from the mundane activities of life and directing us to the presence of the Lord. There is a verse in the Quran and eight ahAdIs on this subject. And if you be ailing or on a journey or one comes from the privy, or you have touched women, and you find no water, then betake yourself to clean earth and wipe your faces and your hands therewith.

One hadIs tells us of the words of AmmAr to Umar: Do you remember, O Commander of the Faithful, when I and you were in a military detachment and we had had a seminal emission and did not find water for taking bath and you did not say prayer, but as for myself I rolled in dust and said prayer, and when it was referred to the Apostle, he said: It was enough for you to strike the ground with your hands and then blow the dust and then wipe your face and palms.

Food and Ablution

Muhammad enjoined that ablution is obligatory for one who takes anything touched by fire. But later on this command was abrogated. The Messenger of Allah took meat of goats shoulder and offered prayer and did not perform ablution.

Ablution is necessary after leaving the privy if you are going to pray but not if you are going to eat. The Apostle of Allah came out of the privy, and he was presented with some food, and the people reminded him about ablution, but he said: Am I to say prayer that I should perform ablution.

MENSTRUATION (HAIZ)

The third book is on menstruation. The subjects of this book and the previous one overlap, for both have to do with ritualistic purity. Therefore, some cross-reference is inevitable. This chapter too, in fact, does not have very much to say on menstruation as such but a great deal on ritualistic ablution and bathing after sexual intercourse.

On the subject of menstruation, Muhammads practice appears, in some respects, different from what was enjoined by the revelation in the Quran. The Quran uses rather strong language on the subject: They ask thee concerning womens courses. Say: They are a hurt and a pollution. So keep away from women in their course, and do not approach them until they are clean.

But perhaps approach here means to have sexual intercourse, for except for coitus all other contacts were permitted by the Prophet. MaimUna tells us: The Messenger of Allah used to lie with me when I menstruated, and there was a cloth between me and him. Umm Salama reports the same. Aisha says: When anyone amongst us menstruated, the Messenger of Allah asked her to tie a waist-wrapper over her and then embraced her.

Other ahAdIs make the same point, besides throwing interesting sidelights on some of the more intimate habits of the Prophet. Aisha reports: The Messenger of Allah would recline in my lap when I was menstruating, and recite the Quran. Rather an unlikely place for svAdhyAya, or scriptural studies.

Carrying the same sexual overtones taught by Freud, Aisha again reports: I would drink when I was menstruating, then I would hand over the vessel to the Apostle and he would put his mouth where mine had been, and drink, and I would eat flesh from a bone when I was menstruating, then hand it over to the Apostle and he would put his mouth where mine had been.

The Prophet would also allow Aisha to comb his hair when she was menstruating and he was supposed to be observing itikAf, technically segregating oneself and staying in a mosque for a certain number of days, especially during the last ten days of the month of RamzAn. The Messenger of Allah put out from the mosque his head for me as he was in itikAf [her room opened on the mosque], and I washed it in the state that I was menstruating, Aisha reports.

All this was opposed to the Jewish practice, which forbade not only sexual intercourse but also kissing and all other forms of physical contact during menstruation. Some Muslims wanted to go whole hog in their opposition to Jewish practice and suggested to Muhammad that he should permit sexual intercourse too since the Jews forbade it. But Muhammad did not go that far.

SEXUAL POLLUTION AND ABLUTION

Aisha reports: Whenever the Messenger of Allah had sexual intercourse and intended to eat or sleep, he performed the ablution of prayer. The commentator explains that this was done so that the soul of man may be transported from the urges of the flesh to its original spiritual domain.

Muhammad enjoined the same on his followers. For example, Umar once went to the Prophet and told him that he became junbi [unclean] during the night. The Messenger of Allah said to him: Perform ablution, wash your sexual organ and then go to sleep. The same advice was conveyed to AlI, who as his son-in-law was shy in putting this question to Muhammad directly. His problem was mazi (prostatic fluid) and not manI (semen). Ablution is obligatory in such a case, he was told.

Ablution was also necessary if one wanted to repeat the intercourse. In the words of Abu Bakr, the narrator of this hadIs, between two acts, there should be an ablution.

BATH (GHUSL)

For the exercise of prayer, the whole body must be washed to absolve it from uncleanliness after certain acts: menses, puerperium, coitus, and pollutio nocturna. This practice is derived from the Quranic verse: If you are polluted, then purify yourselves.

There are over two dozen ahAdIs on the subject of Muhammads own custom in this regard. Aisha says: When Allahs Messenger bathed because of sexual intercourse, he first washed his hands; he then poured water with his right hand on his left hand and washed his private parts....

Muhammads practice was that after the sexual intercourse, sometimes he took a bath and then slept, and sometimes he performed ablution only, postponing the bath till the end of the night before the morning prayer. When Aisha reported this to the narrator of this hadIs, his pious reaction was: Praise be to Allah Who has made things easy for the believers.

The same obligation lay on women. One Umm Sulaim went to Muhammad and asked him: Is bathing necessary for a woman when she has a sexual dream Muhammad replied: Yes, when she sees the liquid [vaginal secretion]. Muhammads wives were scandalized when they learned that Umm Sulaim had put a question to the Prophet which suggested that a woman too could have a sexual dream. You humiliated the women, they told her.

Single Bath for Multiple Coitus

Unlike ablution, the bath need not be repeated after each act of intercourse. Anas reports that the Messenger of Allah used to have sexual intercourse with his wives with a single bath; or in the colorful language of TirmizI: with one bath, the Apostle walked over all his women. The translator explains: The holy prophet did not take a bath after every intercourse; he simply performed ablution and took a bath at the end.

Bathing Together

Many ahAdIs narrate how the Prophet and his wives used to bathe together after sexual intercourse. Aisha reports: The

Messenger of Allah took a bath from the vessel [which contained to pounds of water]. And I and he [the Prophet] took a bath from the same vessel. She reports the same idea with more details in another hadIs: I and the Messenger of Allah took a bath from one vessel and our hands alternated into it in the state that we had sexual intercourse.

Two other wives of Muhammad, Umm Salama and MaimUna, also report that they and Muhammad took their baths together.

The translator feels that the practice of the Prophet needs defense from the likely attacks of hostile critics. He tells us that this bath was quite a modest act. There were no glaring lights; and though the Prophet and his wives on occasion took a bath from the same vessel, it was not a tub-bath where a couple sit together; moreover, they took their bath in pitch darkness, and thus there was no question of their seeing each others bodies.

Conserving Body Heat

If one lost too much body heat during the bath, it could be regained by lying again in the embrace of ones wife. According to a hadIs quoted by TirmizI, Aisha reports: On many occasions it happened that the apostle of Allah came back to me after the bath of purification with the intention of warming up. I wrapped him up round me even though I myself had not taken bath [and was therefore in a state of impurity].

Notwithstanding all these rules and regulations, Muhammad was not bound by them. He had his Apostles privilege, which, in this case, he shared with AlI. According to Abu saId, Muhammad told AlI: O AlI! It is not lawful for anyone except me and thee to go to a mosque in a state of sexual defilement.

PRAYER (SALAT)

The fourth book is the Book of Prayer (SalAt). It is the longest, with, ahAdIs divided into chapters. But in all these pages, one looks in vain for any reference to such problems as self-exploration and self-knowledge, problems of enduring concern for the spirituality of the Indian tradition. There is not even a remote hint of different men endowed with different natures taking different paths toward a divinity differently figured. As there is one Allah, one Guide, one Book, there is also one Prayer, caught and fixed in a single formula.

From the titles of the chapters this book contains, one can see that they all relate to the externals: azAn (the call to prayer), postures like bowing, prostrating and rising, the number and times of the different prayers, the place of imAm in the system of prayers, the merits of prayers at different times, the prayer for rain, the prayer for protection against windstorms and other calamities, the prayer relating to the dead, and so on.

Azan

We are told how the institution of azAn began. In the beginning, in Medina, people forgathered in the mosque without knowing when they were to pray. As a means of calling people to prayer at fixed times, some suggested using a bell, as the Christians did; others a horn, as the Jews did. Some even suggested that a fire should be lighted. All these methods were ruled out. To make the Muslim practice different from that of the Jews, the Christians, and the Fireworshippers, the system of the human voice was introduced. BilAl, who was very loud-throated, and Abdullah b. Umm MaktUm, who later became blind, were the first muazzin (callers).

AzAn is very effective. When Satan hears the call to prayer, he runs away to a distance like that of RauhA, a distance of miles from Medina.

ATTACKS ON NON-MUSLIMS

AzAn became a great indicator. Where it was heard, it meant that everything was not kufr (infidelity). The Messenger of Allah used to attack the enemy when it was dawn. He would listen to the AzAn; so if he heard an AzAn, he stopped. This the commentator finds greatly virtuous in Muhammad. The greatest contribution made by the Holy Prophet in the sphere of warfare is that he elevated it from - the surface of reckless murder or slaughter to the level of humanized struggle for the uprooting of evil in society. The Holy Prophet, therefore, did not allow his Companions to take the enemy unawares under the cover of darkness of night.

BLESSINGS FOR MUHAMMAD

When men hear the muazzin, they should repeat what he says and invoke blessings on Muhammad. They should beg from Allah al-WasIla for me, which is a rank in Paradise fitting for only one of Allahs servants. If any one who asks that I be given the WasIla, he will be assured of my intercession, says Muhammad.

In a variation on this theme, if a man who hears a caller responds by testifying that he is satisfied with Allah as my Lord, with Muhammad as Messenger, and with Islam as dIn [religion] his sins would be forgiven.

In seeking blessings for himself, Muhammad does not forget his wives and progeny. Apostle of Allah, how should we bless you Muhammad is asked. He replies: O Allah! bless Muhammad, and his wives and his offspring.... He who blesses me once, Allah would bless him ten times.

POSTURE DURING PRAYER

Muslim prayer is not carried on in one tranquil posture, sitting or standing; it is accompanied by many bodily movements. These have been codified on the basis of the practice and precepts of Muhammad. There are many ahAdIs on the subject. One narrator saw Muhammad raising his hands opposite the shoulders at the time of beginning the prayer and before bowing down and after coming back to the erect position after bowing, but he did not raise them between two prostrations. Another saw his hands lifted opposite to ears. He also saw that the Prophet then wrapped his hands in his cloth and placed his right hand over his left hand. And when he was about to bow down, he brought out his hands from the cloth, and then lifted them.... And when prostrated, he prostrated between the two palms.

Muhammad was commanded by Allah that he should prostrate on the seven bones and he was forbidden to fold back the hair and clothing. The seven bones are: The hands, the knees, and the extremities of the feet and the forehead. But he asked his followers to observe moderation in prostration and not to stretch out [their] forearms on the ground like a dog.

Originally the practice had been to put ones hands together, palm to palm, and then to put them between ones thighs. But later on this practice was abrogated and the followers were commanded to place them [hands] on the knees.

Another precaution: People should avoid lifting their eyes towards the sky while supplicating in prayer, otherwise their eyes would be snatched away.

The Imam

Muslim prayer is mostly group prayer. It should be led by an imAm. Muhammad enjoins that when there are three persons, one of them should lead them.

Muhammad exhorts his followers to follow their imAm. When he prostrates, you should also prostrate; when-he rises up, you should also rise up, he tells them. He also forbids them to bow and prostrate themselves ahead of the imAm: Does the man who lifts his head before the imAm not fear that Allah may change his face into that of an ass. Also, those who are being led in prayer are required to keep pace with the imAm and are forbidden to recite so loudly as to compete with him. When someone once did this, Muhammad told him: I felt as if [you were] disputing with me... and taking out from my tongue what I was reciting. The imAm is authorized to appoint anyone as his deputy, when there is a valid reason for doing so, just as Muhammad appointed Abu Bakr during his last illness.

The First Mosque: Facing the Qibla

Somebody asked Muhammad which was the mosque first set up on the earth. He answered that it was the Kaba. The second one was the great mosque in Jerusalem.

In the beginning, when Muhammad was trying to cultivate the Jews, he prayed facing their temple in Jerusalem. But later on, the direction (qibla) was changed to Mecca. One tradition says: We prayed with the Messenger of Allah towards Bait-ul-

Maqdis for sixteen months or seventeen months. Then we were made to change our direction towards the Kaba. The followers had no difficulty and adjusted to the new change with alacrity. Some people were praying their dawn prayer and had recited one rakah. Someone told them that the qibla had been changed. They turned towards the new qibla in that very state. The translator assures us that this was a change of far-reaching importance.... It strengthened the loyalty of the Muslims to Islam and the Prophet. It must have made a strong appeal to Arab nationalism.

Allah Allows Muhammad Terror and War Booty

While giving his opinion of the first mosques, Muhammad makes some interesting disclosures. He does not deny that the Jews and the Christians also had their prophets but adds: I have been given superiority over the other prophets in six respects: I have been given words which are concise but comprehensive in meaning; I have been helped by terror (in the hearts of the enemies); spoils have been made lawful to me... ; I have been sent to all mankind; and the line of prophets is closed with me. The whole earth is also made a mosque for him and given to him as a legitimate place of prayer for him and his. This is the idea of the world as a mandated territory bestowed on the believers by Allah. We see here that European imperialism with all its rationalizations and pretensions was anticipated by Islamic imperialism by a thousand years. In Islam we find all the ideological ingredients of imperialism in any age: a divine or moral sanction for the exploitation of the barbarians or heathens or polytheists; their land considered as a lebensraum or held as a mandate; they themselves regarded as the wards and special responsibility (zimma) of the civilizing masters.

Another hadIs mentions Muhammads power of intercession on the Day of Judgment, which other prophets lack. Other ahAdIs mention other points. I have been helped by terror..... and while I was asleep I was brought the keys of the treasures of the earth, says Muhammad. This wealth the followers of the Apostle are now busy in getting them, adds Abu Huraira, the narrator of this hadIs.

Women and Mosques

Women can go to the mosque but they should not apply perfume, a privilege not denied to men who can afford it. They were also told not to precede men in lifting their heads from prostration. The translator explains that this hadIs relates to a period when the Companions were very poor and could not afford proper clothing. The instruction was meant to give them time to adjust their clothing before the women lifted their heads.

Muhammad commanded the believers to take out unmarried women and purdah-observing ladies for Id prayers, and he commanded the menstruating women to remain away from the place of worship of the Muslims. But in a footnote explaining the standpoint of the Islamic sharIah with regard to women joining men in prayer, the translator says: The fact is that the Holy Prophet deemed it preferable for women to say their prayers within the four walls of their houses or in the nearest mosque.

Dos and Donts

There are many dos and donts. For example, to wear shoes while praying is permissible, but clothes having designs and markings on them are distracting and should be avoided. The Prophet commanded the believer that while praying he should not spit in front of him, for Allah is in front of him when he is engaged in prayer. According to another tradition, he forbade spitting on the right side or in front, but it is permissible to spit on the left side or under the left foot.

To eat onion or garlic is not harAm (forbidden), but Muhammad found their odors repugnant and therefore forbade coming to the mosque after eating them, for the angels are harmed by the same things as men.

Curse on the Jews

It is meritorious to build a mosque, for he who builds a mosque for Allah, Allah would build for him a house in Paradise. But it is forbidden to build mosques on graves and to decorate them with pictures. Aisha reports that when the Prophet was about to breathe his last... he uncovered his face and said in this very state: Let there be curse upon the Jews and the Christians that they have taken the graves of their Apostles as places of worship.

Dinner before Prayer

This rule may seem to lack piety but in some ways it is realistic. The believer is told to prefer supper to prayer. When the supper is brought and prayer begins, one should first take food, says Muhammad. First things first.

Prayer in Time of Danger

According to Muslim jurists, there are different forms of prayer for sixteen specific dangerous situations. For example, during a war, one group prays while the other one fights.

Friday Prayer

Friday is a special day. On it Adam was created, on it he was made to enter Paradise, on it he was expelled from heaven.

Every ummah was given the Book before the Muslims. But though Muslims are the last, they shall be the first on the Day of Resurrection. While the Jews and the Christians observe Saturday and Sunday as their respective days, Muslims were fortunate to have Friday as their day, the day prescribed by Allah Himself for them. We were guided aright to Friday, but Allah diverted those who were before us from it.

An interesting story is reported in this connection. One Friday, when the Prophet was delivering a sermon, a caravan with merchandise from Syria arrived. People left the Prophet and flocked toward the caravan. Then this verse was revealed: And when they see merchandise or sport, they break away to it and leave you standing.

Muhammad as a Preacher

Jabir b. Abdullah draws for us a pen-portrait of Muhammad delivering a sermon. He reports: When Allahs Messenger delivered the sermon, his eyes became red, his voice rose, and his anger increased so that he was like one giving a warning against the enemy and saying: The enemy has made a morning attack on you and in the evening too. He would also say: The Last Hour and I have been sent like these two, and he would join his forefinger and middle finger Gust as there is no other finger between these two, similarly there will be no new Prophet between Muhammad and the Day of Resurrection) and would further say: The best of the speech is embodied in the Book of Allah, and the best of guidance is the guidance given by Muhammad. And the most evil affairs are their innovations; and every innovation is error.

There are other eyewitness accounts of Muhammads sermons. One report says: Allahs Messenger stood up [to pray] and we heard him say: I seek refuge in Allah from thee, Then said: I curse thee with Allahs curse three times, then he stretched out his hand as though he was taking hold of something. When asked to throw fight on this unusual behavior, he replied: Allahs enemy IblIs came with a flame of fire to put it in my face. But even though cursed, he did not retreat. Thereafter, I meant to seize him. I swear by Allah that had it not been for the supplication of my brother SulaimAn he would have been bound, and made an object of sport for the children of Medina.

Music, Dance and Sports

Aisha reports: The Messenger of Allah came in my apartment while there were two girls with me singing the song of the Battle of BuAs. He lay down on the bed and turned away his face. Then came Abu Bakr and he scolded me and said: Oh! this musical instrument of the devil in the house of the Messenger of Allah. The Messenger of Allah turned towards him and said: Leave them alone. And when he became unattentive I hinted them [the girls] and they went out, and it was the day of Id. Muhammad added: Abu Bakr, every people have a festival and it is our festival [so let them play on].

This is the only hadIs that can be construed as an instance of Muhammads approving of music. In a large measure he was indulging his child-wife Aisha, but the sufi schools of Islam, in which music plays an important role, make the most of this hadIs.

On the same occasion, Muhammad, with Aishas head resting on his shoulder, was watching some Abyssinians engage in a mock armed fight. Umar came and wanted to drive them away by throwing pebbles at them. But Muhammad told him: Umar, leave them alone.

Prayers for Different Occasions

There are prayers for rain, prayers for protection against windstorms or terrible dark clouds, prayers to be recited at the time of a solar eclipse. However, Muhammad had no friendly eye for nature. He regarded clouds and winds with terror. When there was on any day windstorm or dark cloud its effect could be read on the face of the Messenger of Allah, and he moved forward and backward in a state of anxiety, Aisha tells us. She further says: I asked him the reason of this anxiety and he said: I was afraid that it might be a calamity that might fall on my Ummah.

Muhammad deals with the problem with the help of an incantation. Aisha tells us: Whenever the wind was stormy, the Apostle of Allah used to say: O Allah! I ask Thee for what is good in it, and the good which it contains, and the good of that which it was sent for. I seek refuge with Thee from what is evil in it, what evil it contains, and the evil of that what it was sent for.

Prayers for the Dead

There are also prayers for the dead and the dying. The dying must be treated to a bit of theology. Exhort to recite, There is no god but Allah, to those who are dying, says the Prophet.

When you visit the sick or the dead, supplicate for good, because angels may say amen to whatever you say. Umm Salama tells us: When Abu Salama died, I went to the Apostle of Allah and said: Messenger of Allah, Abu Salama has died. He told me to recite: O Allah! forgive me and him [Abu Salama] and give me a better substitute than he. So I said this, and Allah gave me in exchange Muhammad, who is better for me than him [Abu Salama].

Umm Salama was the widow of Abu Salama, to whom she had borne many children. He died at Uhud, and Muhammad married her four months later.

Weeping Over the Dead

Muhammad discouraged weeping over the dead: The dead is punished because of his familys weeping over it. He also taught haste in the disposal of dead bodies. If the dead person was good, it is a good state to which you are sending him on: but if he was otherwise it is an evil of which you are ridding yourself.

Muhammad himself wept over the death of his loyal followers. Weeping over the dying Sad b. UbAda, he said: Allah does not punish for the tears that the eye sheds or the grief the heart feels, but He punishes for this [pointing to his tongue], meaning loud lamenting. Muhammad also sobbed aloud, according to certain traditions, over his expiring child, who was only eighteen months old. His followers tried to comfort him by reminding him of his own exhortation not to weep. Muhammad replied: It is not this that I forbade, but loud wailing and false laudation of the dead.

Muhammad and His Mother

Muhammad tells us: I sought [Allahs] permission to beg forgiveness for my mother, but He did not grant it to me. I sought permission from Him to visit her grave, and He granted it to me. This was a fine gesture on Muhammads part after sending his mother to hell in fulfillment of the demand for theological consistency.

The Poor Tax (Zakat)

The fifth book is on al-zakAt (charity or poor tax). Every society preaches and to some extent practices charity toward its less-fortunate brothers. Muhammad too stresses the importance of charity, or zakAt, an old Arab practice. But with him it became a tax, an obligatory payment made by the Muslims to the new state that was forming, and to be spent by its representatives. In this form, those who paid zakAt were resentful, and those who spent it actually acquired a new source of power and patronage. Much of the Book of ZakAt is concerned with the question of power. In the beginning, Muhammad had many followers who were needy, and most of them, being migrants, depended a great deal on the goodwill and charity of the people of Medina. Perhaps the rhetoric on charity emanates largely from this situation. There was as yet no universal fellowship as such for a brother in distress, no sense of a larger human brotherhood. ZakAt was solely meant for the brothers in faith, and everyone else was excluded on principle. This has been the Muslim practice ever since.

Uses of Zakat Funds

According to the Quran, the zakAt funds are meant for the poor and the paupers [fuqarA and miskIn], for those in bondage and debt, and for the wayfarers. All these are conventional recipients of charity. The funds are also to be used for the bureaucracy, those who collect and administer the funds. But two other items are also mentioned which deserve special attention. The funds are to be used in the service of Allah (fIsabIlillIAh) and for gaining over [or reconciling, or inclining] the hearts [muallafa qulUbuhum] to Islam.

In the technical vocabulary of Islam, the first phrase, in the service, or way, of Allah, means religious warfare, or jihAd. ZakAt funds are to be spent on buying arms, equipment, and horses. The second phrase, gaining over, or reconciling, hearts, means bribes in unadorned language. The faith of new converts should be strengthened with the help of generous gifts, and that of adversaries should be subverted by the same means. This was an important limb of the Prophets religious offensive and diplomacy, and as the Quranic verse shows, it had for the Prophet, as it still has for his followers, a heavenly sanction.

Exemptions and Incentives

There was a lower exemption limit. No Sadaqa [zakAt] is payable on five wasqs of dates or grain [wasq = about pounds], on less than five camel heads and on less than five uqiyas of silver [uqiya = about tons, or ¼ pound]. Also, No Sadaqa is due from a Muslim on his slave or horse. There was no tax on horses meant for use in a jihAd. The horse which is used for riding in jihAd is exempted from the payment of zakAt.

An Unpopular Tax

There is an interesting hadIs which shows that the zakAt tax was unpopular even with the highest. Umar was appointed the collector. When he reported that KhalId b. WalId (who later became a famous Muslim general) and even the Prophets own uncle, AbbAs, had refused to pay the tax, Muhammad replied: You are unjust to KhalId, for he reserved the armours and weapons for the sake of Allah; and as for AbbAs, I shall be responsible.... Umar, bear in mind, the uncle of a person is like his father. The resentment against zakAt was general. It was particularly strong among the non-Medinan Arab tribes, who shared the burden of the tax but not its benefits. The Bedouins complained to the Prophet that the collectors of Sadaqa come to us and treat us unjustly. Upon this the Messenger of Allah said: Please your collectors.

But things were rougher and not as easily settled as this hadIs seems to suggest. After the conquest of Mecca, when the power of Muhammad became supreme, the collection of the tithe became aggressive. In the beginning of the ninth year of the Hijra (Hegira), parties of collectors were sent out in different directions to realize the tax from the KilAb, GhifAr, Aslam, FazAr, and several other tribes. It seems that the opposition of a section of the tribe of Band TamIm to the collection was somewhat forceful. So Muhammad sent a punitive force consisting of fifty Arab horsemen, who took the tribe by surprise and brought fifty men, women, and children back to Medina as hostages. They had to be ransomed, and after this the tax collection became smoother.

The Quran itself is an eloquent witness to the Arab resentment against the tax. Allah warns Muhammad: Some of desert Arabs look upon their payments as a fine, and they wait a turn of fortune against you; but against them shall a turn of evil fortune be; for God both hears and knows. In fact, the resentment was so great that as soon as Muhammad died, the Arab tribes rose in revolt against the infant Muslim state and had to be reconquered. Their opposition ceased only when they became partners in the growing Muslim imperialism and their zakAt obligation was drowned in the immense gains derived from military conquests and colonization abroad.

DIVINE SANCTIONS

The divine punishment for not paying the poor tax is more gruesome than any secular punishment devised by a human agency. If any owner of gold or silver does not pay what is due on him, when the Day of Resurrection would come, plates of fire would be beaten out for him; these then would be heated in the Fire of Hell and his sides, forehead and his back would be cauterized with them. And when these cool down, the process is repeated during a day the extent of which would be fifty thousand years. And for someone who owns camels and does not pay, a sandy plain would be set for him, as extensive as possible, and his camels will trample him with their hoofs and bite him with their mouths... during a day the extent of which would be fifty thousand years. The same fate awaits the tax-defaulting owner of cows and sheep: They will gore him with their horns and trample him with their hoofs for the same period.

Charity Should Begin at Home

There was a lot of uncoerced charity in its nontax version among the Arabs of pre-Muhammad days. For example, the Arabs of that time would take their camels to a pond every six or seven days and there milk them and distribute the milk among the needy. Muhammads response to this generosity was positive. But he taught, and in some ways wisely, that charity should begin at home. This point is brought out in many ahAdIs. The order in which one should spend his wealth is this: First on ones own self, then on ones wife and children, then on relatives and friends, and then on other good deeds.

Following a common practice, an Arab once willed that his slave was to be freed after his death. When Muhammad heard this, he called him and asked him if he had any other property. The man replied no.

Muhammad then sold the slave for dirhams, gave the money to the owner, and told him: Start with your own self and spend it on yourself, and if anything is left, it should be spent on your family, and if anything is left it should be spent on your relatives. There is another story that makes the same point. A lady set her slave-girl free. When informed about it, Muhammad told her: Had you given her to your maternal uncle, you would have a greater reward. So the morality that Muhammad taught on the question was not particularly heroic, but it agrees with the general practice. Nor was it really revolutionary. The emancipation of slaves was not a matter of justice but only of charity. And even then it should not conflict with the well-being of the family of the believer.

Deeper Aspects

Rather unusual for the HadIs, charity in its deeper aspect is also mentioned in some ahAdIs. People who cannot pay in money can pay in piety and good acts. Administering of justice between two men is also a Sadaqa. And assisting a man to ride upon his beast, or helping him load his luggage upon it, is a Sadaqa; and a good word is a Sadaqa; and every step that you take towards prayer is a Sadaqa, and removing of harmful things from the pathway is a Sadaqa. There are some other passages of equal beauty and insight. Among those whom God affords protection is one who gives charity and conceals it so that the right hand does not know what the left hand has given. In the same vein, Muhammad tells us that if anyone gives as Sadaqa the equivalent of one date... the Lord would accept it with His Right Hand.

And in another hadIs: In every declaration of the glorification of Allah [i.e., saying SubhAn Allah], there is a Sadaqa... and in mans sexual intercourse [with his wife-the omission is supplied by the translator], there is a Sadaqa.

Urgings and Pleadings

Muhammad makes an eloquent plea for aims-giving. Everyone should give charity even if it is only half a date. Abu MasUd reports: We were commanded to give charity though we were coolies.

One hadIs tells us: There is never a day wherein servants [of God] get up at mom, but are not visited by two angels. One of them says: O Allah, give him more who spends, and the other says: O Allah, bring destruction to one who withholds. Was not the first part enough Must a blessing always go along with a curse. The Prophet warns believers to make their Sadaqa and be quick about it, for there would come a time when a person would roam about with Sadaqa of gold but he would find no one to accept it from him. He also adds that a man would be seen followed by forty women seeking refuge with him on account of the scarcity of males and abundance of females. What does this mean The translator finds the statement truly prophetic. By citing the male and female population figures for postwar England and showing their disproportion, he proves the truth of the Prophetic statement.

Theft, Fornication and Paradise

Some of the material included in certain discussions in the various ahAdIs is not in fact relevant to the nominal topic of the discussion. This is true, for instance, of ahAdIs and, which both relate to zakAt but also treat matters that have nothing to do with charity, although in their own way they must be reassuring to believers. For example, Abu Zarr reports that while he and Muhammad were once walking together, Muhammad left him to go some other place, telling him to stay where he was until he returned. After a while Muhammad was out of sight but Abu Zarr heard some sounds. Although he was apprehensive of some possible mishap to the Prophet, he remembered his command and remained where he was. When Muhammad returned, Abu Zarr sought an explanation for the sounds. Muhammad replied: It was Gabriel, who came to me and said: He who dies among your Ummah without associating anything with Allah would enter Paradise. I said: Even if he committed fornication or theft He said: Even if he committed fornication or theft.

Charity and Discrimination

There is a hadIs which seems to teach that charity should be indiscriminate. A man gives charity, with praise to Allah, first to an adulteress, then to a rich man, then to a thief. Came the angel to him and said: Your charity has been accepted. For his charity might become the means whereby the adulteress might restrain herself from fornication, the rich man might perhaps learn a lesson and spend from what Allah has given him, and the thief might thereby refrain from committing theft. One may suppose that the mans acts of charity had these wonderful results because they were accompanied by praise to Allah.

Zakat not for Muhammads Family

ZakAt was meant for the needy of the ummah, but it was not to be accepted by the family of Muhammad. The family included AlI, Jafar, AqIl, AbbAs, and Haris b. Abd al-Muttalib and their posterity. Sadaqa is not permissible for us, said the Prophet. Charity was good enough for others but not for the proud descendants of Muhammad, who in any case needed it less and less as they became heirs to the growing Arab imperialism. But though sadaqa was not permitted, gifts were welcome. BarIra, Muhammads wifes freed slave, presented Muhammad with a piece of meat that his own wife had given her as sadaqa. He took it, saying: That is Sadaqa for her and a gift for us.

War Booty

Within a very short period, zakAt became secondary, and war spoils became the primary source of revenue of the Muslim treasury. In fact, the distinction between the two was soon lost, and thus the Book of ZakAt imperceptibly becomes a book on war spoils. Khums, the one-fifth portion of the spoils of war which goes to the treasury, has two aspects. On the one hand, it is still war booty; but on the other, it is zakAt. When it is acquired, it is war booty; when it is distributed among the ummah, it is zakAt.

Muhammad regards war booty as something especially his own. The spoils of war are for Allah and His Messenger (Quran :). They are put in his hands by Allah to be spent as he thinks best, whether as zakAt for the poor, or as gifts for his Companions, or as bribes to incline the polytheists to Islam, or on the Path of Allah, i.e., on preparations for armed raids and battles against the polytheists.

Abd al-Muttalib and Fazl b. AbbAs, two young men belonging to Muhammads family, wanted to become collectors of zakAt in order to secure means of marrying. They went to Muhammad with their request, but he replied: It does not become the family of Muhammad to accept Sadaqa for they are the impurities of the people. But he arranged marriages for the two men and told his treasurer: Pay so much Mahr [dowry] on behalf of both of them from the khums.

Dissatisfaction

Most of the properties abandoned by the BanU NazIr were appropriated by Muhammad for himself and his family. Other funds at his disposal for distribution were also increasing. This new money was hardly zakAt money but war booty. Its distribution created a lot of heart-rending among his followers. Many of them thought they deserved more-or at any rate that others deserved less-than they got. Muhammad had to exercise considerable diplomacy, combined with threats, both mundane and celestial.

Gaining Hearts by Giving Gifts

The principle of distribution was not always based on need, justice, or merit. Muhammad had other considerations as well. I give [at times material gifts] to persons who were quite recently in the state of unbelief, so that I may incline them to truth, says Muhammad.

To gain hearts (mullafa qulUbhum) for Islam with the help of gifts is considered impeccable behavior, in perfect accord with Quranic teaching. Muhammad made effective use of gifts as a means of winning people over to Islam. He would reward new converts generously but overlook the claims of Muslims of long standing. Sad reports that the Messenger of Allah bestowed gifts upon a group of people.... He however left a person and did not give him anything and he seemed to me the most excellent among them. Sad drew the Prophets attention to this believing Muslim, but Muhammad replied: He may be a Muslim. I often bestow something on a person, whereas someone else is dearer to me than he, because of the fear that he [the former] may fall headlong into the fire, that is, he may give up Islam and go back to his old religion. The translator and commentator makes the point very clear by saying that it was with a view to bringing him nearer and making him feel at home in the Muslim society that material gifts were conferred upon him by the Holy Prophet. There are other instances of the same type. Abdullah b. Zaid reports that when the Messenger of Allah conquered Hunain he distributed the booty, and he bestowed upon those whose hearts it was intended to win. He bestowed costly gifts on the Quraish and Bedouin chiefs, many of them his enemies only a few weeks before. Traditions have preserved the names of some of these elite beneficiaries, like Abu SufyAn b. Harb, SafwAn b. Umayya, Uyaina b. Hisn, Aqra b. HAbis, and Alqama b. Ulasa. They received a hundred camels each from the booty. Muhammad did the same with the booty of some gold sent by AlI b. Abu TAlib from Yemen. He distributed it among four men: Uyaina, Aqra, Zaid al-Khail, and the fourth one was either Alqama b. UlAsa or Amir b. Tufail.

Pacification

But this course was not without its problems. It created quite a lot of dissatisfaction among some of his old supporters, and Muhammad had to use all his powers of diplomacy and flattery to pacify them. Dont you feel delighted that [other] people should go with riches, and you should go back with the Apostle of Allah, he told the ansArs with great success when, after the conquest of Mecca, they complained about the unjust distribution of the spoils. They had grumbled: It is strange that our swords are dripping with their blood, whereas our spoils have been given to them [the Quraish].

Muhammad added other words of flattery and told the ansArs that they were his inner garments (i.e., were closer to him), while the Quraish, who had received the spoils, were merely his outer garments. To cajolery, he added theology, telling them that they should show patience till they meet him at Hauz Kausar, a canal in heaven. The ansArs were happy.

Muhammad Ruffled

According to another tradition, Muhammad gave a hundred camels each to Abu SufyAn, SafwAn, Uyaina, and Aqra, but less than his share to AbbAs b. MirdAs. AbbAs told Muhammad: I am in no way inferior to anyone of these persons. And he who is let down today would not be elevated. Then Muhammad completed one hundred camels for him.

In other cases when similar complaints were made, Muhammad could not always keep his temper. One man complained that this is a distribution in which the pleasure of Allah has not been sought. On hearing this, Muhammad was deeply angry... and his face became red; he found comfort in the fact that Moses was tormented more than this, but he showed patience.

The Khwarij

AlI sent some gold alloyed with dust from Yemen to Muhammad. In its distribution, Muhammad showed favoritism. When some people complained, Muhammad demanded: Will you not trust me, whereas I am a trustee of Him Who is in the heaven The news comes to me from the heaven morning and evening. This silenced the men, but one of them, a man with deep-sunken eyes, prominent cheekbones, thick beard, and shaven head, stood up, and said: Messenger of Allah, fear Allah and do justice. This angered Muhammad, and he replied: Woe be upon thee, who would do justice if I do not do justice Umar, who was present, said to Muhammad: Messenger of Allah, permit me to kill this hypocrite. Though the man was spared, he and his posterity were denounced. Muhammad said: From this very persons posterity there would arise people who would recite the Quran, but it would not go beyond their throat; they would kill the followers of Islam but would spare the idol-worshippers.... If I were to find them I would kill them like Ad [a people who were exterminated root and branch].

These men, who later on were called the khwArij, took some of the slogans of Islam seriously. It was about them, according to AlI, that Muhammad said: When you meet them, kill them, for in their killing you would get a reward with Allah on the Day of Judgment. These were the anarchists and purists of the early days of Islam. The injunction about them was: Pursue them as they are routed and kill their prisoners and destroy their property.

3

Fasting and Pilgrimage

The sixth and seventh books relate respectively to fasting (al-sawm) and pilgrimage (al-hajj). Both of these practices are accounted among the pillars of Islam.

FASTS

There are many kinds of fasts in Islam, but the fast during the month of RamzAn (Ramadan) is considered the most important. Enjoined in the Quran, it is compulsory. When there comes the month of RamzAn, the gates of mercy are opened, and the gates of Hell are locked and the devils are chained.

Fasting in the Muslim tradition is rather different from fasting in many other religious traditions. In Islam, there is no uninterrupted fasting (saum wisal), because Muhammad forbade this practice out of mercy for his Companions. During fasts eating is prohibited in the daytime but permitted at night. This has its disciplinary role, but nonetheless there is an attempt to make things easy. One is advised to eat as late as possible before sunrise, and to break the fast as soon as possible after sunset. Take meal a little before dawn, for there is a blessing in taking meal at that time ; and the people will continue to prosper as long as they hasten the breaking of the fast.

This approach distinguished the Muslims from the Jews and the Christians, who ate early and broke their fasts late, waiting for the stars to appear. The difference between our fasting and that of the People of the Book is eating shortly before dawn, says Muhammad. The translator explains the advantages that accrued to the ummah from maintaining this difference. It distinguishes the Ummah of the Islam from other Ummahs, and hammers into its consciousness the sense of its separate entity which is the first step towards prosperity of any nation. In addition, taking a meal late in the dawn and breaking fast early at the sunset indicate the fact that one feels the pangs of hunger.... This feeling inculcates in one a spirit of humility rather than of stoic pride.

SEXUAL INTERCOURSE ALLOWED DURING RAMZAN

The Prophet softens the rigor of the fast somewhat by proclaiming that eating and drinking in forgetfulness does not break the fast. Kissing and embracing too are permissible. Aisha, Hafsa, and Salama, Muhammads wives, all report that the Prophet used to kiss them and embrace them while fasting. Aisha narrates: The Messenger of Allah kissed one of his wives while he was fasting, and then she [Aisha] smiled.

The translator elucidates: It is one of the great favours of Allah upon humanity that He has guided us in every sector of our life through his Prophet Muhammad. Prior to Islam, the man observing fast separated himself completely from his wives. Islam did not approve this practice.

Sexual intercourse is also permitted during the night of the fast. It has a divine sanction. It is made lawful for you to go to your wives on the night of the fast, says the Quran. In fact, even if one gets up in a state of seminal emission and the dawn overtakes him without giving him time for the ordained bath, he should still go on with his fast. The state of janabah (in which one is unclean and cannot perform a religious act or join in religious assemblies) does not break the fast. Aisha and Salama, Muhammads wives, report: The Messenger of Allah at times got up in the morning in a state of Junub on account of having a sexual intercourse... in the month of RamzAn, and would observe fast. There are other ahAdIs on the same subject.

This hadIs was checked and rechecked by Abu Bakr himself. At first Abu Huraira thought differently, but when the matter was clarified by Aisha and Salama, he said, They have better knowledge, and retracted his previous position.

Sexual intercourse during the daytime in the month of RamzAn could be atoned for either by freeing a slave or, failing that, by observing a two-month fast or, failing that, by feeding sixty poor men-but during the Prophets lifetime, a poor man who violated this prohibition got his expiation at no cost to himself. Muhammad gave him a basket of dates and told him: Go and give it to your family to eat. Missed fasts could be completed later on at any time of the year. Women do not fast during the days of menses but are required to complete the fast the following year before the commencement of the next RamzAn (in the month of ShabAn).

FASTING NOT OBLIGATORY UNDER CERTAIN CIRCUMSTANCES

Under certain circumstances fasting was optional. For example, a fast during a journey could be broken. Fast if you like and break it if you like, Muhammad told a questioner on the subject. There is even a reward for not observing the fast if you are engaged in the Way of Allah, i.e., in the act of jihAd. You are going to encounter the enemy in the morning and breaking of the fast would give you strength, so break the fast, Muhammad tells the believers. Women sometimes abstained from fasts so that they could perform their duties to their husbands unhindered. Aisha reports: I had to complete some of the fasts of RamzAn, but I could not do it... due to my duties to the Messenger of Allah. Aisha reports the same about Muhammads other wives. If one amongst us had to break fasts [of RamzAn due to natural reasons, i.e., menses] during the fife of the Messenger of Allah, she could not find it possible to complete them so long as she had been in the presence of Allahs Messenger till ShabAn [the eighth month] commenced. The translator explains that every wife of Muhammad was so much devoted to him that she avoided fasting lest it should stand in her way in the performance of her duty as a wife to him.

It was not only from devotion but also because of Muhammads injunction that the wives did not fast. No woman should observe fast when her spouse is present [in the house] but with his permission. And she should not admit any mahram in his house, while the husband is present, but with his permission. A mahram is a near relative with whom it is unlawful to marry. A woman can feel free in his presence and thus need not observe purdah. The translator gives us the rationale for this injunction. Such is the regard which Islam gives to the natural instinct of man that it enjoins upon women not to observe (voluntary) fasts, and not to admit even those relatives of theirs in their apartments who are maharam to them so that they may not stand in the way of the husbands to satisfy their sexual urge.

OTHER FASTS

Several other fasts are mentioned. One is the Ashura fast, observed on the tenth day of Muharram. The Ashur day was one which the Jews respected and they treated it as Id, and in the pre-Islamic days, Quraish used to fast on this day ; but after Muhammad migrated to Medina he made it optional for his followers. Other voluntary fasts are mentioned, but we need not go into them here. One interesting thing about these fasts is that one could declare ones intention of observing them in the morning but break them without reason in the evening. One day, Muhammad asked Aisha for some food, but nothing was available. Thereupon Muhammad said: I am observing fast. After some time, some food came as gift, and Aisha offered it to Muhammad. He asked: What is it Aisha said: It is hais [a compound of dates and clarified butter]. He said: Bring that. Aisha further narrates: So I brought it to him and he ate it; and then he said: This observing of voluntary fasts is like a person who sets apart Sadaqa out of his wealth. He may spend it if he likes, or he may retain it if he so likes.

THE MERITS OF FASTING

There are many merits in observing the fasts. The breath of the observer of fast is sweeter to Allah than the fragrance of musk, Muhammad tells us. On the Day of Resurrection, there will be a gate called RayyAn in Paradise, through which only those who have fasted will be allowed to enter-and when the last of them has entered, it would be closed and no one would enter it. The recompense of one who combines fasting with jihad will be immense. Every servant of Allah who observes fast for a day in the way of Allah, Allah would remove, because of this day, his face from the Fire of Hell to the extent of seventy years distance.

PILGRIMAGE

The book on hajj (setting out) is full of ceremonial details which have little interest for non-Muslims. Its ninety-two chapters contain minute instructions on the rites and rituals of the pilgrimage, providing useful guidance to a hajji (pilgrim) but of dubious value to a traveler of the Spirit.

An Idolatrous Idea

Considered from the viewpoint of Muslim theology, the whole idea of pilgrimage to Mecca and the Kaba is close to being idolatrous. But it has great social and political importance for Islam. Even the very first Muslim pilgrimage to Mecca under the leadership of Muhammad was perhaps more of a political demonstration and a military expedition than a religious congregation. In the sixth year of the Hijra, Muhammad started out for Mecca to perform the umrah ceremony (the lesser pilgrimage), the very first after coming to Medina. He headed a pilgrim force of fifteen hundred men, partially armed. In order to swell the number, he had appealed to the desert Arabs to join him, but their response was lukewarm, for no booty was promised and they thought, as the Quran puts it, that the Apostle and the believers would never return to their families.

Even so, fifteen hundred was an impressive number, and anyone could see that this was hardly a band of pilgrims. The Meccans had to enter into a treaty with Muhammad, called the Treaty of Hodeibia. Muhammad regarded this as a victory for himself, and a victory it turned out to be. Two years later, by a kind of delayed action, Mecca succumbed. In this year of victory, pilgrimage, or hajj, was declared one of the five fundamentals of Islam.

Two years later, in March A.D., Muhammad undertook another pilgrimage; it turned out to be his last and is celebrated in the Muslim annals as the Farewell Pilgrimage of the Apostle. Great preparations were made for the occasion. It was meant to be more than an assembly of believers. It was to be a demonstration of the power of Muhammad. Messengers were sent to all parts of Arabia inviting people to join him in this great Pilgrimage. After the fall of Mecca, Muhammads power was unrivaled, and the Bedouin tribes understood that this summons was more than an invitation to a pilgrimage of the type they had formerly performed on their own, at their own convenience and for their own gods. It was also, they knew, a call to submission. Thus, unlike the last time, their response on this occasion was great. As the caravan moved on, the number of participants swelled, until, according to some of the narrators, it reached more than, Everyone was in a hurry to jump on the bandwagon.

The State of Ihram

The Book of Pilgrimage deals with the pilgrims attire and with the place where he puts on the garments of a pilgrim, entering into the state of ihrAm (prohibiting), in which he is forbidden to do certain things till he has completed his worship at Mecca. For his dress, he is forbidden to put on a shirt or a turban, or trouser or cap. The use of perfume is disallowed during the state of ihrAm, but not before and after. I applied perfume to the Messenger of Allah as he became free from IhrAm and as he entered upon it, says Aisha. The best of perfume, she adds in another hadIs.

Hunting

Hunting too is forbidden to a muhrim (one in a state of ihrAm). Somebody once presented Muhammad with the flesh of a wild ass, but he declined it, saying: If we were not in a state of IhrAm, we would have accepted it from you. But if the animal is killed by a non-muhrim, its flesh is acceptable to a muhrim. The leg of a wild ass killed by a non-muhrim Companion was presented to Muhammad. The Messenger of Allah took it and ate it.

Though hunting of a sort is forbidden to a muhrim, this does not make him a Jain or a Vaishnava. Four are the vicious beasts he should still kill: kite, crow, rat and voracious dog. But what about a snake somebody asks. Muhammad replies: Let it be killed with disgrace.

Circumambulation and Kissing

After a man has put on the pilgrims robe, two seamless wrappers, he should not shave or pare his nails. He should now proceed toward Mecca singing the pilgrims song, Talbiyah, Labbaika! Allahumma! (I stand up for thy service, O Allah). After arriving in Mecca, he performs ablutions in the Masjidul HarAm and kisses the Black Stone (al-hajarul-aswad), then makes seven circuits round the Kaba (tawAf). Muhammad himself circumambulated on the back of his riding camel... so that people should see him, and he should be conspicuous. For the same reason, he touched the Corner (Black Stone) with a stick. I saw Allahs Messenger circumambulating the House, and touching the Corner with a stick that he had with him, and then kissing the stick, reports Abu Tufail.

The practice of kissing the Stone is idolatrous. Umar said: By Allah, I know that you are a stone and if I were not to see Allahs Messenger kissing you, I would not have kissed you. Following the lead of Christian theologians who distinguish between veneratio and adoratio, Muslim scholars argue that the Kaba and the Black Stone are objects of veneration and not of worship. Another important rite is that the pilgrim runs from the top of Mount as-SafA to the summit of Mount al-Marwah, the two Signs of Allah, according to the Quran. Muhammad says that Allah does not complete the Hajj of a person or his Umra if he does not observe Sai [i.e., run between al-SafA and al-Marwa]. Each time the pilgrim is on the top of these mounts, he recites the following: There is no deity but Allah.... He hath performed His promise, and hath aided His servant [Muhammad] and bath put to flight the hosts of infidels by Himself alone. Muhammad never relaxes. At every turn, he instills an unrelenting enmity toward the infidels.

Casting the Pebbles

Another important ceremony is ramyur-rijAm, the casting of the pebbles. On the tenth day, also the Day of Sacrifice, the pilgrim throws seven pebbles at Jamrat al-Aqaba, also known as ShaitAnuul KabIr, the Great Devil. While doing this, he chants: In the name of God, the Almighty, I do this, and in hatred of the Devil and his shame. Allah and Devil are somehow

inseparable in certain theologies. This ceremony celebrates an ancient event when the Devil successively met Adam, Abraham, and Ishmael, and was driven away by the simple method which Gabriel taught them of throwing seven small pebbles. The three pillars at MinA represent the three occasions when this happened; therefore, the pilgrim casts seven stones at each of the three pillars.

There are several ahAdIs on the merits of throwing pebbles, on their size and number, and on the best time for throwing them. The pebbles should be small- I saw Allahs Apostle throwing stones like pelting of small pebbles. The best time for throwing them is after sunrise on the Day of Sacrifice- Allahs Messenger flung pebbles at Jamra on the Day of Nahr after sunrise, and after that-on the th, th and th of Dhul-Hijja -when the sun had declined. Their number should be odd. Odd number of stones are to be used for cleaning the private parts after answering the call of nature, and the casting of pebbles at the Jamrat is to be done by odd numbers (seven), and the number of circuits around al-SafA and al-Marwa is also odd (seven), and the number of circuits around the Kaba is also odd (seven), says the Prophet.

Animal Sacrifice

Next comes the sacrifice of the idul-azhA. The hAjji (pilgrim) could sacrifice a goat or a sheep, or a cow or a camel, The Messenger of Allah sacrificed a cow on behalf of Aisha. It is permissible for seven persons to join in the sacrifice of a cow or a camel. While sacrificing the camel, the hAjji should not make his camel kneel down but slaughter it in a standing posture and in a fettered condition according to the Sunnah of the Holy Prophet. Its left foreleg should be tied to its hindlegs. Cows and goats should be sacrificed after making them lie down.

One who cannot go for hajj can send a sacrificial animal to al-Haram and earn merit thereby. Aisha reports: I wove the garlands for the sacrificial animals of Allahs Messenger with my own hands, and then he marked them, and garlanded them, and then sent them to the House, and stayed at Medina and nothing was forbidden to him which was lawful for him before.

As Muhammads affluence increased, the scale of his sacrifices also increased. On his umrah pilgrimage in the sixth year, his biographers tell us, he sacrificed seventy camels at Hodeibia. On a similar pilgrimage the next year, he sacrificed sixty camels. On the Farewell Pilgrimage in the tenth year, we are told by JAbir, the total number of those sacrificial animals brought by AlI from Yemen [where he had gone on a campaign against the Bani Nakha] and those brought by the Apostle was one hundred. A little further on in the same hadIs we are told that Muhammad then went to the place of sacrifice, and sacrificed sixty-three camels with his own hands. Then he gave the remaining number to AlI who sacrificed them.... He then commanded that a piece of flesh from each animal sacrificed should be put in a pot, and when it was cooked, both of them [AlI and Muhammad] took some meat out of it and drank its soup. To his followers, Muhammad said: I have sacrificed the animals here, and the whole of MinA is a place of sacrifice; so sacrifice your animals at your places. Even Jehovah, the God of the Jews, whose Temple was a veritable slaughterhouse, had declared that He desired mercy, and not sacrifice (Hosea :); but Muhammads Allah expresses no such sentiment. Because Islam is so preponderantly Muhammadism, one of the consequences of the Prophets offering sacrifices is that sacrificing has become a sacred institution in Islam. Thus we find in Islam none of that generous movement of the spirit against animal sacrifice that we find in some measure in most cultures.

Drink

Muhammad also drank water from the well of Zamzam as part of the ritual. Coming to the tribe of Abd al-Muttalib (also his own tribe), he said: Draw water, O BanI Abd al-Muttalib; were it not that people would usurp this right of supplying water from you, I would have drawn it along with you. So they handed him a basket and he drank from it. KAtib al-WAqidI, the Prophets biographer, gives us one further detail which would be considered unhygienic by the impious. Muhammad took part of the content, then rinsed his mouth in the pitcher and directed that the water remaining in it should be thrown back into the well. That was his way of invoking a blessing on a well-by spitting into it. Many such wells are mentioned in the traditions. He also did not forgo his favorite beverage, nabIz, a soft drink. Though the nabIz offered him had been fouled by many hands, he took it, declining the offer of a cleaner and purer one. The orthodox pilgrims of every generation have continued the practice.

Shaving: Muhammads Hair

After the sacrifice, the ceremony of pilgrimage concludes, and the hAjji has himself shaved and his nails pared and his pilgrim garment removed. Shaving should begin from the right side. Anas reports that Allahs Messenger went to Jamra and threw pebbles at it, after which he went to his lodging in Mind, and sacrificed the animal. He then called for a barber and, turning his right side to him, let him shave him; after which he turned his left side. He then gave these hairs to the people ; the hairs became important Islamic relics. Now the pilgrimage is over, but the pilgrim should spend another three days in Mecca to rest after the hectic four days of ceremony. Before leaving Mecca, he should again go round the Kaba seven times and throw stones at the satanic pillars at MinA seven times. Before returning home, he should go to Medina to pay his homage at the tomb of Muhammad.

Kaba Closed to Non-muslims

The Kaba, which had been open to all in pre-Islamic times, whether they were worshippers of Al-LAh or Al-LAt, was closed to all except Muslims after Muhammad conquered Mecca. After this year no polytheist may perform the Pilgrimage, it was declared on his behalf. This was Allahs own command. The Quran says: O you who believe! those who ascribe partners to God are impure, and so they shall not approach the sacred House of worship from this year onward. Most religions build houses or temples for their gods out of their own labor, but Islam conquered one for its god, Allah, from others. The difference is striking. A worthy habitation for any worthwhile god is the one built by his devotees with the love of their hearts and the labor of their hands. Any other house is a monument of imperialist greed and aggrandizement and is not acceptable to the gods of the purified spirit.

4

Marriage and Divorce

The eighth book is entitled the Book of Marriage; one section of it also discusses divorce (al-talaq).

Muhammad forbids celibacy. Those among you who can support a wife should marry, for it restrains eyes from casting evil glances and preserves one from immorality. One of his Companions wanted to live in celibacy, but Muhammad forbade him to do so.

In fact, Muhammad discouraged self-denial in general. One of his Companions said, I will not marry women; another said, I will not eat meat; and yet another said, I will not lie down in bed.

Muhammad asked himself: What has happened to these people that they say so and so, whereas I observe prayer and sleep too; I observe fast and suspend observing them; I marry women also And who turns away from my Sunnah, he has no relation with me.

A woman is a great safety valve, but if even that fails and a man is aroused by some other woman, he should come home and cohabit with his wife. Allahs Messenger saw a woman and so he came to his wife, Zainab, as she was tanning a leather and had sexual intercourse with her.

He then went to his Companions and told them: The woman advances and returns in the shape of a devil, so when one of you see a woman, he should come to his wife, for that will repel what he feels in his heart. We are all too ready to see the devil in others, but not in our own selves.

TEMPORARY MARRIAGE (MUTAH)

Muhammad allowed temporary marriages. Abdullah b. Masud reports: We were on an expedition with Allahs Messenger and we had no women with us. We said: Should we not have ourselves castrated The Holy Prophet forbade us to do so. He then granted us permission that we should contract temporary marriage for a stipulated period giving her a garment [for a dowry]. At this Abdullah felt happy and remembered the Quranic verse: The believers do not make unlawful the good things which Allah has made lawful for you, and do not transgress. Allah does not like transgressors.

JAbir reports: We contracted temporary marriage giving a handful of dates and flour as a dower. He told another group: Yes, we had been benefiting ourselves by this temporary marriage during the lifetime of the Holy Prophet, and during the time of Abu Bakr and Umar. IYas b. Salama reports, on the authority of his father, that Allahs Messenger gave sanction for contracting temporary marriage for three nights in the year of AutAs [after the Battle of Hunain] and then forbade it.

Sunni theologians regard this form of marriage as no longer lawful, but the Shias differ and still practice it in Persia. The Shia theologians support this with a Quranic verse: Forbidden to you also are married women, except those who are your hands as slaves.... And it is allowed you, besides this, to seek out wives by means of your wealth, with modest conduct, and without fornication. And give those with whom you have cohabited their dowry. This is the law. But it shall be no crime in you to make agreements over and above the law. Verily, God is knowing, Wise.

Prohibitions

The law appears to be quite indulgent, but it is not entirely so. There are many restrictions on grounds of number, consanguinity, affinity, religion, rank, etc. For example, a man cannot marry more than four free women at a time-there is no restriction on the number of slave concubines. Also, one cannot marry ones wifes fathers sister nor her mothers sister. It is also forbidden to marry the daughter of ones foster brother, or even the sister of ones wife if the wife is alive and not divorced. It is also forbidden to marry an unbeliever. Later on, this restriction was relaxed, and a male Muslim could then marry a Jew or a Christian. Under no circumstances could a female Muslim marry a nonbeliever.

Marriage is also disallowed when the parties are not equal in rank or status (kafaah), though what is rank is differently understood by different people. Generally speaking, an Arab is considered higher than a non-Arab, the Prophets relatives being the highest. One who had committed a portion of the Quran to memory was considered a qualified match by Muhammad himself. A woman came to him and entrusted herself to him. He cast a glance at her from head to foot... but made no decision about her. Then a Companion who was there stood up and said: Messenger of Allah, marry her to me if you have no need for her. But the man possessed nothing, not even an iron ring for a dowry. He was turning away in disappointment when Muhammad asked him if he knew any verses of the Quran and could recite them. The man said yes. Then Muhammad decided and said: Go, I have given her to you in marriage for the part of the Quran which you know.

One should also not outbid ones brother. A believer is the brother of a believer, so it is not lawful for a believer to outbid his brother, and he should not propose an agreement when his brother has thus proposed until he gives it up.

ShighAr marriage is also prohibited. This is the marriage which says: Marry me your daughter or sister, and in exchange I will give you in marriage my daughter or sister.

One should also not marry when one has put on the ritual garb of pilgrimage. A Muhrim should neither marry nor make the proposal of marriage, reports UsmAn b. AffAn, quoting the Prophet. But this point is controversial, for Muhammad himself married MaimUna while he was a Muhrim.

One cannot remarry ones divorced wife unless she subsequently married someone else and the new husband had sexual intercourse with her and then divorced her. A divorcee married but then decided to go back to her old husband. Seeking the Prophets permission, she told Muhammad that all the new husband possessed was like the fringe of a garment (i.e., he was sexually weak). The Prophet laughed but withheld the permission. You cannot do that until you have tasted his [the new husbands] sweetness and he has tasted your sweetness, he told her.

The Husbands Rights

A husband has complete sexual rights over his wife. Your wives are your tilth; go then unto your tilth as you may desire. The same idea is also found in the Quran. Another hadIs in the same group tells the husband that if he likes he may have intercourse being on the back or in front of her, but it should be through one hole, which means vagina only, as the commentators tell us.

It is the duty of a wife to be responsive to all of her husbands overtures. When a woman spends the night away from the bed of her husband, the angels curse her until morning.

Womens Rights

In return, a woman has her rights. She is entitled to a lawful maintenance (nafaqah); if the husband fails to provide it, she can seek a divorce. She is also entitled to a dowry (mahr), or what the Quran in some verses calls her hire (ujUrat). She can claim it when divorced.

She is also to be consulted in the choice of her partner. A woman who has been previously married (Sayyib) has more right to her person than her guardian. And a virgin should also be consulted, and her silence implies her consent. Theoretically, a Muslim woman is entitled to make the marriage contract herself, but in practice it is her nearest kinsman, the guardian (walI), who does it.

The father and the grandfather are even called compelling walIs. According to some schools, a minor girl given in marriage by a guardian other than her father or grandfather can seek dissolution of the marriage when she attains her majority.

Al-azl

Coitus interruptus is permitted, but it is useless if the object is to prevent conception, for that is in the hand of Allah. Abu Sirma reports: We went out with Allahs Messenger on the expedition.... and took some excellent Arab women; and we desired them... but we also desired ransom for them. So we decided to have sexual intercourse with them but by observing azl. They consulted Muhammad, and he advised: It does not matter if you do not do it, for every soul that is to be born up to the Day of Resurrection will be born.

Captive Women

Adultery and fornication are punished according to Muhammads law, but not if you commit them with the women that your right hands possess, that is, those women, whether married or unmarried, who are captured by the Muslims in jihAd, or holy war. A Quranic verse fortifies this position: Also prohibited are women already married except those whom your right hands possess.

AhAdIs - tell us that this verse descended on the Prophet for the benefit of his Companions. Abu SaId reports that at the Battle of Hunain Allahs Messenger sent an army to AutAs.... Having overcome them [the enemies] and taken them captives, the Companions of Allahs Messenger seemed to refrain from having intercourse with captive women because of their husbands being polytheists. Then, Allah, Most High. sent down [the above verse].

The followers had a feeling of delicacy in the matter, based on an old moral code, but Allah now gave a new one.

Cast a Glance at the Woman you Want to Marry

It is permissible to cast a glance at the woman one wants to marry, from head to foot. A believer came to Muhammad, informing him that he had contracted a marriage with an ansAr woman and wanted him to contribute toward the dowry payment. Did you cast a glance at her, for there is something in the eyes of the AnsArs, Muhammad asked. The man replied: Yes. For what dower did you marry her, Muhammad inquired.

For four Uqiyas, the man replied. For four Uqiyas It seems as if you dig out silver from the side of the mountain (that is why you are prepared to pay so much dower). We have nothing which we should give you. There is a possibility that we may send you to an expedition where you may get booty. The man was sent on an expedition marching against the BanU Abs.

But this permission actually originated in a different incident. An Arab woman named Umra, the daughter of one Jaun, was mentioned before Allahs Messenger. By now the Prophet was an important man in Arab politics, so he commanded an official of his named Abu Usaid to send a messenger to the woman. She was brought and she stayed in the fortresses of BanU SAidah. Allahs Messenger went out until he came to her to give her a proposal of marriage. She was sitting with her head downcast. They saw each other, and Muhammad talked to her. She told him: I seek refuge with Allah from you. Meanwhile the Prophet had arrived at his own conclusion. He told her: I have decided to keep you away from me. Then Muhammad retired with his host and told him: Sahl, serve us drink.

It is in this hadIs that one finds it permissible to cast a glance at the woman whom one intends to marry.

Deportment Toward Ones Wives

Ticklish problems arise if one has more than one wife and if one marries often. One of the problems, for example, is how many nights one should spend with ones newly wed wife The answer is seven days if she is a virgin, and three days if she is a widow.

Umm Salama, one of the wives of Muhammad, tells us that when Muhammad married her, he spent three nights with her. When he intended to leave, she caught hold of his garment. But the Prophet told her: If you wish I can stay with you for a week, but then I shall have to stay for a week with all my wives.

Though a husband should divide his days equally among all his wives, one wife could make over her day to another. AhAdIs - tell us that when Sauda became old, she made over her day to Aisha. So Allahs Messenger allotted two days to Aisha. But sometimes the Prophet himself would ask a wife to forgo her day. One wife told him: If I had the option in this I would not have allowed anyone to have precedence over me.

Eventually the rule of rotation was withdrawn altogether by a special dispensation of Allah: Thou may defer the turn of any of them that thou pleasest, and thou may receive any thou pleasest; and there is no blame in thee if thou invite one whose turn thou hast set aside. Allah is very accommodating. Aisha, for whose benefit He really spoke, taunted Muhammad: It seems to me that your Lord hastens to satisfy your desire.

Night Sessions

We have one important hadIs which provides another indulgence to the believers and also throws some light on the Prophets sexual code. In order to be impartial, a believer should visit his wives by turn. But while he is in bed with one of them, he is allowed to have his other wives around. Anas, one of the servants of Muhammad, reports that all the wives of the Messenger of Allah used to gather every night in the house of one where he [the Apostle] had to come.... It was the night in the house of Aisha, when Zainab came there. He [the Holy Prophet] stretched his hand towards her [Zainab], whereupon she [Aisha] said: it is Zainab. Allahs Apostle withdrew his hand. There was an altercation between the two until their voices became loud. When the morning prayer was announced, Abu Bakr came to get Muhammad; hearing their voices, he said: Messenger of Allah, come for prayer, and throw dust in their mouths.

On Marrying a Virgin

In other ahAdIs, the Prophet touches upon the excellence of marrying a virgin. JAbir reports: The Apostle of Allah said: JAbir, have you married I said, yes. He said: A virgin or one previously married I said: with one previously married, whereupon he said: Why did you not marry a virgin with whom you could sport, or who might amuse you and you might amuse her.

Tastahidda

Muhammad also made effective use of what are known in literary criticism as vulgar expressions. Once the Prophet and his party returned from an expedition rather late, and his Companions wanted to hurry to their homes. But the Prophet told them to wait till the woman with dishevelled hair may comb it, and the woman whose husband had been away may get herself clean; and when you enter, you have the enjoyment.

The translator tells us that the Arabic word for get herself clean is tastahidda, which literally means to remove the hairs on the private parts, but it is here used metaphorically in the sense of getting ready for the husbands company.

The Original Sin

Had it not been for Eve, woman would have never acted unfaithfully towards the husband, the Prophet tells us.

Muhammads Marriages

Some incidents relating to the Prophets marriages with SafIyya and Zainab hint Jahsh are mentioned.

Safiyya

Muhammads wars and raids not only fed his coffers, they also swelled his harem. SafIyya, a beautiful girl of seventeen years, was the wife of the chief of a Jewish clan inhabiting Khaibar. Muhammads custom was to make surprise attacks. Khaibar was invaded in the same fashion. Anas narrates: We encountered the people at sunrise when they had come out with their axes, spades and strings driving their cattle along. They shouted in surprise: Muhammad has come along with his force! The Messenger of Allah said: Khaibar shall face destruction. There is even a Quranic verse relating to Muhammads sudden sweep on the valley and the fate of its people: But when it descends [nazala] into the open space, before them evil will be the morning for those who were warned.

In any case, many people were butchered, and many others were taken prisoners. We took Khaibar by force, and there were gathered the prisoners of war, according to Anas. SafIyya, the daughter of Huyayy b. Akhtab, the chief of the Quraiza and al-NazIr, was one of them. Her husband, KinAna, was put to a cruel death.

Anas continues: She first fell to the lot of Dihya in the spoils of war. (Incidentally, Dihya was strikingly handsome. Muhammad used to see Gabriel in his form.) But Anas adds that people praised her in the presence of Allahs Messenger and said: We have not seen the like of her among the captives of war. Muhammad took her away from Dihya, Gabriel or no Gabriel, and even took her to his bed the same night her husband was killed, in violation of his own command, which enjoined the believers to wait until the beginning of the next menstrual cycle in their captive women.

Rihana and Juwairiya

SafIyya was no exception. Many other women, among them RIhAna and JuwairIya, were taken in and treated as part of the war booty. RIhAna was a Jewish girl of the BanU Quraizah. After her husband was beheaded in cold blood along with eight hundred other male members of her tribe in the genocide at Medina, Muhammad kept her as his concubine. We shall touch upon this massacre again in our discussion of jihAd.

JuwairIya, another of these unfortunate girls, was the daughter of the chief of the Banul Mustaliq. She was captured in the fifth or sixth year of the Hijra along with two hundred other women. The Messenger of Allah made a raid upon BanU Mustaliq while they were unaware and their cattle were having a drink at the water. He killed those who fought and imprisoned others. On that very day, he captured JuwairIya bint al-HAris.

In the division of the booty, she fell to the lot of SAbit ibn Qays. He set her ransom price at nine ounces of gold, beyond the power of her relatives to pay. Aishas reaction when she saw this beautiful girl being led into the presence of Muhammad is recounted in these words: As soon as I saw her at the door of my room, I detested her, for I knew that he [Muhammad] would see her as I saw her. And indeed, when Muhammad saw JuwairIya he paid her ransom and took her for his wife. JuwairIya was at that time about twenty, and she became the seventh wife of the Prophet. The whole story is given by Ibn IshAq, the Prophets biographer.

There was another girl, named Zainab, again Jewish, who had seen her father, husband, and uncle killed. She poisoned the roasted lamb she was ordered to prepare for Muhammad. Suspecting something wrong, Muhammad spat out the very first morsel. He was saved, and she was immediately put to death, according to some authorities.

Zainab bint Jahsh

Here we shall mention another Zainab, whose affair was not cruel but scandalous. She was the wife of Muhammads adopted son, Zaid, and therefore, in the eyes of the Arabs, as good as his own daughter-in-law. Muhammad went to her house when her husband was away, saw her in a state of seminudeness, and was aroused. When Zaid heard about it, he offered to divorce her, but Muhammad, fearing a public scandal, told him to keep his wife for himself.

At this point Allah spoke and decided the matter. He chided Muhammad for telling Zaid, Retain thou in wedlock thy wife, and for hiding in his heart that which God was about to make manifest. Allah told Muhammad: Thou feared the people, but it is more fitting that thou should fear God; and He revealed His plan, present and future, to Muhammad thus: We joined her in marriage to thee, in order that in future there may be no difficulty to the believers in the matter of marriage with the wives of their adopted sons. He now also addressed Himself to the Muslims of all generations: It is not fitting for a believer, man or woman, when a matter has been decided by God and His Apostle to have any option about their decision. If anyone disobeys God and His Apostle, he is indeed clearly on a wrong path.

Thus reassured, Muhammad made Zaid himself go to his wife with his marriage proposal. Allahs Messenger said to Zaid to make a mention to her about him. The marriage ordered from above was celebrated with unusual festivity. Allahs Messenger gave no better wedding feast than the one he did on the occasion of his marriage with Zainab.

Divorce (Talaq)

TalAq literally means undoing the knot, but in Islamic law, it now means annulment of marriage by the pronouncement of certain words.

The marriage and divorce laws of Islam derive from the Prophets own practice and pronouncements. According to the Shias, the Prophet had twenty-two wives, two of whom were bondswomen; but that was a special divine dispensation for him alone. The other believers are allowed only four wives at a time, exclusive of slave concubines, who do not count. The total of four wives at one time cannot be exceeded, but individual wives can be replaced through talAq. The procedure is not difficult; once a man says the word talAq three times, the divorce becomes operative.

Yet there are certain restrictions. For example, it is forbidden to divorce a woman during her menstrual period. Abdullah, the son of Umar, the future KhalIfa, divorced his wife while she was in a state of menses. When Umar mentioned this to Muhammad, the latter ordered: He [Abdullah] should take her back, and when she is pure he may divorce her.

Three Pronouncements

The word talAq has to be pronounced three times before talAq becomes operative. But opinions differ as to whether it has to be pronounced on three separate occasions, after three successive menses, or whether three times at one sitting is enough. According to the translator, traditions are not lacking in which three pronouncements at one sitting were held as irrevocable divorce even during the time of the prophet.

With such easy conditions of divorce, the limitation of wives to four at a time was not unduly self-denying. Wives were constantly replaced. Abdar-RahmAn, a senior Companion, adviser, and friend of Muhammad, Abu Bakr, and Umar, had children by sixteen wives besides those from concubines. Somewhat later, Hasan, the son of AlI and grandson of Muhammad, married seventy-some say ninety-times. People in his day called him the Divorcer.

It is no wonder that women had no sanctity. Wives could be easily disposed of by gifting or divorce. For example, on emigrating to Medina, Abdar-RahmAn was adopted by Sad, son of RabI, as a brother in faith-in accordance with the arrangement made by Muhammad to join every Emigrant to an ansAr in brotherhood. As they sat together at supper, the host said: Behold my two wives and choose one you like the best. One wife was divorced on the spot and gifted away.

Zihar and Ila

There were two other forms of separation not amounting to legal divorce prevalent among the Arabs at the time of Muhammad: zihAr and IlA. In zihAr, the husband vowed that his wife would be unto him as the back (zahr) of his mother and then stayed away from her for a specified period. This was a customary vow of abstinence among the Arabs, and according to some traditions, Muslims also took it during the period of fasting. The purpose of the abstinence could be penitential or devotional, or the vow might be taken in a fit of anger. The same formula was also used as a form of divorce. Muhammad condemned divorce by zihAr and allowed a husband who had taken the vow to go back to his wife. The broken vow could be expiated by making a kaffArah (literally, that which covers a sin), which in this case is either a fast for two months or the feeding of sixty poor men and women.

There was another form of separation called IlA (to swear). In this form, the husband swore an oath to abstain from sexual intercourse with his wife. In the pre-Islamic period, the Arabs regarded IlA as a form of divorce, but it did not fully dissolve the marriage. The oath of IlA was sometimes taken to penalize the wife and extort ransom from her. Muhammad forbade this. A man who had taken such a vow was to go back to his wife without any blame to himself; if not, the marriage was ipso facto legally dissolved at the end of four months. The broken vow could be expiated. When a man declares his wife as unlawful for himself that is an oath which must be atoned.... There is in the Messenger of Allah a model pattern for you. In due course, the two forms of separation died away in Islam.

Muhammads Separation from His Wives

IlA is a temporary separation from ones wife. In this sense of the term, the believers are indeed fortunate in having a model pattern in an example provided by the Prophet.

Muhammad himself had to undergo separation from his wives for a period which lasted twenty-nine days. The SahIh Muslim narrates this incident in several ahAdIs; but before we take them up, let us provide some background information.

In visiting his numerous wives, Muhammad observed a rough-and-ready rule of rotation. In fact, the days in his life were known by the name of the wife he was visiting. One day Muhammad was supposed to be with Hafza, but instead she found him with Mary, the beautiful Coptic concubine. Hafza was furious. In my room, on my day and in my own bed, she shouted. Muhammad, trying to pacify her, promised never to visit Mary again, but he wanted Hafza to keep the incident a secret.

Hafza, however, told Aisha, and very soon everybody knew about it. Muhammads Quraish wives detested Mary and were jealous of the servile wretch, who had even given Muhammad a son. Soon the harem was filled with gossip, excitement, and jeering. Muhammad was very angry, and he told his wives that he would have nothing to do with them. He separated himself from them, and soon the news was afloat that he was divorcing them all. In fact, in the eyes of the believers this rumor was more newsworthy and significant than the reports that Medina was soon to be attacked by GhassAn (the Arab auxiliaries of Byzantium).

In a long hadIs, Umar b. al-KhattAb (Hafzas father) reports: When Allahs Apostle kept himself away from his wives, I entered the mosque, and found the people striking the ground with pebbles and saying: Allahs Messenger has divorced his wives. Umar decided to find out what was actually happening. First he asked Aisha if she had gone to the extent of giving trouble to Allahs Messenger. Aisha told him to mind his own business. I have nothing to do with you. You should look to your own receptacle [Hafza]. Umar next sought out Hafza and chided her. You know that Allahs Messenger does not love you, and had I not been your father he would have divorced you, he told her. She wept bitterly.

Then Umar sought permission to be admitted into the presence of Muhammad. The request was disregarded, but he insisted. O RahAb, seek permission for me from Allahs Messenger. I think that Allahs Messenger is under the impression that I have come for the sake of Hafza. By Allah, if Allahs Messenger would command me to strike her neck, I would certainly do that, he told RahAb, Muhammads doorman. He was admitted.

As Umar entered, he saw the signs of anger on his [Muhammads] face, so he tried to calm him down. He told him how we the people of Quraish had domination over women but when we came to Medina we found people whom their women dominated. So our women began to learn from their women.

He also told him: Messenger of Allah, what trouble do you feel from your wives, and if you had divorced them, verily Allah is with you, His angels, Gabriel, Mikail, I and Abu Bakr and the believers are with you.

Muhammad relaxed. I went on talking to him until the signs of anger disappeared on his face... and he laughed, Umar narrates. In this new mood, the famous verses descended on the Prophet, freeing him from his oath respecting Mary, threatening his wives with divorce, and incorporating Umars asSurance that all the angels and believers supported him: O Prophet! said Allah. Why do you prohibit thyself what God has made lawful to you, craving to please thy wives... Allah has already ordained for you the dissolution of your oaths. Allah also told the Prophets wives in no uncertain terms that his Lord if he divorces you will give him in exchange wives better than you. Allah warned them, particularly Aisha and Hafza, in the following terms: If ye both turn repentant unto God,-for your hearts have swerved!-but if you back each other up against him, verily, Allah, He is the sovereign; and Gabriel, and the righteous of the believers, and the angels after that will back him up. Allah also told them that if they misbehaved, being the Prophets wives would avail them nothing on the Day of

Judgment. God strikes out a parable to those who misbelieve: the wife of Noah and the wife of Lot; they were under two of our righteous servants, but they betrayed them: and they availed them nothing against God; and it was said, Enter the Fire with those who enter.

The matter blew over, and they became his wives again. The Holy Prophet had taken an oath of remaining away from them [his wives] for a month, and by now only twenty-nine days had passed, [but] he visited them. Aisha mischievously reminded the Prophet that it was not yet one month but only twenty-nine days, to which Muhammad replied: At times, the month consists of twenty-nine days.

Now Umar stood at the door of the mosque and called out at the top of his voice: The Messenger of Allah has not divorced his wives. A verse chiding his followers for so readily believing in rumors also descended on Muhammad: And if any matter pertaining to peace or alarm comes within their ken, they broadcast it. But if they had only referred it to the Apostle, or to those charged with authority among them, the proper investigators would indeed know it.

Option of Divorce Different from Divorce

It seems there were other occasions of domestic discord, some of them centering round money. These must have occurred in the early days at Medina, when Muhammad lacked funds. Once Abu Bakr and Umar went to Muhammad and found him sitting sad and silent with his wives around him. He told the two fathers: They [his wives and their daughters] are around me as you see, asking for extra money. Then Abu Bakr got up, went to Aisha and slapped her on the neck; and Umar stood up and slapped Hafza.

On this occasion, the Prophet also gave his wives the option of a goodly departure if they cared more for this world and its adornments than for Allah and His Apostle and the abode of the Hereafter. The wives chose the latter.

The moral of these ahAdIs as drawn by the translator is that mere giving option to women to divorce does not make the divorce effective, but when it is really intended.

No Maintenance Allowance for a Divorcee

FAtima hint Quais was divorced by her husband when he was away from home. She was very angry and went to Muhammad, who told her: There is no lodging and maintenance allowance for a woman who has been given irrevocable divorce. But he mercifully helped her to find another husband. She had two suitors, Abu Jahm and MuAwiya. Muhammad advised against them both, for the former did not put down his staff from his shoulder (i.e., he beat his wives), and the latter was poor. In their place, he proposed the name of UsAma b. Zaid, the son of his slave and adopted son, Zaid.

Later on a more generous sentiment prevailed. Umar ruled that husbands should provide their divorced wives with a maintenance allowance during the period of idda on the ground that the true purpose of the Prophets words had been misunderstood by FAtima, a mere woman. We cannot abandon the Book of Allah and the Sunnah of our Apostle for the words of a woman.

Idda is a period of waiting during which a woman cannot remarry. It normally lasts four months and ten days but ends sooner if the woman gives birth to a child. Once idda has ended, the woman can contract another marriage.

Having to provide an allowance for four months at the most was not very difficult. Thus, since husbands had almost no fear of any future burden, and could get rid of their wives so easily, the threat of divorce hung heavily on Muslim women.

Mourning

A woman whose husband dies must abstain from all adornment during the idda period, but mourning for other relatives should not last for more than three days. Abu SufyAn, the father of Umm HabIba, one of Muhammads wives, died. She sent for some perfume and rubbed it on her cheeks, observing: By Allah, I need no perfume but for the fact that I heard Allahs Messenger say, It is not permissible for a woman believing in Allah and the Hereafter to mourn for the dead beyond three days, but in the case of the death of the husband it is permissible for four months and ten days.

Lian (Invoking Curse)

If a man finds his wife in adultery, he cannot kill the adulterous man, for that is forbidden; nor can he make an accusation against his wife, for unless he has four witnesses, he receives eighty stripes for making a false accusation against the chastity of a woman. But if the witnesses are not always forthcoming, which is most likely in such a case, what should he do This was the dilemma confronting the believers. An ansAr posed the problem to Muhammad: If a person finds his woman along with a man, and if he speaks about it, you would lash him; and if he kills, you will kill him, and if he keeps quiet, he shall have to consume anger. Muhammad supplicated God: Allah, solve this problem. And a verse descended on him which gives us the practice of liAn. The word literally means oath, but technically it stands for that particular form of oath which brings about separation between husband and wife with the help of four oaths and one curse. A husbands solitary evidence can be accepted if he bears witness four times with an oath by Allah that he is solemnly telling the truth and then invokes the curse of Allah upon himself if he is lying. Similarly, the wife can solemnly deny the accusation four times and then invoke the wrath of Allah on herself if her accuser is telling the truth. One of them must be lying, but this closes the chapter, and they are wife and husband no more.

Emancipating a Slave

For some unexplained reason, a few chapters at the end of the book dealing with marriage and divorce are on slaves. This may be due to a faulty method of classification, or it may be that emancipating a slave was considered a form of talAq, which literally means freeing or undoing the knot; or it may be that the subject really belongs to the next book, which is on business transactions-a slave, after all, was no more than a chattel.

Modern Muslim writers trying to boost Islam as a humane ideology make much of the sayings of Muhammad on the emancipation (itq) of slaves. But the fact remains that Muhammad, by introducing the concept of religious war and by denying human rights to non-Muslims, sanctioned slavery on an unprecedented scale. Pre-Islamic Arabs, even in their wildest dreams, never imagined that the institution of slavery could take on such massive proportions. Zubair, a close companion of the Prophet, owned one thousand slaves when he died. The Prophet himself possessed at least fifty-nine slaves at one stage or another, besides thirty-eight servants, both male and female. Mirkhond, the Prophets fifteenth-century biographer, names them all in his Rauzat-us-Safa. The fact is that slavery, tribute, and booty became the main props of the new Arab aristocracy. Slaves continued to suffer under the same old disabilities. They were the property of their master (saiyid), who could dispose of them as he liked, selling them, gifting them away, hiring them out, lending them, mortgaging them. Slaves had no property rights. Whatever they acquired became the property of their masters. The master had the right to live in concubinage with his female slaves if they confessed Islam or belonged to the People of the Book. The Quran (Sura) permitted this. Slavery was interwoven with the Islamic laws of sale, inheritance, and marriage. And though the slaves fought for their Muslim masters, they were not entitled to the spoils of war according to Muslim religious law.

Emancipation of Slaves

The emancipation of slaves was not unknown in pre-Islamic Arabia. Slaves could gain their freedom in several ways. One way, and a very common one, of course, was that they were ransomed by their relatives. Another was when a master granted his slave a free and unconditional emancipation (itq). There were two other forms of emancipation: tadbir and kitabah. In the first, the master declared that on his death his slaves would be free. In the second, slaves who were not ransomed by their relatives obtained their masters permission to earn their ransom by work.

We have already seen how HakIm b. HizAm freed one hundred slaves even before he became a Muslim. We have also observed that it was an old custom among the Arabs of more pious disposition to will that their slaves would be freed at their death, a practice which was opposed in some cases by Muhammad because he did not want such emancipations to take place at the expense of the heirs and relatives of the masters. On the whole, however, Muhammads response to the practice was positive, but this did not make him into a Messiah of the slaves. On the other hand, he saw the time when the meek and the lowly would inherit the earth as a portent of the approaching end of the world. When the slave-girl will give birth to her master, when the naked, barefooted would become the chiefs of the people-these are some of the signs of Doom, according to him.

To Muhammad, the freeing of a slave was an act of charity on the part of the master, not a matter of justice. In any case, a slave should not seek his emancipation by running away. The slave who fled from his master committed an act of infidelity so long as he would not return to him, says Muhammad.

Which Slaves Deserve Emancipation

Only a believing slave deserves freedom. Someone once slapped his maid-slave in anger and then, in contrition, wanted to free her. When Muhammad was consulted, he said: Bring her to me. She was brought. Muhammad asked her: Where is Allah She replied: He is in the heaven. Muhammad asked: Who am I Thou art the Messenger of Allah, she answered. Muhammad gave his verdict: Grant her freedom, she is a believing woman.

Thus there is merit in freeing a slave. A Muslim who emancipates a Muslim [slave], Allah will save from Fire every limb of his for every limb of the slave, even his private parts for his.

One could also emancipate a jointly owned slave to the extent of ones share in him. For the rest a fair price for the slave was to be fixed, and the slave will be required to work to pay for his freedom, but must not be overburdened.

Who Inherits a Slaves Property

Even if a slaves person was freed, any property he might have or come to have was inherited by the emancipator. Aisha was ready to help a slave-girl, BarIra, to purchase her freedom on the condition that I shall have the right in your inheritance. But the owner, though ready to free her for cash money, wanted to retain the right of inheritance for himself. Muhammad gave his judgment in favor of Aisha: Buy her, and emancipate her, for the right of inheritance vests with one who emancipates. Muhammad then admonished: What has happened to the people that they lay down conditions which are not found in the Book of Allah.

Other Disabilities

A freed slave is subjected to several other disabilities. He cannot seek any new alliance, nor can he offer himself as an ally without the permission of his former owner. One who took the freed slave as an ally without the consent of his previous master, there is upon him the curse of Allah and that of His angels and that of the whole mankind.

Slavery Has its Own Reward

Beyond all that may be said or done, the condition of a slave is no great evil. It has its own reward. When a slave looks to the welfare of his master and worships Allah well, he has two rewards for him.

Proper Peading for Muhammads Descendants

We close the Book of Marriage and Divorce by quoting one of the very last ahAdIs. It is on a different subject but interesting. AlI, the Prophets son-in-law, says: He who thinks that we [the members of the Prophets family] read anything else besides the book, of Allah and the SahIfa [a small book or pamphlet that was tied to the scabbard of his sword] tells a lie. This SahIfa contains problems pertaining to the ages of the camels and the recompense of injuries, and it also records the words of the prophet.... He who innovates or gives protection to an innovator, there is a curse of Allah and that of his angels and that of the whole humanity upon him.

Speculation Forbidden

Muhammad forbids speculation. He who buys food grains should not sell it until he has taken possession of it. During

Muhammads own lifetime, as the control of Arabia passed into his hands, his injunctions became state policy. SAlim b. Abdullah reports: I saw people being beaten during the lifetime of Allahs Messenger in case they bought the food grain in bulk and then sold them at that spot before taking it to their places.

Because of their speculative nature, Muhammad also disallowed futures transactions. He forbade selling ahead for years and selling of fruits before they become ripe. Transactions with the help of documents (probably the hundi or bill of exchange system), were also made unlawful. The injunction was implemented with the help of the police. I saw the sentinels snatching these documents from the people, reports SulaimAn.

Outbidding

Muhammad also forbade outbidding. A person should not enter into a transaction when his brother is already making a transaction and he should not make a proposal of marriage when his brother has already made a proposal except when he gives permission. He also forbade brokerage, the selling of goods by a townsman on behalf of a man of the desert.

Contracts

Muhmmad recognized the contract system. Unless otherwise laid down in the contract, he who buys a tree after it has been fecunded, its fruits belongs to one who sells it.... and he who buys a slave, his property belongs to one who sells him.

Tenancy

Muhammad also forbade the leasing of land. He who has land should cultivate it, but if he does not find it possible, he should lend it to his Muslim brother, but he should not accept rent from him.

The Prophet as a Landlord

Several ahAdIs show that Muhammads own business practices could be sharp. Abdullah, the son of Umar, reports that when Khaibar had been conquered, it came under the sway of Allah, that of his Messenger and that of the Muslims.

Muhammad made an agreement with the Jews of Khaibar that they could retain the date-palms and the land on the condition that they worked them with their own wealth (seeds, implements) and gave half of the yield to Allahs Messenger. Out of this half, Allahs Apostle got the fifth part, and the rest was distributed. This lends credence to the common observation that those who control the funds, whether in the name of Allah or the state or the poor, are apt to spend them first on themselves.

These acquisitions enabled Muhammad to give each of his wives wasqs (wasq = about English pounds), wasqs of dates, and wasqs of barley per year. When Umar became the KhalIfa he distributed the land and gave the wives of Allahs Apostle the option of taking the land or the yearly wasqs. Their reactions to this offer differed. Aisha and Hafza, two wives of the Prophet, opted for land and water.

Improper Earnings

Muhammad also forbade the charging of price of the dog, and earnings of a prostitute and sweets offered to a Kahin [soothsayer]. He said that the worst earning is the earning of a prostitute, the price of a dog and the earning of a cupper.

Muhammad had a great dislike for dogs. He said: It is your duty to kill the jet-black [dog] having two spots [on the eyes], for it is a devil. Abdullah, Umars son, tells us that the Prophet ordered to kill dogs, and he sent men to the corners of Medina that they should be killed.... and we did not spare any dog that we did not kill. Later on, on representation, an exception was made in the case of dogs meant for hunting and for protecting the herds. With the exception of these dogs, anyone who kept a dog lost two qIrAt [the name of a measure] of reward every day. Muhammad also forbade the sale of wine, carcasses, swine, and idols. May Allah the Exalted and Majestic destroy the Jews; when Allah forbade the use of fat of the carcass for them, they melted it, and then sold it and made use of its price.

Barter Disapproved

In some matters, the Prophet was modern. He disapproved of the barter system and in its place stood for money-exchange.

The collector of the revenues from Khaibar once brought Muhammad some fine dates. Muhammad asked whether all the dates of Khaibar were of such fine quality. The collector said: No. We got one sA [of fine dates] for two sAs [of inferior dates]. Muhammad disapprovingly replied: Dont do that; rather sell the inferior quality of dates for dirhams [money], and then buy the superior quality with the help of dirhams.

Riba

Muhammad also forbade Riba, which includes both usury and interest. He cursed the accepter of interest and its payer, and one who records it, and the two witnesses; and he said: They are all equal.

Though he forbade interest, Muhammad himself sent Abu Bakr to the QainuqA tribe of Medina with a message bidding them to lend to God at good interest, using the very words of the Quran, to lend to God a goodly loan. When they rebuffed him, their fate was sealed, and they were driven away from their homes.

Inheritances, Gifts, and Bequests

The next three books are the Book of Inheritances (al-faraid), the Book of Gifts (al-hibAt), and the Book of Bequests (al-wasIyya). In some ways, they are interrelated. The laws deriving from them are complicated, and we need not go beyond mentioning them here.

Gifts

Anything given as a gift or charity should not be taken back. Umar had donated a horse in the Path of Allah (i.e., for jihAd). He found that the horse was languishing in the hands of the recipient, who was very poor, and considered buying it back. Dont buy it back.... for he who gets back the charity is like a dog which swallows its vomit, Muhammad told him.

Waqf

Muhammad favored waqf, i.e., the dedication of the corpus of a property to Allah. Umar told Muhammad: I have acquired land in Khaibar [the land of the defeated Jews, which had now been conferred on the Companions]. I have never acquired property more valuable for me than this, so what do you command me to do with it Thereupon, Allahs Apostle said: If you like, you may keep the corpus intact and give its produce as sadaqa.... Umar devoted it to the poor, to the nearest kin, and to the emancipation of slaves, and in the way of Allah and guests.

Two-third for Legal Heirs

The estate of a deceased person can be distributed after certain obligations, such as funeral expenses and debts incurred by the deceased, have been met. A person who professes a religion other than Islam cannot inherit anything from a Muslim, and vice versa. Another principle of inheritance is that the male is equal of the portion of two females.

Muhammad says that one can will only one-third of ones property; the remaining two-thirds must go to the legal heirs. Muhammad visited Sad b. AbI WaqqAs, on his deathbed. Sad had only one daughter. He wanted to know whether he could will two-thirds or half of his property in sadaqa (charity). The Prophet replied: Give one third, and that is quite enough. To leave your heirs rich is better than to leave them poor, begging from people.

Debts

Muhammad was scrupulous about the debts of the deceased. That was the first charge on the property of a deceased person after the funeral expenses. In cases where the property was not sufficient to meet the debt obligations, money was raised through contributions. But when Muhammad became rich through conquest, he himself met these charges. When Allah opened the gateways of victory for him, he said: I am nearer to the believers than themselves, so if anyone dies leaving a debt, its payment is my responsibility, and if anyone leaves a property it goes to his heirs.

Muhammads Last Will

On a certain Thursday when his illness took a serious turn, Muhammad said: I make a will about three things: Turn out the polytheists from the territory of Arabia; show hospitality to the foreign delegations as I used to do. The third the narrator forgot.

Muhammad also wanted to write a will in his last moments. Come, I may write for you a document; you would not go astray after that, he said, asking for writing materials. But Umar, who was present, said that the people already had the Quran. The Book of Allah is sufficient for us, he asserted, and thus it was unnecessary to tax Muhammad in his critical state. When those who were gathered around his bed then began to argue among themselves, Muhammad told them to get up and go away.

Umar might have been moved by genuine concern for the dying man, but the supporters of AlI later claimed that Muhammad in his last will had wanted to appoint AlI as his successor, and that Umar, in league with Abu Bakr, had prevented him from doing so by a dirty trick.

Vows and Oaths

The twelfth and thirteenth books, on vows (al-nazar) and oaths (al-aiman), respectively, can be treated together. Muhammad discourages taking vows, for a vow neither hastens anything nor defers anything. Allah has no need of a mans vows. A man once took a vow to walk on foot to the Kaba, but Muhammad said that Allah is indifferent to his inflicting upon himself chastisement, and commanded him to ride.

Muhammad also forbids believers to swear by LAt or UzzA or by their fathers. Do not swear by idols, nor by your father, says Muhammad. But he allows you to swear by God, something which Jesus forbade. He who has to take an oath, he must take it by Allah or keep quiet, Muhammad says.

Abrogation of an Oath

Allah Himself allowed abrogation of oaths if need be. God has already ordained for you the dissolution of your oaths.

A vow which is in disobedience to Allah or which is taken for un-Islamic ends is not to be fulfilled. Muslim jurists differ as to whether a vow taken during the days of ignorance (i.e., before one embraces Islam) is binding or not. Some hold that such a vow should be fulfilled if it is not against the teachings of Islam.

An oath can be broken, particularly if the oath-taker finds something better to do. He who took an oath, but he found something else better than that, should do that which is better and break his oath, says Muhammad. Some people once asked Muhammad to provide them with mounts. Muhammad swore: By Allah, I cannot provide you a mount. But immediately after they were gone, he called them back and offered them camels to ride. Muhammad explained: So far as I am concerned, by Allah, if He so wills, I would not swear, but if later on, I would see better than it, I would break the vow and expiate it and do that which is better.

The God Willing Clause

If one includes the proviso God willing (InshA Allah) when taking an oath, the vow must be fulfilled. SulaimAn (Solomon) had sixty wives. One day he said, I will certainly have intercourse with them during the night and everyone will give birth to a male child who will all be horsemen and fight in the cause of Allah. But only one of them became pregnant, and she gave birth to a premature child. But if he had said InshA Allah he would have not failed, observes Muhammad. In other ahAdIs about the same story, the number of wives increases from sixty to seventy and then to ninety.

Crime and Punishment (Qasamah, Qisas, Hadud)

The fourteenth, fifteenth, and sixteenth books all relate to the subject of crime: the forms and categories of crime, the procedure of investigating them, and the punishments resultant from having committed them.

Muslim fiqh (law) divides punishment into three heads: hadd, qisAs, and tazIr. Hadd (pl. HadUd) comprises punishments that are prescribed and defined in the Quran and the HadIs. These include stoning to death (rajm) for adultery (zinA); one hundred lashes for fornication; eighty lashes for slandering an honorable woman (husun), i.e., accusing her of adultery; death for apostatizing from Islam (irtidAd); eighty lashes for drinking wine (shurb); cutting off the right hand for theft (sariqah, Quran); cutting off of feet and hands for highway robbery; and death by sword or crucifixion for robbery accompanied by murder. The law also permits qisAs, or retaliation. It is permitted only in cases where someone has deliberately and unjustly wounded, mutilated, or killed another, and only if the injured and the guilty hold the same status. As slaves and unbelievers are inferior in status to Muslims, they are not entitled to qisAs according to most Muslim faqIhs (jurists).

In cases of murder, the right of revenge belongs to the victims heir. But the heir can forgo this right and accept the blood-price (diyah) in exchange. For the death of a woman, only half of the blood-price is due. The same applies to the death of a Jew or a Christian, but according to one school, only one-third is permissible in such cases. If a slave is killed, his heirs are not entitled to qisAs and indemnity; but since a slave is a piece of property, his owner must be compensated with his full value. The Muslim law on crime and punishment is quite complicated. Though the Quran gives the broad outline, the HadIs alone provides a living source and image.

Qasamah

The fourteenth book is the Book of Oaths (al-qasAmah). QasAmah literally means taking an oath, but in the terminology of the sharIah, it is an oath of a particular type and taken under particular conditions. For example, when a man is found slain, and the identity of his slayer is unknown, fifty persons from the nearest district take an oath that they neither killed the man nor knew who did it. This establishes their innocence.

This was apparently the practice among the pre-Islamic Arabs, and Muhammad adopted it. Once a Muslim was found slain. His relatives accused the neighboring Jews. Muhammad told them: Let fifty persons among you take oath for leveling the charge of murder against a person among them, and he would be surrendered to you. They declined to take the oath since they had not witnessed the murder. Then Muhammad told them that the Jews will exonerate themselves by fifty of them taking this oath. They replied: Allahs Messenger, how can we accept the oath of unbelieving people Then Muhammad paid the bloodwite of one hundred camels for the slain man out of his own funds. Another hadIs specifically tells us that Allahs Messenger retained the practice of QasAma as it was in the pre-Islamic days.

Death Penalty for Apostasy Rebellion

One can accept Islam freely, but one cannot give it up with the same freedom. The punishment for apostasy-for giving up Islam-is death, though not by burning. Once a group of men apostatized from Islam. Ali burnt them to death. When Ibn AbbAs heard about it, he said: If I had been in his place, I would have put them to sword for I have heard the apostle say, Kill an apostate but do not burn him for Fire is Allahs agency for punishing the sinners. Eight men of the tribe of Ukl became Muslims and emigrated to Medina. The climate of Medina did not suit them. Muhammad allowed them to go to the camels of sadaqa and drink their milk and urine (urine was considered curative). Away from the control of the Prophet, they killed the shepherds, took the camels and turned away from Islam.

The Prophet sent twenty ansArs after them with an expert tracker who could follow their footprints. The apostates were brought back. He [the Holy Prophet] got their hands cut off, and their feet, and put out their eyes, and threw them on the stony ground until they died. Another hadIs adds that while on the stony ground they were asking for water, but they were not given water. The translator gives us the verse from the Quran according to which these men were punished: The just recompense for those who wage war against Allah and His Messenger and strive to make mischief in the land is that they should be murdered, or crucified or their hands and their feet should be cut off on opposite sides, or they should be exiled.

Qisas

Qisas literally means tracking the footsteps of an enemy; but technically, in Muslim law, it is retaliatory punishment, an eye for an eye. It is the lex talionis of the Mosaic law.

A Jew smashed the head of an ansar girl and she died. Muhammad commanded that his head be crushed between two stones. But in another case, which involved the sister of one of the Companions, bloodwite was allowed. She had broken someones teeth. When the case was brought to Muhammad, he told her that QisAs [retaliation] was a command prescribed in the Book of Allah. She made urgent pleas and was allowed to go free after paying a money compensation to the victims next of kin.

A Muslim and the Death Penalty

A Muslim who bears testimony to the fact that there is no God but Allah, and I [Muhammad] am the Messenger of Allah, can be punished with the death penalty only if he is a married adulterer, or if he has killed someone (i.e., someone who is a Muslim, according to many jurists), or if he is a deserter from Islam. The translator tells us that there is almost a consensus of opinion among the jurists that apostasy from Islam must be punished with death. Those who think such a punishment is barbarous should read the translators justification and rationale for it.

Diyat (Indemnity)

Muhammad retained the old Arab practice of bloodwite. Thus, when a woman struck her pregnant co-wife with a tent-pole, causing her to have a miscarriage, he fixed a male or female slave of best quality as the indemnity for what was in her womb.

An eloquent relative of the woman pleaded for the cancellation of the indemnity, arguing: Should we pay indemnity for one who neither ate, nor made any noise, who was just Eke a nonentity Muhammad brushed aside his objection, saying that the man was merely talking rhymed phrases like the rhymed phrases of desert Arabs.

Hadud

Hadud, the penal law of Islam, is dealt with in the fifteenth book. The ahAdIs in this book relate to measures of punishment defined either in the Quran or in the Sunnah. The punishments include the amputation of limbs for theft and simple robbery; stoning to death for adultery; a hundred stripes for fornication; eighty stripes for falsely accusing a married woman, and also for drinking wine; and death for apostasy, as we have already seen.

Punisment for Theft

Aisha reports that Allahs Messenger cut off the hands of a thief for a quarter of dInAr and upwards. Abu Huraira reports the Prophet as saying: Let there be the curse of Allah upon the thief who steals an egg and his hand is cut off, and steals a rope and his hand is cut off. The HadIs merely confirms the Quran, which also prescribes: And as for the man who steals and the woman who steals, cut off their hand as a punishment for what they have done, an exemplary punishment from Allah, and Allah is Mighty and Wise. The translator, in a long two-page note, tells us that it is against the background of this social security scheme envisaged by Islam that the Quran imposes the severe sentence of hand-cutting as deterrent punishment for theft.

Aisha reports a similar case. At the time of the victorious expedition to Mecca, a woman committed some theft. Although UsAma b. Zaid, the beloved of Muhammad, interceded in her behalf, her hand was cut off. Hers was a good repentance, Aisha adds. The translator assures us that after the punishment There was a wonderful change in her soul.

Adultery and Fornication

Adultery is severely punished. UbAda reports the Prophet as saying: Receive teaching from me, receive teaching from me. Allah has ordained.... When an unmarried male commits adultery with an unmarried female, they should receive one hundred lashes and banishment for one year. And in case of a married male committing adultery with a married female, they shall receive one hundred lashes and be stoned to death. Umar adds his own emphasis: Verily Allah sent Muhammad with truth and He sent down the Book upon him, and the verse of stoning was included in what was sent down to him. Umar is emphatic because in the Quran there is no punishment for adultery as such, though there is one for the larger category of zinA, which means sexual intercourse between parties not married to each other. In this sense, the term includes adultery as well as fornication. And the punishment provided for both is one hundred stripes and not stoning to death as enjoined in the Sunnah for adultery. The whore and the whoremonger. Flog each of them with a hundred stripes, preaches the Quran.

Umar was apprehensive that people might neglect the Sunnah and appeal to the Book as grounds for a lenient punishment for their adultery. Therefore, he said quite emphatically: I am afraid that, with the lapse of time, the people may forget it and may say, We do not find the punishment of stoning in the Book of Allah, and thus go astray by abandoning this duty prescribed by Allah. Stoning is a duty laid down in Allahs Book for married men and women who commit adultery.

Self-confessed Adultery

There are some gruesome cases. A fellow named MAiz came to Muhammad and told him that he had committed adultery. He repeated his confession four times. Confessing four times stands for the four witnesses who are required to testify in case of adultery. Upon finding that the man was married and also not mad, Muhammad ordered him to be stoned to death. I was one of those who stoned him, says JAbir b. Abdullah, the narrator of this hadIs.

After this incident Muhammad harangued his followers: Behold, as we set out for JihAd in the cause of Allah, one of you lagged behind and shrieked like the bleating of a male goat, and gave a small quantity of milk. By Allah, in case I get hold of him, I shall certainly punish him. The translator explains that by the metaphor of goat and milk, the Prophet means sexual lust and semen. Similarly, a woman of GhAmid, a branch of Azd, came to Muhammad and told him that she had become pregnant as a result of fornication. She was spared till she had given birth to her child.

An ansAr took the responsibility of suckling the infant and she was then stoned to death. Another hadIs tells us how it was done. She was put in a ditch up to her chest and he [Muhammad] commanded people and they stoned her. Other traditions tell us that the Prophet himself cast the first stone.

Fornication and Adultery Joined

In a case of zinA in which one party is married and the other party unmarried, the former is punished for adultery and the latter for fornication. Abu Huraira narrates one such case involving a man and woman belonging to desert tribes. A young bachelor found employment as a servant in a certain household and committed zinA with the masters wife. His father gave one hundred goats and a slave-girl in ransom, but when the case was brought before Muhammad, he judged it according to the Book of Allah. He ordered the slave-girl and the goats to be returned and punished the young man for fornication with one hundred lashes and exile for one year. The woman was punished for adultery. Allahs Messenger made pronouncement about her and she was stoned to death.

Model Persecution

These cases provide a model for all future persecutions. When a woman is to be stoned, a chest-deep hole is dug for her, just as was done in the case of GhamdIya (the woman of GhAmid), so that her nakedness is not exposed and the modesty of the watching multitude is not offended. No such hole need be dug for a man, as no such hole was dug for MAiz, the self-confessed adulterer whose case we have just narrated. The stoning is begun by the witnesses, followed by the imAm or qAzI, and then by the participating believers. But in the case of a self-confessed criminal, the first stone is cast by the imAm or qAzI, following the example of the Prophet in the case of GhamdIya. And then the multitudes follow. The Quran and the Sunnah, in fact, enjoin the believers to both watch and actively participate in the execution. Do not let pity for them take hold of you in Allahs religion.... and let a party of the believers witness their torment, the Quran urges while prescribing punishment for the fornicators.

Mosaic Practice Revived

The punishment of stoning to death (rajm) is Mosaic. The Old Testament prescribes it for adultery and fornication, and also for those who serve other gods. Muhammad retained it for adultery but prescribed death by other means for crimes like apostasy. Among the Jews themselves, by the time of Muhammad, stoning had fallen into disuse. According to one tradition, a Jew and a Jewess who had committed adultery were brought to Muhammad. He asked the Jews what their Torah prescribed for such offenses. The Jews replied: We darken their [the culprits] faces and make them ride on a donkey with their faces turned to the opposite direction. Muhammad said: Bring the Torah. The prescribed punishment was found to be stoning to death. So Allahs Messenger pronounced judgment about both of them and they were stoned, says Abdullah, the son of Umar. I was one of those who stoned them, and I saw him [the Jew] protecting her [the Jewess] with his body, he adds. Another hadIs gives more details about the same incident. The Jews sent the two accused to Muhammad, telling their chiefs: Go to Muhammad; if he commands you to blacken the face and award flogging as punishment, then accept it; but if he gives verdict for stoning, then avoid it. Muhammad was grieved at this softening of the Scriptures. But Allah comforted him: O Messenger, the behaviour of those who vie with one another in denying the truth should not grieve you. Allah also told him that they who do not judge in accordance with what Allah has revealed-they are indeed wrongdoers, they are the iniquitous. The man and woman were stoned to death at Muhammads order, and he was happy and thanked Allah: O Allah, I am the first to revive thy command when they had made it dead.

A Ṣlave Adulteress

A more lenient view was taken in cases of adultery involving slave-women. A slave-woman, even if she was married, was not to be stoned to death, and if she was unmarried, she was liable to half the penalty (fifty strokes). If a slave-girl is unprotected (unmarried) and commits adultery, then flog her and if she commits adultery again, then flog her and then sell her even for a rope of hair.

Flogging Could be Postponed

If a woman has just delivered and there is an apprehension that flogging might kill her, she may be spared until she is alright. AlI says: O people, impose the prescribed punishment upon your slaves, those who are married and those not married, for a slave-woman belonging to Allahs Messenger had committed adultery, and he committed me to flog her. But she had recently given birth to a child and I was afraid that if I flogged her I might kill her. So I mentioned that to Allahs Messenger and he said You have done well. The Prophet was a merciful man. On the basis of this hadIs, Muslim jurists conclude that flogging can be spread over several days, depending on the physical condition of the offender; and if he is sick, the flogging can be postponed until he recovers.

Punishment for Drinking

The punishment for drinking is equally harsh. Muhammad prescribed forty stripes with two lashes. So did Abu Bakr, but Umar came and prescribed eighty stripes. A man charged with drinking was brought before UsmAn, the third KhalIfa, and UsmAn ordered AlI to lash him. AlI in turn ordered Hasan and then Abdullah b. Jafar to lash him. While Abdullah was flogging the victim, AlI counted the stripes. When the number forty was reached, AlI said: Stop now. Allahs Messenger gave forty stripes, and Abu Bakr also gave forty stripes, and Umar gave eighty stripes, and all these fall under the category of the Sunnah, but this one [forty stripes] is dearer to me.

Tazir

HadUd punishments are prescribed by the Quran and the HadIs. But there is another class of punishment, called tazIr, in which the judge can use his own discretion. In such cases, none should be given more than ten lashes. But the majority of later Muslim jurists think differently. They hold that the number of stripes is to, be determined on the basis of the enormity of the crime.

Punishment Has its Reward

At the end, Muhammad assures the believer that if he committed a crime, and-upon him is imposed the prescribed punishment and that is carried out, that is his expiation for that sin.

Judicial Decisions

The sixteenth book deals with judicial decisions (aqdiyya). It is small in size and discusses such matters as the qualities of a good judge and a good witness. A judge should not judge between two persons when he is angry. If he does his best and also gives the right judgment, he has two rewards. If he does his best but errs, he still has one reward. The excellent witness is he who produces his evidence before he is asked for it.

According to the Quran, a womans testimony (shahadah) has half the weight of a mans. In a dispute regarding property or debt, the evidence of two men or of one man and two women is required. In cases involving hadUd, the evidence of a woman is not considered at all. Nor is the testimony of Jews, Christians, and unbelievers considered in a strictly Islamic law court.

A few other matters that are not connected with judicial decisions, such as hospitality, are also discussed in this book. Muhammad says that one should show hospitality to guests but wisely adds that hospitality extends for three days, and what is beyond that is Sadaqa [charity].

Crime with Impunity

The Islamic laws on crime and punishment seem to be foolproof and ironclad, but apparently this is not really so. According to some, Maulana Mohammad Matin Hashmis book Islamic HadUd, recently published in Pakistan, is as good as a manual on how to steal without attracting extreme penalties under Islamic law. Hashmi says that the theft of many articles, such as books, birds, and bread, is not covered by Islamic law. Fresh vegetables, fruit and firewood, meat and chicken and musical instruments can be stolen with impunity. Also exempt are bricks, cement, marble, glass, mats, and carpets from mosques, and loaded camels and merchandise from trade centers.

5

Religious Wars

JihAd is a divinely ordained institution in Islam. By many authorities it is counted as one of the pillars of Islam. Theologically, it is an intolerant idea: a tribal god, Allah, trying to be universal through conquest. Historically, it was an imperialist urge masked in religious phraseology.

Three Options

Muhammad told those whom he made chiefs of his raiding par-ties: Fight in the name of Allah and in the way of Allah. Fight against those who disbelieve in Allah. Make a holy war; do not embezzle the spoils.

He also told them to offer their enemies three options or courses of action: Invite them to accept Islam; if they respond to you, accept it from them.... Then invite them to migrate from their lands to the land of MuhAjirs [i.e., Medina; in the early days of Muhammads stay in Medina, living there was a sign of acceptance of Islam and loyalty to Muhammad], and inform them that, if they do so, they shall have all the privileges and obligations of the MuhAjirs.

If they refuse to migrate, tell them that they will have the status of Bedouin Muslims and will be subjected to the Commands of Allah like other Muslims, but they will not get any share from the spoils of war or Fai..... If they refuse to accept Islam, demand from them the JizyA..... If they refuse to pay the tax, seek Allahs help and fight them. Allah, the spoils of war, the jizyA-all beautifully and profitably interwoven.

Raid without Warning

It is not always necessary to give warning or offer options in advance. If need be, this requirement can be waived. Religious con-version is likely to ensue from a military victory followed by pillage and plunder. The Messenger of Allah made a raid upon BanU Mustaliq while they were unaware and their cattle were having a drink at the water. He killed those who fought and imprisoned others. All is fair in love and war, particularly a war fought in the Way of Allah. As the Prophet says, war is a stratagem, or, as some others have translated it, cunning.

Children of the Polytheists

In jihAd, all arms-bearing males of the enemy are killed, but Muhammad disapproved of the killing of women and children. They are generally taken prisoners and then enslaved or sold or released after ransom is exacted. But if they are killed, no song need be made about it. Sab b. JassAma said to Muhammad: Messenger of Allah, we kill the children of polytheists during the night raids. He [Muhammad] said: They are from them.

Justification of Burning Trees

Muhammad surrounded a Jewish tribe called BanU NazIr, residing in the vicinity of al-Madina, and ordered their date-palms to be burnt and cut. Since destroying palm trees was something of a sacrilege in Arabia, this shocked the Arabs. So Allah hastened to speak through Muhammad: Whatever trees you have cut down or left standing on their trunks, it is with the permission of Allah so that he may disgrace the evil-doers.

Fortified by this revelation, Muhammad cut down and burned the celebrated vineyards of the enemy at at-TAif in the eighth year of the Hijra. That was another contribution by Muhammad to the new ethics of war, unknown to the Arabs before.

Spoils of War

The plundering of infidels and polytheists is a central concept in the Muslim religion, and was the linchpin in the economy of the ummah for centuries. Allah made war booty lawful for the Muslims. Eat ye the spoils of war, it is lawful and pure, says the Quran.

One hadIs tells us that the spoils were made lawful especially for the ummah. The spoils of war were not lawful for any people before us. This is because Allah saw our weakness and humility and made them lawful for us.

Division

Essentially, the spoils belong to Allah and His Apostle. They ask thee concerning the spoils of war. Say: The spoils of war are for Allah and the Apostle. But since the mujAhid does not live by Allah alone, and also as a favor and extra incentive, he is given a share in it.

The translator explains: A mujAhid fights to uphold the cause of righteousness and for the supremacy of Islam, and if in this fight he gets a share in the spoils of war, it is an extra favour to him.

Abdullah Yusuf AlI, translator and commentator of the Quran, in commenting on this verse puts the matter still more eloquently. He says that booty taken in a lawful and just war does not belong to any individual. If he fought for such accessory rewards, he fought from wrong motives. It belongs to the Cause, in this case the cause of God, as administered by his Apostle. Any portion given out to individuals are accessory gifts, windfalls from the bounty of the Commander.

A Great Motivating Force

Despite the pious rhetoric, material incentives had to be provided. The lure of plunder was a great motivating force, all the more powerful because of the religious phraseology. In fact, Muhammad fully satisfied this motive and constantly appealed to it. He reminded the believers of how they slew a part [of their enemies] and another part made captive; and how Allah gave them their [enemies] land, and their dwellings, and their property for an inheritance.

In fact, providing opportunities for easy booty was Muhammads way of rewarding his followers. Denying such opportunities to the lukewarm was his way of punishing them. For example, the desert Arabs did not participate in his expedition to Hudaibiyeh, where resistance was expected to be stiff. Muhammad told them that the next time, when it would be easy to win booty, they would say, Permit us to follow you, but he would answer, Ye shall by no means follow us. The recalcitrant should earn their reward the hard way. Allah Himself directed Muhammad to say to the desert Arabs who lagged behind that ye shall be called out against a people given to vehement war.... then if you obey, Allah will give you a goodly hire.

Muhammad was as good as his word. Within a few months, he set out on an expedition against Khaibar, which he took by surprise. The booty was very large, but Muhammad distributed it only among those who had accompanied him on the previous occasion.

Muhammad Accused of Concealing Spoils

The spoils of war were most welcome, but the process of allocating the plunder was rarely easy sailing. The occasions when the spoils were distributed were, in fact, pretty rough. The atmosphere was charged with expectation and excitement, and was full of claims, grievances, recriminations, suspicion, and accusations. Even Muhammad was once accused of concealing spoils (TirmizI, vol. II, hadIs), and supernal intervention had to take place in order to quiet the suspicion. It is not for a prophet to cheat or be false to his trust. If any person is so false, he shall, on the Day of Judgment, restore what he misappropriated, said Allah (.-). Commenting on this verse, the translator of the Glorious Quran, Abdullah Yusuf AlI, assures us that those low suspicions were never believed in by any sensible person, and they have no interest for us now.

The distribution of the booty was always a passionate issue. Ibn IshAq reports that on one such occasion, after the capture of Hunain, Muhammad was mobbed by the men. Divide our spoil of camels and herds among us,' the mujAhids demanded, surrounding Muhammad until they forced him back against a tree and his mantle was tom from him. He cried: Give me back my mantle. I swear by Allah that if I had as many sheep as the trees of Tilham I would distribute them among you. You have not found me niggardly or cowardly or false.

Al-ghanimah and Fai

There are two forms of war gains: al-ghanImah and fai. The first includes spoils which fall to the lot of the Muslims after an armed conflict; the other accrues when the non-Muslims surrender without offering resistance. If you come to a township which has surrendered without a formal war and you stay therein, you have a share [in the form of an award] in [the properties obtained from] it. If a town disobeys Allah and the Messenger [and fights against the Muslims] one-fifth of the booty seized there from is for Allah and His Apostle and the rest is for you.

The Quranic sanction for this principle of the division of the booty is contained in the following verse: Know that of that which you seize as spoils [ghanImah], a fifth-part [khums] belongs to Allah, to His Apostle, his family, the orphans, the poor, the traveller.....

The fai, gains from a war not actively fought, on the other hand, belongs wholly to the Prophet. Along with the khums, it is entirely at his disposal. The very word and the principle of its disposal derive from the Quran: What Allah gives [afaa] to His Apostle of the people of the cities belongs to Allah, His Apostle, his family, orphans, the poor, and the traveller. This is based on the divine principle that all the possessions of the unbelievers must revert to Muhammad and his family and, when they are no more, to the Muslims in general.

In due course, the rules relating to the distribution of booty and the disposal of fai were codified by the various fiqh schools. According to this code, it was unlawful for a Muslim conqueror to leave anything in the hands of the infidels. Such property must be carried away and four-fifths of it distributed among the soldiers. During a retreat, any such property that cannot be carried away, including the cattle, should be destroyed.

From the beginning of Muhammads sojourn in Medina, all prisoners, whether men, women, or children, were regarded as legitimate items of plunder. They were either distributed among the believers as slaves or sold into slavery or held against payment of ransom by their relatives. Thus prisoners were a rich source of revenue. When seventy men were captured in the Battle of Badr, Muhammad consulted Abu Bakr and Umar about their treatment. Abu Bakr took a view that was more economic and also more humane. They are our kith and kin. I think you should release them after getting from them ransom. This will be a source of strength to us against the infidels, he advised. But Umar took a view that was more theological and also more cruel. He advised that they should be put to death, for they were leaders of the disbelievers and veterans amongst them. The economic view prevailed, at least in this case.

A Muslim chief who conquered a territory was at liberty to leave the land in the possession of the conquered, provided that they paid tribute and became tenants on their own land. This provision was supported by Muhammads own example. When the Jews of Khaibar were defeated, they were allowed for some time to continue cultivating their land on the payment of half the harvest. The chief was also at liberty to distribute the land among his soldiers, but more often this was not done. The land was considered fai and declared to be part of the public domain. It was used in the interest of the whole Muslim community (for the payment of troops and officers, and for the building of bridges, forts, and mosques), and kept as a permanent source of income for future generations.

Another imposition, called jizyA, also belongs to the fai. It was a poll tax levied on all unbelievers of certain categories and on payment of this tax they were allowed freedom in the exercise of their faith. At first this benefit was limited to the Jews and Christians, but later on, as the Muslim empire grew, it was extended to other subject peoples. These peoples were called zimmIs, responsibility of the Muslims. Imperialism has the same language in every age.

The institution of jizyA derives from the Quran: Fight those who believe not in God and in the last day, and... those to whom the Book has been brought, until they pay the tribute [jizyA] in abasement. In abasement is an active clause and includes many humiliating provisions. The zimmIs are to carry no weapons; they are not to ride on horseback; they are to wear a special kind of girdle (zunnAr) and are to fasten a piece of colored cloth (ghiyAr)-Jews a yellow one and Christians a blue one-on their clothes to make it easy to distinguish them from Muslims. They are not to build new churches and temples, though they can repair old ones; they cannot engage in public worship; they are not to give offense to the Muslims by ringing church or temple bells; in short, they are not to do anything that would display their infidelity in the face of the tokens of Islam, such as their public prayers and festivals. There are many other disabilities of the same kind.

Main Source of Livelihood

After Muhammad established himself in Medina, the main source of livelihood for his Companions for quite some time was loot from raids on non-Muslim tribes. TirmizI tells us that a goatherd belonging to the BanU SalIm once passed by a group of the Companions of the Apostle. When he greeted them in the Muslim fashion, they said among themselves: This man has saluted us in this way with a view to protect himself. Then they got up and killed him and took away his goats. Muhammad sent out his men to waylay non-Muslim tribes and to make raids on them. He gave the belongings of anyone who was killed to the Muslim who killed him as a sort of encouragement to the Muslims to participate in jihAd, as the translator puts it.

Abu Qatada reports that while accompanying the Prophet on an expedition in the year of the Battle of Hunain, he killed a polytheist enemy and was awarded his belongings. I sold the armour (which was a part of my share of the booty) and brought with the sale proceeds a garden in the street of BanU Salam. This was the first property I acquired after embracing Islam, he says. Umar tells us: The prophet sent an expedition to Najd and I was among the troop. They got a large number of camels as booty. Eleven or twelve camels came to the lot of every fighter and each one of them also got one extra camel. He also tells us that he acquired land in Khaibar that had belonged to the defeated Jews, a property more valuable than anything he had ever possessed. Khaibar was a populous valley inhabited by the Jews. They were raided and captured and their property confiscated.

As the amount of war booty increased, Muhammad and the other Emigrants became rich enough to pay the ansArs for their help and gifts. Anas reports that after Muhammads migration to Medina, a person placed at his [Muhammads] disposal some date-palms... until the lands of Quraiz and NazIr were conquered. Then he began to return to him whatever he had received. So did the others. When the Messenger of Allah had finished the war with the people... the MuhAjirs [Emigrants] returned to the AnsArs [Helpers] all the gifts they had given them.

Muhammads Share

In the distribution of the booty, the Prophet received a fifth of all the spoils taken from the enemy. As a chief, he also had the first choice in everything, whether slaves or women or property. Spoils obtained without a battle went entirely to him. The properties of the exiled BanU NazIr, a Jewish tribe of Medina, were confiscated by Muhammad. He distributed some of them among his Quraish followers, to the exclusion of the ansArs, but kept a large part for himself. As Umar says: The properties abandoned by BanU NazIr were the ones which Allah bestowed upon His Apostle for which no expedition was taken either with cavalry or camel. These properties were particularly meant for the Holy Prophet. He would meet the annual expenditure of his family from the income thereof, and would spend what remained for purchasing horses and weapons as preparation for JihAd.

One plot of land from the confiscated properties Muhammad turned into what is known as the summer garden of Mary, his Coptic slave-wife. He also had seven other gardens in Medina, which according to some were bestowed on him by a Jew named MukhayrIq, but according to others were a portion of the confiscated estates of the BanU NazIr. Similarly, he had properties at Khaibar, part of the spoils that accrued to him when the Jewish community there was defeated.

The Quarrel over Muhammads Properties

After Muhammad died, there was a quarrel over the inheritance of his property. Aisha tells us that Muhammads other wives sent UsmAn, the son-in-law of the Prophet and a future KhalIfa, to Abu Bakr to demand from him their share from the legacy of the Holy Prophet. But, Aisha sided with her fathers faction and not with her co-wives. She told them what Muhammad is supposed to have said: We prophets do not have any heirs; what we leave behind is charity.

It was not much of charity, though, for as Abu Bakr says, the household of the Messenger of Allah will [continue to] live on the income from these properties, but there was no formal transfer of ownership. Instead, the properties were placed under the joint management of AbbAs, the Prophets uncle, and AlI, the Prophets son-in-law. The denial of this property so angered FAtimA, the Prophets daughter, that she never spoke to Abu Bakr again for the rest of her life.

In due course, Abbas and Ali themselves quarreled over the property which they jointly managed. They took their dispute to Umar, who had succeeded Abu Bakr as KhalIfa. Commander of the Faithful, decide between me and this sinful, treacherous, dishonest liar [AlI], petitioned AbbAs.

Raids and Battles

The book refers to many forays, raids, and battles of the Muslims. These are of two kinds, ghazwAt and sariya. A ghazwAt is a military expedition led by the rasUl or imAm himself; a sariya is one led by his appointed lieutenant. The total number of expeditions was eighty-two, two every three months during Muhammads stay in Medina. Twenty-six are the GhazwAt in which the Holy Prophet himself participated and fifty-six are the Sariya. Nine of the twenty-six ghazwAt expeditions were armed conflicts. So Muhammads share of the booty must have been considerable.

There are other traditions too, more or less in confirmation of the above. According to Zaid b. Arqam, the Prophet personally led nineteen expeditions, in seventeen of which the narrator himself participated. According to JAbir b. Abdullah, the number was twenty-one, and he himself participated in nineteen of them. Another narrator participated in seven military expeditions led by the Messenger and nine led by his lieutenants including Abu Bakr and UsAma b. Zaid.

Many battles, not always in the order in which they were fought, are described by name; for example, the Battle of Hunain, the Battle of TAif, the Battle of Badr, the Battle of AhzAb, or as it is popularly known, the Battle of the Ditch, the Battle of Uhud, and the Battle of Khaibar. The conquest of Mecca is also mentioned.

Miracles

In the accounts of these battles, several miracles are mentioned. On many an occasion, angels came and fought on the side of the Muslims. In most of the battles, Muhammads own role was planning and praying. For example, at the Battle of Badr, Muhammad stretched out his hands and supplicated Allah in these words: O Allah, accomplish for me what Thou hast promised to me. O Allah, if this small band of Muslims is destroyed, Thou will not be worshipped on this earth.

People who accompanied the Prophet on these expeditions report several miracles. Ibn Salama tells us that when they arrived at Hudaibiya fourteen hundred in number, they found that the water in the local well was insufficient for such a large company. The Messenger of Allah sat on the brink of the well. Either he prayed or spat into the well. The water welled up. We drank and watered the beasts as well. Another tradition in the same vein is quoted by Mirkhond, author of the Prophets Persian biography. During the Battle of the Ditch, JAbir b. Abdullah slaughtered a young goat and placed its flesh in a pot, then ground one measure of barley into flour and leavened it, and invited Muhammad to a humble repast. To the consternation of JAbir and his family, Muhammad came with the whole army, numbering one thousand men. But Muhammad approached in his holy person the pot and leaven, throwing into each of them some of the saliva of his Kausar-like mouth, and the meat and the loaves sufficed for the whole assembly.

On another occasion, when people failed to respond to Muhammads call to become Muslims, the angel in charge of the mountains greeted the Prophet and said: I am the Angel in charge of the mountains, and thy Lord has sent me to thee.... If thou wishest that I should bring together the two mountains that stand opposite to each other at the extremities of Mecca to crush them in between, I would do that. This was told to Aisha by the Prophet himself.

Expulsion of the Jews and Christians

I will expel the Jews and Christians from the Arabian Peninsula and will not leave any but Muslims, Muhammad declared to Umar.

Abu Huraira reports: We were sitting in the mosque when the Messenger of Allah came and said: Let us go to the Jews. We went out.... The Messenger of Allah called out to them: O ye assembly of Jews, accept Islam and you will be safe. When the answer was unsatisfactory, he told them: You should know that the earth belongs to Allah and His Apostle, and I wish that I should expel you from this land.

Muhammads expulsion plan began with the Jews of Medina and was implemented with great cruelty. He played on their hopes and fears and took them one by one. He first expelled BanU NazIr, and allowed Quraiza to stay on, and granted favour to them until they too fought against him. Then he killed their men, and distributed their women, children and properties among the Muslims.... The Messenger of Allah turned out all the Jews of Medina, BanU QainuqA, and the Jews of BanU HArisa and every other Jew who was in Medina, we are told by Abdullah, the son of Umar.

The Banu Quraiza

The fate of the BanU Quraiza was rather gruesome. Muhammad said that Allah had commanded him to destroy the Quraiza. According to Aisha, the Prophet had hardly laid down his arms after returning from the Battle of the Ditch when Gabriel appeared and told him: You have laid down arms. By God, we havent laid down ours. So march against them. Where

Muhammad asked. Then Gabriel pointed to the BanU Quraiza. So the Messenger of Allah fought against them... they surrendered... those of them who can fight [were] killed, their women and children taken prisoners and their properties distributed among Muslims.

A Quranic verse put Allahs seal on the fate of this tribe of the People of the Book: God did take them down from their strongholds, and cast terror into their hearts; [so that] some ye slew, and some ye made prisoners. And He made you heirs of their lands, their houses, and their goods.

Commanded by Allah through Gabriel, Muhammad approached the fort of the Quraiza, where they had gathered for shelter. He told them: O ye brothers of monkeys and swines, we have arrived, Allah has disgraced you and brought His vengeance upon you. The Apostle besieged them for twenty-five nights until they were sore pressed and God cast terror into their hearts. They surrendered unconditionally and were taken captive. Traditions and the pious biographies of the Prophet tell gleefully and in detail about the fate of the prisoners. We give the story as summarized by W. Muir in his Life of Mahomet.

The men and women were penned up for the night in separate yards.... [they] spent the night in prayer, repeating passages from their scriptures, and exhorting one another in constancy. During the night graves or trenches... were dug in the market-place.... when these were ready in the morning, Mahomet, himself a spectator of the tragedy, gave command that the captives should be brought forth in companies of five and six at a time. Each company was made to sit down by the brink of the trench destined for its grave, and there beheaded. Party after party they were thus led out, and butchered in cold blood, till the whole were slain.... For Zoheir, an aged Jew, who had saved some of his allies of the Bani Aus... SAbit intervened and procured a pardon.... But what hath become of all our chiefs-of KAb, of Huwey, of OzzAl, the son of Samuel asked the old man.... He received to each inquiry the same reply;-they had all been slain already-Then of what use is life to me any longer Leave me not to that bloodthirsty man who has killed that are dear to me in cold blood-But slay me also, I entreat thee. Here take my sword, it is sharp; strike high and hard. SAbit refused, and gave him over to another, who under AlIs orders beheaded the aged man.

Having sated his revenge, and drenched the market-place with the blood of eight hundred victims, and having given command for the earth to be smoothed over their remains, Mahomet returned from the horrid spectacle to solace himself with the charms of RIhAna, whose husband and all whose male relatives had just perished in the massacre. He invited her to be his wife, but she declined, and chose to remain (as, indeed, having refused marriage, she had no alternative) his slave or concubine. She also declined the summons to conversion and continued in the Jewish faith.

The booty was divided into four classes-land, chattels, cattle, and slaves; and Muhammad took a fifth of each. There were (besides little children, who were counted with their mothers) a thousand captives; from his share of these, Mahomet made certain presents to his friends, of female slaves and servants; and then sent the rest of the women and children to be sold among the Bedouin tribes of Najd, in exchange for horses and arms; for he kept steadily in view the advantage of raising around him a body of efficient horses.

The whole story in all its gruesomeness is narrated by Ibn IshAq, TabarI, and Mirkhond, Muhammads biographers. TabarI quotes WAqidI, an earlier biographer, to the effect that Muhammad himself had deep trenches dug up, took his seat there, and AlI and Zubair did the killing in his presence. Ibn HishAm, another biographer, provides some material omitted in the other accounts. One of his stories shows how Muhammad utilized local conflicts to his own advantage. The two most important non-Jewish tribes of Medina were the Aus and the BanU Khazraj. The Quraiza were allied to the Aus, and therefore were not well liked by the BanU Khazraj. Thus, when Muhammad ordered the Jews beheaded, the Khazraj began to cut off their heads with great satisfaction. The Apostle saw that the faces of Khazraj showed pleasure, but there was no such indication on the part of the Aus, and he suspected that that was because of the alliance that had existed between them and

BanU Quraiza. When there were only twelve of them left he gave them over to Aus, assigning one Jew to every two of Aus, saying, Let so-and-so strike him and so-and-so finish him off.

Those who follow the Prophet must become new men with a new conscience and new loyalties. They must be hardened in the difficult school of Islam. They must become participants in its blood-rites. They must become parties to an act which is effective in the measure that it is compromising. A man who still has some integrity is un-safely independent. In any case the followers should not be allowed to feel superior and to refrain from an act simply because they regard it as iniquitous or cruel. They must learn to have a conscience equal to their prescribed part and acts and to be worthy of their new role.

Besides the aged Zoheir, Ibn IshAq and Mirkhond mention another case touching in its bravery. Huyayy b. Akhatab, a Jewish leader, was known affectionately among his people as the grandee of the town, the friend of the destitute and the poor, and the prince of the desert and the sown. He too was brought before Muhammad, with his hands bound to his neck with a rope. Muhammad exultantly told him: O enemy of Allah, at last the Most High and Glorious has given thee into my power, and has made me thy judge. Huyayy replied: I do not blame myself for having borne enmity to thee... but God the most High has given thee victory, and there is no remedy.... He who forsakes God will be forsaken... Gods command is right. A book and a decree, and massacre have been written against the Sons of Israel. Then he sat down, and at a signal from Muhammad, his head was struck off. He had come in a shirt so torn and tattered that it was not worth taking as a spoil. In fact, before dying, he told AlI, his executioner: I beseech thee not to take off my robe from my body.

There is a similar tale about a woman who was beheaded in the same fashion. Aisha says of her, I shall never forget my wonder at her good spirits and loud laughter when all the time she knew that she would be killed.

Muhammads court poets duly celebrated his victory. HassAn sang:

Quraiza met their misfortune

And in humiliation found no helper.

A calamity worse than that which fell BanU al-Nazir befell them

The day that Gods Apostle came to them like a brilliant moon,

With fresh horses bearing horsemen like hawks,

We left them with the blood upon them like a pool They having accomplished nothing.

They lay prostrate with vultures circling round them.

The Conquest of Mecca

Though Muhammad and the Meccans had entered into a ten-year truce, he made secret preparations to invade Mecca. O God, take eyes and ears from Quraish so that we may take them by surprise, he prayed to Allah, and stealthily advanced on Mecca with ten thousand men. Ibn IshAq tells us that when the Apostle reached Marr al-ZaharAn, the Quraish were completely ignorant of the fact and did not even know what he was doing. He took Mecca by surprise.

Muhammad knew how to use men and utilize their psychology. In fighting the Meccans, he gave the pride of place to the ansArs, who were from Medina, and not to the Emigrants, who were themselves Meccans and therefore might be somewhat inhibited. He called the ansArs and said to them: O ye Assembly of AnsArs, do you see the ruffians of the Quraish... When you meet them tomorrow, wipe them out. Abu Huraira adds: Whoever was seen by them that day was put to death. But on representation by Abu SufyAn, Muhammad dealt with them leniently, so much so that the ansArs murmured: After all the man has been swayed by tenderness towards his family and love for his city.

Eventually Muhammad entered the city and destroyed the idols around the Kaba, declaring: Truth has come and falsehood has vanished. Wonderful! To say the least, the sentiment was merely optimistic and lacked true spiritual insight. It takes more than an invading army of crusaders or a demolition squad with sledgehammers to establish the domain of Truth. Truth cannot be ushered in by replacing one godling with another, say Al-lAt with Al-lAh. To win something of the spiritual light requires self-work, self-churning, self-shedding, self-discovery. The enemy on the path is not the multiplicity of god-symbols but the unregenerate heart and the wanderings of a diffused mind, or what the Yogas call the mUdha and the vikshipta consciousness.

Similarly, it is not that easy to get over falsehood according to Hinduism, a more psychological and mystical religion. Spiritual darkness, or falsehood, has a source deep in our being; it is rooted in the dualities of the mind (dvandva), in egoistic life (aham, asmitA), and in a deeper nescience (avidyA). It is easy to demolish stone or copper gods on the altars, but more difficult to demolish false gods enshrined in ones own heart. True, spiritual demolition involves the demolition of the desire-gods and the ego-gods, the demolition of the false gods that reside in conceited theologies, in pretentious revelations and fond beliefs. According to the Yogas, the real difference is not between one god and many gods but between an ordinary mind and an awakened mind. A fixed and fanatic idea of God is worse than a plurality of god-forms. A gentle god-form which exists in harmony with other god-forms is to be preferred to a Leviathan-God, whether Jehovah or Allah.

After the conquest of Mecca, Muhammad declared: No Quraishite will be killed bound hand and foot from this day until the Day of Judgment. But this did not save the Meccans from other forms of killing as sure and disgraceful as this one, and that too at the hands of their fellow Muslims.

Assassination

Assassination, like jihAd, is an extension of a fanatic creed and psychology. Muhammad had at his disposal a band of hatchet men ready to do his bidding. Through them, he got inconvenient elements eliminated, particularly those who questioned his apostolic inspiration and had the ability to put their opposition into poetry and satire. Who will kill Kab. b.

Ashraf He has maligned Allah, the Exalted, and His Messenger, said Muhammad. Volunteered one Muhammad b. Maslama: Messenger of Allah, do you wish that I should kill him The Prophet replied: Yes. Then the assassin sought Muhammads permission to talk to the intended victim as he thought best-even to talk ill of the Prophet in order to win his confidence. The permission was given. Then the assassin, accompanied by some accomplices, went to Kabs house at night. Posing as a disgruntled follower of the Prophet, he lured his intended victim outside. Kabs wife warned: I bear a voice which sounds like the voice of murder. But Kab replied: It is only Muhammad b. Maslama and his foster brother, Abu MAila. When a gentleman is called at night even if to be pierced with a spear, he should respond to the call. He went down and was killed. Very soon, Kabs head was flung at the feet of the Prophet.

Further details are available in various other accounts, such as the Sahih BukhAri, and the biographies of Muhammad by Ibn IshAq and TabarI. Ibn IshAq also quotes from the poems written by Muhammads court poets to celebrate the event. Another Kab, a poet, sang:

Of them Kab was left prostrate there;

Sword in hand we cut him down

By Muhammads order when he sent secretly by night

Kabs brother to go to Kab;

He beguiled him and brought him down with guile.

HassAn b. Sabit, another poet, describes the assassins bold as lions, travelling by night with their light swords, who made the victim taste his death with their deadly swords, seeking victory for the religion of their prophet. Another tradition quoted by Ibn IshAq says that our attack upon Gods enemy cast terror among the Jews, and there was no Jew in Medina who did not fear his life.

Jihad Takes Precedence Over Prayer

Returning from the Battle of AhzAb, Muhammad announced that nobody would say his zuhr prayer (the afternoon prayer, recited when the sun has begun to decline) but in the quarters of the BanU Quraiza, the unlucky victims of his aggression, as we have seen. Some, fearing that the time for the prayer might be over, said the prayer before reaching the street of the BanU Quraiza. Others did not say it at all for fear of losing time and not reaching the spot in time. On learning this, Muhammad did not blame anyone from the two groups.

Help From a Polythist in Jihad

The last hadIs of this book is about a man who approached Muhammad and said: I have come so that I may follow you and get a share from the booty. Muhammad asked him if he believed in Allah and His Messenger. When the man said he did not, Muhammad declined his offer till he corrected his theology..

The translator makes an interesting comment on this hadIs. He says that it apparently contradicts some other ahAdIs from which we learn that the Holy Prophet accepted help offered by non-Muslims in his military campaigns. For example, SafwAn b. Ummaya fought on his side at the Battle of Hunain, and QuzmAn was present on the day of Uhud, and both were polytheists. According to the translator, these two instances go to prove that the help of a non-Muslim can be accepted when it is essential.

Government (Al-Imara)

The eighteenth book is the Book on Government (al-imAra). It is not a treatise on the theory and practice of government as understood today. The spirit and informing principles are very different.

An Islamic state is necessarily a theocracy. The function of a truly Islamic government is not merely to maintain law and order but to enforce the law of sharIah, with which we have been making acquaintance to some extent in these pages. SharIah does not pertain merely to prayer, general morality, zakAt, and pilgrimage; rather, it enters intimately into every detail of the believers life: his modes and manners, food, dress, marriage, and so on. It includes all his beliefs and affairs. God has given a prototype for imitation in Muhammad. We [Allah] put thee [Muhammad] in the right way concerning affairs. The function of an Islamic state is to enforce this model as best it can. Has not Allah sent His apostle with guidance and the religion of Truth, to make it prevail over every other religion.

An Islamic state is totalitarian in the philosophic sense. A closed politics or civics is a necessary corollary of a closed theology. In Islam, the concept of ummah dominates over the concept of man or mankind. So in a Muslim polity, only Muslims have full political rights in any sense of the term; non-Muslims, if they are allowed to exist at all as a result of various exigencies, are zimmIs, second-class citizens.

The Supremacy of the Quraish

At the very beginning, in thirteen ahAdIs, the Book on al-ImAra establishes the supremacy of the Quraish, the tribe to which Muhammad belonged, in all matters, political and intellectual. People are subservient to the Quraish: the Muslims among them being subservient to the Muslims among them, and the disbelievers among them, being subservient to the unbelievers among them, says Muhammad. In another version, people are the followers of Quraish in good as well as evil.

Only a Quraish May be Khalifa

The Caliphate will remain among the Quraish even if only two persons are left on the earth, Muhammad says. This principle has been held very high in the Muslim world, though the Shias limit the office still further to the descendants of Muhammad, and specifically to the branch descended from AlI, the Prophets cousin and son-in-law, and his wife FAtima, the Prophets daughter.

As a result, for six hundred years, though the center of power of Islam shifted from Mecca to Damascus to Baghdad, the Caliphate remained with the Quraish till HalAku, the grandson of Genghis Khan, put to death the last KhalIfa at Baghdad. Later, a shadowy Caliphate, shorn of temporal power yet still Quraish, emerged in Egypt. Then it passed on to the Turkish SultAn UsmAn (A.D), who added to his many titles three others: Protector of the Two Lands (al-HijAz and Syria, the holy lands of Islam), Successor of the Apostle of God, and

Ruler of the Faithful. But the sentiment that the KhalIfa should be a Quraish or at lout an Arab was so strong that the SultAn of Turkey was never given universal recognition by Muslim theologians. The present-day Sauds, helped by petrodollars, may one day revive this idea. At present they are busy laying the first, necessary foundations, strengthening fundamentalism and pan-Islamism, and buying up political support in Muslim countries and among Muslim populations. There can be no Arab Caliphate (a euphemism for Arab imperialism) without Muslim fundamentalism. Muslim fundamentalism feeds pan-Islamism under the Arab aegis.

Thanks to Muhammad, the Arabian Quraish became a most durable caste with not many parallels in history. They were warriors, rulers, financial tycoons, and scholars. A branch of them, the Saiyids, who are supposed to be descendants of the Prophet, are held in very high esteem and their persons are considered sacred.

Rulers

Islamic rulers should be just to the ummah and follow Muhammads sharIah faithfully. O God, who happens to acquire some kind of control over the affairs of my people and is hard upon them-be Thou hard upon him, and he who acquires control over the affairs of my people and is kind to them-be Thou kind to him, Muhammad prays to Allah.

There are other conventional exhortations. A man should not seek a position of authority. An official should not accept gifts, for as we know, gifts are given to the office, not to the officer. A man in charge of sadaqa comes to Muhammad and says: This wealth is for you, and this is a gift presented to me. Muhammad told him: Why didnt you remain in the house of your father and mother to see whether gifts were presented to you or not.

War booty is sacred; it is a religious obligation, but misappropriation of booty is a serious offense. I shouldnt find that any of you should come on the Day of Judgment.... and should appeal to me for help, Muhammad warns misappropriators of booty.

Obedience to Rulers

Closed theologies claiming a perfected revelation and denying a place to mans ever-living reason, and to his moral and spiritual sense, have to invoke God at every step; but they end by establishing the tyranny of men. Muhammad establishes the following chain of command: Whoso obeys the commander [appointed by me] obeys me, and whoso disobeys the commander disobeys me. Allah Himself enjoins this chain. O you who believe, obey Allah, His Apostle, and those in authority from amongst you. Some exceptions are mentioned. It is obligatory upon a Muslim that he should listen to the ruler appointed over him and obey him whether he likes it or not, except that he is ordered to do a sinful thing. This is a big loophole which was fully used. But other ahAdIs try to fill this gap.

Warning Against Schism

Muhammad tells his followers that after him there will be no prophet but many KhalIfas. Somebody asks him what to do when there are more KhalIfas than one. Muhammad says: The one to whom allegiance is sworn first has a supremacy over the others. In fact, When oath of allegiance has been taken for two KhalIfas, kill the one for whom the oath was taken later. Very thorough.

This injunction was followed to the letter by Umar. As he lay dying, he appointed a board of six electors to choose the new KhalIfa after him. Some of the guiding principles he laid down for the council were:

- If the electors choose someone unanimously, then that person is designated as the KhalIfa.
- If any five of them agree on one man and the sixth disagrees, then the dissenter should immediately be killed.
- If any four of them agree on one person and two disagree, then those two should be killed.
- If there is an equal division, then the deciding vote would be that of Abdullah b. Umar, his own son and one of the electors.

Solidarity and Single Leadership

Anyone who tries to disrupt the affairs of this Ummah while they are united you should strike him with the sword. Kill him, enjoins the next hadIs. Hold on to a single leader in order to ensure solidarity. When you are holding to one single man as your leader, you should kill him who seeks to undermine your solidarity or disrupt your unity.

Warning against Bad Times

Muhammad warns against the coming bad days when people will arise who will adopt ways other than mine and seek guidance other than mine and yet they will be a people having the same complexion as ours and speaking our language. What should a believer do if he lives in those times He should stick to the main body of the Muslims and their leader.

In those days there will be leaders who will not be led by my guidance and will not adopt my ways. There will be among them men who will have the hearts of devils in the bodies of human beings. Under the circumstances, answering a follower, Muhammad says: You will listen to the AmIr [ruler] and carry out his orders; even if your back is flogged and your wealth is snatched, you should listen and obey.

A crisis psychology indispensable for any dictatorship. A theology which teaches unceasing war against the peoples of the Darul Harb (territories not held by Muslims) makes a complete somersault and now teaches patient submission to the authorities of Darul Islam (territories under Islam) and to all its Ulul-amr, men of authority. These include not only its administrators but its divines.

There is also a warning not only against schismatics and innovators but also against false prophets. Is not Muhammad the final prophet But before the Day of Judgment, there will appear a number of impostors. You are to guard against them.

Horses and Archery

There are sixteen ahAdIs on horses, among them two on horse racing. Muhammad used to have a horse race between two particular points six miles apart. The translator assures us that it was not a horse race used for betting as in modern times. There is almost a consensus of opinion amongst the jurists that it is an act of great piety to break the horses for JihAd and for other useful purposes and there is no harm if there is a competition of race in them.

There are also some ahAdIs on archery. Beware, strength consists in archery, Muhammad repeated thrice in a sermon from the pulpit. Again, Lands shall be thrown open to you and Allah would suffice you, but none of you should give up playing with his arrows. Yet again, Who learnt archery and then gave it up is not from us or he has been guilty of disobedience to Allahs Apostle.

The Age of Majority

The son of Umar went to fight in the Battle of Uhud when he was fourteen, but the Prophet did not accept him. The next year, when he was fifteen, he went to fight in the Battle of Khandaq, and this time he was accepted. That decided the issue. One of fifteen years is considered an adult, and one below fifteen is a minor.

But the translator tells us that in Islamic law the age of majority differs with different conditions and circumstances. For example, for purposes of marriage, the puberty of a boy is established by other criteria, such as nocturnal emission and his capacity for impregnation. Similarly, the puberty of a girl is established by menstruation, nocturnal emission, or pregnancy.

JIHAD

Jihad appears again. In a book on government containing ahAdIs, are on jihAd and mujAhids (crusaders) and martyrs. This is understandable, for jihAd is central to Islam and mujAhids are its Army of Liberation. Without jihAd, there is no Islam. JihAd is a religious duty of a Muslim state. All lands not belonging to the territory of Islam (dAr al-islAm) must be conquered by the Muslims, and are therefore called the territory of war (dAr al-harb). But it is left to the discretion of the imAm to decide when the attack should begin. According to some fiqh schools, one campaign at least must be undertaken against the unbelievers every year, but since this is not always practical, it is enough if he keeps his army in preparedness and trains it for jihAd.

Jihad as Proof of True Conversion

After Muhammad migrated to Medina from Mecca, prospective converts to Islam used to come to Medina to swear fidelity to him and as a proof of their sincerity would leave their hometowns and settle in Medina. Having no home and no livelihood, and being uprooted from their old loyalties, they became desperate, and motivated soldiers of Islam. After the conquest of Mecca, when the power of Muhammad was fully vindicated, there must have been a rush of people wanting to become Muslims. So the rules were changed. The proof of a sincere conversion was no longer migration but jihAd. Muhammad told someone who intended to settle in Medina: There is no Hijra now, but only JihAd and sincerity of purpose; when you are asked to set out [on an expedition under-taken for the cause of Islam] you should [readily] do so.

The Merits of Jihad

Allah has undertaken to look after the affairs of one who goes out to fight in His way believing in Him and affirming the truth of His Apostles. He is committed to His care and He will either admit him to Paradise or bring him back to his home with a reward or booty. if he dies in the Way of Allah, his body will not decay. Every wound received by a Muslim in the Way of Allah will appear on the Day of Judgment in the same condition as it was when it was inflicted.... and the colour [of its discharge] will be the colour of blood, but its smell would be smell of musk.

Jihad for the spread of Islam is most meritorious and the easiest gateway to Paradise. Paradise is under the shadows of the swords, Muhammad tells his followers.

Think not of those who are slain in Allahs way as dead. In fact, the souls of the martyrs live in the bodies of green birds who have their nests in chandeliers hung from the throne of the Almighty. They eat the fruits of Paradise from wherever they like. They have no other desire except to be reborn so that they can be slain in Thy [Allahs] way once again. Muhammad had the same desire for himself. I love to fight in the way of Allah and be killed, to fight and again be killed and to fight and again be killed.

The Superiority of Jihad to Other Acts

The spiritual merits that accrue to the believer for participating in jihAd are equal to the merits he can obtain by performing all the other religious duties required by Islam, such as fasting, praying, and going on pilgrimage. One who goes out for jihAd is like a person who keeps fasts, stands in prayer constantly and obeys Allahs verses in the Quran.

Some people disputed the excellence of different virtues. One said: I do not care, if after embracing Islam, I do not do any good except distributing drinking water among the pilgrims. Another thought that maintainers of service to the mosque were superior. Yet a third wanted only to be a mujAhid. Muhammad was consulted. Allah sent him a verse: Do ye make the givers of drink to pilgrims, or the maintainers of the Sacred Mosque equal to the believers in Allah and the Last Day [yauml-Akhirat], and the crusaders [jAhid] in the cause of God They are not comparable in the sight of God. And God guides not those who do wrong.

There is more reward in jihAd than in anything this world has to offer. Leaving for jihAd in the way of Allah in the morning or in the evening will merit a reward better than the world and all that is in it.

THE HIGHEST GRADE OF HEAVEN IS RESERVED FOR THE MUJAHID

The rewards of being a Muslim are great, but the rewards of being a mujAhid are immensely greater. The Prophet said: Whoever cheerfully accepts Allah as his Lord, Islam as his religion and Muhammad as his Apostle is necessarily entitled to enter Paradise... [yet] there is another act which elevates the position of a man in Paradise to a grade one hundred [higher], and the elevation between one grade and the other is equal to the height of the heaven from the earth.... What is that act... JihAd in the way of Allah! JihAd in the way of Allah. But even the delights of this grade of paradise are no attraction to a martyr (ShahId). Therefore, the martyr will desire to return to this world and be killed ten times for the sake of the great honour that has been bestowed upon him.

The Story of a Martyr

The promise of heaven was tempting. On the way to the Battle of Uhud, one believer asked Muhammad: Messenger of Allah, where shall I be if I am killed He [Muhammad] replied: In paradise. The man threw away the dates he had in his hand and fought until he was killed.

Brain-teasers

Muslim theology is not without its brain-teasers. Two men, one the slayer and the other the slain, both go to Paradise. The Companions ask Muhammad: How He replied: One is slain in the Way of Allah [in jihAd] and dies a martyr. Then Allah turns in mercy to the murderer who embraces Islam; he too fights in the Way of Allah and dies a martyr.

Another puzzle seeking solution. Two men, again one of them a slayer and the other the slain, go to hell but never gathered together. Who are they the Companions ask Muhammad. He answers: A disbeliever and a believer. But how The translator clarifies: A believer goes to hell for some great sin, and a disbeliever goes there as a matter of course. But there is still a great difference between the two. A sinful believer and a disbeliever are not the same in the eyes of Allah. So a believer would not be kept there [in hell] for ever as is the case with the disbeliever;... [and also] a disbeliever would be made to occupy the most terrible place in Hell, whereas the sinful believer would be in a comparatively less tormenting situation and thus they would not be together in Hell.

We may give here another paradox, taken from tradition quoted by Ibn IshAq. A man goes to the Muslim Paradise without ever having offered a single Muslim prayer! He was

Al-Aswad, a shepherd who was called to participate in jihAd as soon as he became a Muslim, without having had the time to say a single prayer. In the engagement, a stone struck him and he died a martyr. Muhammad visited his corpse and delicately averted his face. Asked to explain why, he said: He has with him now his two wives from the dark-eyed houris.

An Earthly Note

After all this Paradise-mongering, the book ends on a more down-to-earth note. JAbir reports: We accompanied the Messenger of Allah on an expedition. When we came back to Medina and were going to enter our houses, he said: Wait and enter your houses in the later part of the evening so that a woman with dishevelled hair may have used the comb, and a woman whose husband has been away may have removed the hair from her private parts.

Another tradition forbids a mujAhid to come to his family like an unexpected night visitor doubting their fidelity and spying into their lapses. One interpretation is that the mujAhids have been away so long that their return is not expected, and thus their wives may be with their paramours. In such instances, let them not be taken by surprise, and let there be no avoidable breaking of homes. Give them time to separate. Homely wisdom.

Two men did not heed this command. And the result: they both found their wives with other men, according to Ibn Abbas.

Hunting, Food and Drink

The nineteenth book is the Book of Game and the Animals Which May Be Slaughtered and the Animals That Are to Be Eaten.

Muhammad did not set much store by the many Jewish restrictions on the subject of food (taAm), and softened them a good deal. O ye who believe! eat of the good things wherewith we have pro-vided you, says the Quran, repeating the sentiment in another verse. Yet some ritualistic restrictions were still there from the very beginning. Some animals were considered halUl (lawful), some mubAh (permitted), some makrUh (disapproved but not penalized), and some were altogether harAm (forbidden). Animals that are clean must be hunted and slaughtered in a particular way, with the help of a particular incantation, for their flesh to be lawful food. When slaughtering an animal, one should draw the knife across its throat, cutting the windpipe, and at the same time repeat the words Bismillahi, Allahu akbar (In the name of Allah, Allah is great). However, if an animal is slaughtered in this way by an idolater or an apostate from Islam, its flesh is not lawful.

Game

There are similar restrictions on game. It is not enough to recite the formula Bismillah-i-Allah-o-Akbar over game caught and killed by ones trained dog before eating it. One must also recite Allahs name over the dog that one sets off to catch a game animal. When you set off your trained dogs having recited the name of Allah, then eat what these hounds have caught for you, even if the game is killed, provided the hunting dog has not eaten any part of the game. When someone asks: What if I find along with my dog another dog, and do not know which of them caught [the game] Muhammad answers: Then dont eat it. What applies to the hunting dog applies to any animal used for hunting-a falcon, a cheetah. The test of a trained dog is that it catches a game animal three times without eating it. The test of a trained hawk is that it returns to its master in response to his call. The same holds true for game animals shot with an arrow. When you shoot your arrow, recite the name of Allah, and if the arrow killed [the game] then eat, except when you find it [the prey] fallen into water, for in that case you do not know whether it is water that caused its death or your arrow.

Dos and Donts

If you are in the land of the People of the Book [Jews and Christians], do not eat from their utensils. But if it cannot be avoided, then wash them before using them.

Flesh Lawful and Unlawful

The eating of all fanged beasts of prey and of all birds having talons is prohibited, but it is permissible to eat water animals even if they die of natural causes. There is a story behind this particular permission. JAbir gives us an eyewitness account. Allahs Messenger sent us on an expedition so that we might intercept a caravan of the Quraish, he says. During the journey, supplies ran short and they were on starvation rations when they saw rising before them on the coast of the sea something like a big mound. It was a whale called al-Anbar. The beast was dead. But as they were sent by the Messenger of Allah in the path of Allah, and as they were hard pressed, they ate even the dead animal. It fed them, three hundred of them, for a month till they grew bulky. I saw how we extracted pitcher after pitcher full of fat from the cavity of its eye, and sliced from its compact piece of meat equal to a bull.... Abu Ubaid [the chief] called forth thirteen men from us and he made them sit in the cavity of its eye, JAbir tells us. When they came back and mentioned this to Muhammad, he said that it was a special provision which Allah had brought forth for them. Is there any piece of meat left with you Muhammad inquired. They gave him one and he ate it.

Asses

It is unlawful to eat the flesh of domestic asses, for they are loathsome or impure, and their flesh is a loathsome evil of Satans doing. The prohibition came on the day of Khaibar, when the earthen pots of the Companions were boiling with the flesh of domestic asses.

Throw away your pots, came the order. Some thought at first that the prohibition was temporary, since one-fifth of the booty has not been given to the treasury, as is legally required. The point is that no personal use can be made of any spoils of war unless the booty has been properly distributed and one-fifth made over to the treasury. To illustrate, we give another tradition, narrated by RAfi b. KhadIj: We got hold of goats and camels. Some persons amongst us made haste and boiled the flesh of goats and camels in their earthen pots. He [the Prophet] then commanded and these were turned over. The translator tells us that it is permissible to make use of these spoils in Dar-ul-Harb [in the territory of the enemy], but it is not allowed in Daru-ul-IslAm.

Horses

The flesh of a horse is lawful.

Lizards, Locusts, Hares

The flesh of lizards is not forbidden, but to eat it is against the high standard of piety. A roasted lizard was sent to the Prophet. He did not accept it, saying: I neither eat it, nor do I prohibit it. His reason for not eating it: It is not found in the land of my people, and I feel that I have no liking for it.

The eating of locusts is permissible. We went on seven expeditions with Allahs Messenger and ate locusts, report Ibn Abu AufA and Abu Bakr.

Similarly, the flesh of hares is lawful. Anas reports that he and his companions chased a hare, caught and slaughtered it, and sent its haunch and two hind legs to Allahs Messenger.... and he accepted them.

Kill with a Good Attitude

The Prophet was not without compassion. ShaddAd b. Aus reports: Two are the things which I remember Allahs Messenger having said: Verily Allah has enjoined goodness to everything; so when you kill, kill in a good way and when you slaughter, slaughter in a good way. So every one of you should sharpen his knife, and let the slaughtered animal die comfortably.

Sacrifices

Intimately connected with the above is the next book, the Book of Sacrifices (Kitab al-Azahi).

The Quran uses many words for animal sacrifice. AzAhi itself derives from the root zabh, which means to split or pierce. Another word used is nahr, which means to injure the jugular vein; the word stands for stabbing the breast of a camel as in a sacrifice, and hence derivatively for the sacrifice itself.

In many religious traditions, compassion for all living beings is a strong element, which itself has its basis in a deeper vision of the unity of all fife. But this feeling and this vision are rather conspicuous by their absence in Semitic religions.

Some portions of the Old Testament read almost like a manual of animal slaughter. The menu of the early Christians also did not exclude flesh food, except for flesh of a particular kind and flesh obtained in a particular way. They were only required to abstain from meats offered to idols, and from blood, and from things strangled. The Holy Ghost wanted to lay upon them no greater burden than was necessary.

In Islam, too, animal sacrifice is highly meritorious. Muhammad tells his Companions that there is reward annexed to every hair of the animal sacrificed; verily its blood reacheth the acceptance of God, before it falleth upon the ground (TirmizI, vol. I, hadIs). But in order to be meritorious, the sacrifice should be made to Allah, not to Al-lAt or Al-UzzA or Al-ManAt. Let only theology change but facts remain the same for this miracle to happen. Among the people whom Allah cursed, Muhammad tells us, are those who sacrificed for anyone besides Allah, and those who accommodated an innovator in religion.

Some people talk glibly about what the Holy Ghost wants or what Allah wills but are deaf to the voice of conscience and compassion within the human heart.

The Proper Time for Sacrifice

The proper time for sacrificing an animal on the day of Idul AzA is after the morning prayer. In Muhammads lifetime, many slaughtered their animals before Muhammad had said his prayer. They were asked to slaughter other ones in their stead. People should not sacrifice an animal before Allahs Messenger had sacrificed [his animal].

Proper Age

As there is a proper time for sacrificing, so there is also a proper age for the sacrificial animal. Sacrifice only a grown-up animal, unless it is difficult for you, in which case sacrifice a ram [of less than a year, but more than six months age].

Proper Agency

It is meritorious to sacrifice the animal with ones own hand as Muhammad did. Muhammad commanded that a ram with black legs, black belly and black circles round the eyes should be brought to him. He then said to Aisha, Give me the large knife, and told her to sharpen it on a stone. When she did, he took the knife and the ram; he placed it on the ground and then sacrificed it. Another hadIs adds that when Muhammad sacrificed rams, he placed his foot on their sides.

While sacrificing, Muhammad recited: In the name of Allah, O Allah, accept [this sacrifice] on behalf of Muhammad and the family of Muhammad and the Ummah of Muhammad.

The proper instrument for slaughtering an animal is a sharp knife. Muhammad is informed by a Companion: Allahs Messenger, we are going to encounter the enemy tomorrow, but we have no knives with us. (The knives were not required for use against the enemy but for slaughtering the animals which might fall to their lot as spoils of war, the translator explains.) The Prophet answered: Make haste or be careful [in making arrangements for procuring knives] which would let the blood flow, [and along with it] the name of Allah is also to be recited.

The same hadIs tells us that no nail or bone should be used in slaughtering an animal. As for the nail, it is bone, and the bone is the knife of the Abyssinians.

Sacrifice is Compulsory

The translator in a note quotes a hadIs to show that animal sacrifice on the day of Idul AzA is compulsory for every Muslim adult. According to Abu Huraira, Muhammad said: He who can afford sacrifice but does not offer it, he should not come near our place of worship.

This is understandable, for is not animal sacrifice Allahs own command Allah ordains: The sacrificial camels, we have made for you as among the symbols from God... then pronounce the name of Allah over them as they line up for sacrifice, and when they are down on their sides eat of them.... We made animals subject to you, that you may be grateful.

Pot and Piety

On the ordinary level of consciousness on which religions operate, there is nothing exceptionable in the Muslim institution of sacrifice. We offer to our gods what we ourselves eat. In animal sacrifice, the flesh comes to us, and we like to believe that the piety of the act (whatever it may be) goes to God. It is not their meat nor their blood, that reaches Allah, it is your piety.

Let it be so if you like. But when a deeper consciousness dawns, all this changes. We realize that this unregenerate piety is not good enough. We experience a new togetherness, a new reverence for all living beings. We realize that an animal sacrifice can never be a fit-ting and acceptable offering to any god worthy of man.

Drinks

The twenty-first book is the Book of Drinks (Ashriba). Muhammad forbade all intoxicating liquors, all liquors in the various stages of fermentation.

It seems that the habit of drinking was quite popular with the Companions of Muhammad. Many ahAdIs in this book show Abu Talha, Abu AyyUb, Abu DujAna, MuAz b. Jabal, Sahil b. BaiadA, Abu Ubaida, and Ubayy b. Kab drinking. The worst case is that of Hamza b. Abd al-Muttalib, the Prophets uncle. AlI, the Prophets son-in-law, narrates an interesting story. There fell to my lot a she-camel out of the spoils of war on the day of Badr, and Allahs Messenger gave me another on that day out of the khums [the fifth reserved for Allah and His Messenger]. Some business took AlI to the house of an ansAr, and he brought his camels along. He tied them up outside, but when he returned, he found their humps were chopped off and their haunches had been cut off and their livers had been taken out. When AlI asked who had done this, people said, Hamza and he is in this house dead drunk in the company of the AnsArs with a singing girl.

AlI reported the matter to Muhammad, who put on his mantle, went to where Hamza was, and began to reprimand him. Hamzas eyes were red. He cast a glance at Allahs Messenger and then looked towards his knees, and then lifted his eyes and cast a glance at his waist and then lifted his eyes and saw his face. And then Hamza said: Are you anything but the slaves of my father Allahs Messenger came to know that he was intoxicated, and he thus turned upon his heels, and came out. Liquor was forbidden.

Nabiz

Also forbidden was nablz, a kind of wine made by mixing fresh dates and unripe dates together. Muhammad also forbade its preparation in varnished jars, gourds, green pitchers, or hollow stumps.

Muhammad and Drinking

There are many ahAdIs to show that the Prophet himself drank nablz. Aisha reports: We prepared nablz for him [Muhammad] in a waterskin.... We prepared nablz in the morning and he drank it in the evening and we prepared the nablz in the night, and he would drink it in the morning. Ibn AbbAs, the Prophets cousin, reports: Nablz was prepared for Allahs Messenger in the beginning of the night and he would drink it in the morning and the following night and the following day and the night after that up to the afternoon. If anything was left out of that he gave it to his servant, or gave orders for it to be poured out.

How to reconcile the Prophets prohibition with his indulgence The theologians are not at a loss, They say: This prohibition is not a complete prohibition but it implies disapproval. So long as nablz does not turn into liquor, it is not forbidden. For ImAm Abu HanIfa and QAzi Abu YUsuf, there is not even a disapproval, but the prohibition was valid only in the early period of Islam when the people had to be trained for the prohibition of liquor.

Milk

Muhammad approved of drinking milk. I milked for him [the Prophet] a small quantity of milk and brought it to him and he drank it, reports Abu Bakr.

Table Manners

Etiquette relating to eating and drinking is also given. Muhammad says: None of you should eat with his left hand

and drink with the left hand, for Satan eats with the left hand and drinks with that hand. In another tradition, he tells Umar, the son of his wife Umm Salama by her first husband: Boy, mention the name of Allah, and eat with your right hand and eat from what is near you.

One should not drink water while standing, but one could do so with water from Zamzam (the well-known well within the precincts of the mosque at Mecca) as Muhammad himself did. In ordinary course, if one drinks water standing, one must vomit. It is also meritorious to lick ones fingers after taking ones food. Abdullah b. Kab reports that the Messenger of Allah used to eat food with three fingers, and he licked his hand before wiping it. The injunction is: When anyone of you eats food he should not wipe his hand until he had licked it or got it licked by someone else.

Pumpkins and Cucumbers

It is meritorious to eat pumpkin and also cucumber with dates, because Muhammad did so. Anas reports: I saw Allahs Messenger going after the pumpkin round the dish, so I have always liked the pumpkin since that day.

Garlic

Muhammad himself did not eat garlic because of its odor, but it is permissible for other Muslims. Still, it should be avoided when one has to talk to eminent persons. Abu AyyUb AnsArI tells us that the holy prophet did not take garlic as he was visited by angels who brought him the message of Allah.

Miraculous Feeding

Miraculous feeding after the fashion of Jesus is repeated in Islam too. The roasted liver of one sheep and two cups containing soup and meat suffice, with the blessing of the Prophet, for feeding persons.

Do Not Find Fault

Do not find fault with the food served to you. It is said about the Prophet that if he liked anything, he ate it and if he did not like it, he left it. A laudable practice. In fact, a man should eat with thankfulness in his heart-thanks for the gods that reside in his food, thanks for the elements that have gone into making it, thanks for the farmer who produced it, and thanks for the mothers, sisters and wives, and cooks who lovingly cooked it and served it.

However, it is not enough to thank our Father who art in heaven for giving us this day our daily bread. Let us pray that this bread is also honest. What Lord Buddha calls Right Livelihood (samyak AjiviikA) is a great spiritual truth. Food derived from the spoils of war and tribute is a negation of this insight. Though we may placate Him with soulful praises and pious thanks, no God can legitimize it.

Similarly, it is self-deception to believe that we adore or glorify God by reciting Allah-o-Akbar (Allah is Great) while killing an animal. That way we really profane Him, negate Him. Be a meat-eater if you like, but one ought not to feel so pious about it.

Clothing, Decorations, General Behavior, Greetings, Magic, Poetry, Visions, Dreams

The twenty-second book pertains to clothing and decorations (KitAb al-LibAs wal-ZInah). The book begins with ahAdIs which forbid the use of gold and silver vessels. He who drinks in the vessel of silver in fact drinks down in his belly the fire of Hell.

Silk

Silk is also forbidden. Do not wear silk, for one who wears it in the world will not wear it in the Hereafter.

It is also not permissible for a man to wear clothes of yellow color, for these are the clothes usually worn by the non-believers. A man was wearing clothes dyed in saffron; finding that the Prophet disapproved of them, he promised to wash them. But Muhammad said: Burn them.

The mantles of Yemen, on the other hand, were considered excellent. These were striped and made of coarse cloth.

It is permissible to use carpets.

Sandals

Sandals are recommended. JAbir reports that during an expedition in which we all participated, the Prophet said: Make a general practice of wearing sandals, for a man is riding as it were when he wears sandals.

Hair

Not only clothes, but the hair too should not be dyed in saffron.

On the day of the conquest of Mecca, Abu QuhAfA, the father of Abu Bakr, a veteran old man of one hundred years, met the Prophet to pledge his loyalty to him. His head and his beard were white like hyssop. The Prophet said: Change it with something but avoid black.

But why this change or dyeing at all The Prophet gives the reason: The Jews and Christians do not dye their hair, so oppose them.

Dogs

Many ahAdIs tell us that angels do not enter a house in which there is a dog. In fact, Gabriel himself told this to the Prophet. The angel had promised a rendezvous with Muhammad but did not turn up because meanwhile a puppy had gotten into his house and was sitting under a cot. Then on that very morning, he [Muhammad] commanded the killing of the dogs until he announced that the dog kept for the orchards should also be killed, but he spared the dog meant for the protection of extensive fields [or big gardens], reports MaimUna, one of the wives of the Prophet.

Pictures and Statues

The same is true of statues and pictures in any form, whether of birds or animals or men. They effectively keep out the angels. Aisha tells us: We had a curtain which had portraits of birds upon it.... The Messenger of Allah said to me: Change them, [they bring] to my mind [the pleasures on the worldly life. On seeing portraits on a curtain, he told Aisha: The most grievous torment from the Hand of Allah on the Day of

Resurrection would be for those who imitate Allah in the act of His creation. On that day Allah would ask these imitators: Breathe soul into what you have created.

False Hair and Facial Culture

Some of Muhammads prohibitions relate to practices which are surprisingly modern. He forbade women to add false hair to their head, or to pluck their eyebrows. The Prophet cursed the woman who adds false hair and the woman who asks for it.

We are also told that Allah has cursed those women who tattooed and who have themselves been tattooed, those who pluck hair from their faces and those who make spaces between their teeth for beautification changing what God has created. Abdullah, the son of Umar, tells us that if he found any of these things in his wife, he would have never slept with her in the bed.

Muhammad tells us also of women wearing see-through dresses: women who would be dressed but appear to be naked will not enter paradise.

Muhammad also disapproved of qaza, i.e., having a part of a boys head shaved and leaving a part unshaven. This may have been an old ritualistic practice or a thoughtless current fashion.

General Behavior and Salutations

The twenty-third and twenty-fourth books are the Book of General Behavior (al-AdAb) and the Book on Salutations and Greetings (as-Salam).

Personal Names

Curiously, the book on AdAb starts with personal names. Muhammad took great interest in this matter. He said that ugly personal names should be replaced with good ones. He changed the name of Umars daughter Asiya (disobedient) to JamIla (good and handsome). But he also changed the name of one of his wives from Barra to JuwairIya. Barra means pious, and it is a perfectly good name.

Muhammad said that the dearest names to Allah are SubhAn Allah (Hallowed be Allah), and al-Hamidulillah (praise be to Allah). But he forbade giving the following four names to servants: Aflah (successful), RabAh (profit), YasAr (wealth), and NAfi (beneficial).

The vilest name in Allahs sight is Malik al-AmlAk (king of kings). So is the appellation ShahinshAh, having the same meaning.

Naming Infants After Muhammad

People who wanted to name their sons after Muhammad were only allowed to use his personal name (Muhammad), but not his kunya (a name descriptive of some quality or attribute), QAsim. JAbir narrates that a man named his newborn babe Muhammad. When other Muslims objected, he went to Muhammad for clarification. Muhammad said: Give him my name but do not give him my kunya, for I am QAsim in the sense that I distribute [the spoils of war] and the dues of ZakAt amongst you.

Tahnik

TahnIk is the practice of blessing a newborn infant with religious piety. AzAn and IqAma are recited in its right and left cars, and some chewed dates are rubbed over its palate. AsmA, the daughter of Abu Bakr, gave birth to a baby. The baby was taken to Muhammad. Muhammad called for some dates, chewed them and then put his saliva in his [the infants] mouth.

The first thing that entered his stomach was the saliva of Allahs Messenger.... He then rubbed him and blessed him and gave him the name of Abdullah. He [Abdullah] went to him [the Holy Prophet] when he had attained the age of seven or eight years in order to pledge allegiance to Allahs Messenger.

Asking Permission Before Entering A House

One should not enter anybodys house without his permission. When a man seeks permission three times, and it is not granted, he should come back.

Dont Peep into Anoumr Mans House

It is forbidden to peep into the house of another person. A man peeped through a hole in the door at Allahs Messenger, who was using a pointed object of some kind to arrange the hair on his head. Allahs Messenger said to him: If I were to know that you had been peeping, I would have thrust it into your eyes. Then Muhammad pronounced: He who peeped into the house of people without their consent, it is permissible for them to put out his eyes.

Salutations and Greetings

Six are the rights of a Muslim over another Muslim... When you meet him, offer him greetings; when he invites you to a feast accept it; when he seeks your counsel give him; and when he sneezes and says: All praise to Allah, you say, May Allah show mercy to you; and when he falls ill visit him; and when he dies follow his bier.

When the People of the Book (Jews and Christians) offer you salutations, you should say: The same to you. Some Jews once made a pun and greeted Muslims by saying as-sAm-u-alaikum (death be upon you) instead of the usual as-salAm-u-alaikum (peace be upon you). Muhammad teaches his followers to respond by saying: Let it be upon you. The Prophet himself followed this practice.

First Greetings

The rider should first greet the pedestrian, and the pedestrian the one who is seated. And all should greet the children. Muhammad also taught his followers to avoid sitting on the paths; or if that cannot be helped, then give the path its due right. But it is different with the People of the Book. Do not greet the Jews and the Christians before they greet you and when you meet any one of them on the roads force him to go to the narrowest part of it.

Veil

Umar wanted Muhammad to ask his women to wear the veil, but Muhammad did not respond. One day, when the

Prophets wife SaudA, who was tall in stature, went out to the fields in the dark to ease herself, Umar called out: SaudA, we recognize you. He did so with the hope that the verses pertaining to veil would be revealed. His hope was fulfilled. Allah, the Exalted and Glorious, then revealed the verses pertaining to veil, says Aisha.

Also, beware of getting into the houses and meeting women. But what about the husbands brother, an ansAr asked. Husbands brother is like death, the Prophet replied.

Magic and Spells

With rather slovenly classification, the Book of Salutations and Greetings also contains many ahAdIs on magic, spells, medicine, poisons, and incantations.

The Prophet believed that the influence of an evil eye is a fact. A bath is prescribed as its remedy. When you are asked to take a bath from the influence of an evil eye, you should take a bath.

Muhammad also believed in witchcraft. In fact, he believed that he himself had once been put under a spell by a Jew and his daughters. During this period, he lost his appetite and even became impotent; or, in the language of Ibn IshAq, could not come at his wives. And under the influence of the charm, he also felt that he had been doing something whereas in fact he had not been doing that. But two angels came and revealed everything: the nature of the sickness, those who had brought it about, and the way they did it. The angels told Muhammad that the spell has affected him, and that it was LabId b. Asam [who cast the spell]. The angels explained that hairs combed from the head of the Prophet had been stolen, tied in eleven knots around a palm branch, and deposited at the bottom of a well. The effect of the charm was transmitted by the comb and by the hair stuck to the comb and the spathe of the date-palm-[and that it was] in the well of Zi ArwAn. Muhammad sent his men there and they found it at the very spot revealed by the angels. Muhammad told Aisha: Aisha, by Allah, its [the wells] water was yellow like henna and its trees [i.e., the trees around the well] were like heads of the devils.

As the knots were untied, the Prophet got well. He sought refuge with the Lord of the Dawn from the mischief of women who blow on knots [i.e., practice the secret art of casting spells] (Quran Sura). In the same Sura, the Prophet also seeks refuge from the mischief of darkness as it overspreads. Has this prayer to do with his fear of darkness His biographers say he was afraid of the dark and would not sit in a dark room unless a lamp was brought for him.

On another occasion, a Jewish woman gave Muhammad poisoned mutton, but, of course, it had no power over him. The Jewish woman was none other than the unfortunate victim who had seen her father and husband killed in the Prophets raid on Khaibar and whom he was now contemplating to marry. She poisoned the mutton she was asked to cook for Muhammad. He had just taken a morsel and finding the taste unusual spat it out. This saved him for the time being, but the poison had a delayed effect, and according to some traditions, it caused his last illness.

Cures by Incantation

Muhammad used to cure people with the help of incantations. Among others, he treated cases of evil eye and snakebite. He even granted the sanction of treating snakebite with incantation to a family of ansArs.

Aisha reports: When any person fell ill with a disease or he had any ailment or he had any injury, the Apostle of Allah placed his forefinger upon the ground and then lifted it by reciting the name of Allah and said: The dust of our ground with the saliva of any one of us would serve as a means whereby our illness would be cured with the sanction of Allah.

The translator extends the area from the Prophets four walls and household to the whole of Medina. He says that according to some Muslim scholars, the word dust in the hadIs refers to the sacred dust of Medina on which had fallen the saliva of the pious Muslims.

On another occasion, a Companion of the Prophet cured a man bitten by a poisonous scorpion with the help of Sura al-FAtiha, reinforced by the application of his saliva.

No Evil Omen, No Hama. No Infection

Muhammad said that there are no ill omens, no ghouls, and no star promising rain. There is also no hAma. According to the Arab belief of that time, the soul of a slain man took the form of a bird known as hAma, which kept crying for the blood of the slayer until the slayer was killed.

Muhammad also taught that there is no infection, no epidemic disease. About the plague he said: When you hear that it has broken out in a land, dont go to it, and when it has broken out in the land where you are, dont run out of it. The fever is due to the intense heat of the Hell. Cool it down with water, Muhammad says.

Leprosy

Dont mix with lepers. A delegation that included a leper once came to pay homage to Muhammad. The Prophet would not meet the leper but sent him a message: We have accepted your allegiance, so you may go.

Luck

Though Muhammad did not believe in divination, he believed in good omens and luck. There is no transitive [i.e., epidemic] disease, no divination, but good omens please me, he says.

About luck he says: If a bad luck is a fact, then it is in a horse, the woman and the house. According to the translator, the unluckiness of a horse is that the horse is used not for JihAd but for evil designs.

Kahins

Muhammad was against kahins, i.e., augurs, soothsayers, and fortune-tellers. The reason for this opposition was personal as well as ideological; personal because he himself was accused of being no better than a kahin but wanted to be known as a prophet. Allah had assured him that by the favour of the Lord, thou art neither a soothsayer [kahin], nor one possessed or mad [majnun]. His other ground of opposition was of a more general nature. Muhammad believed that Gabriel was the true source of the knowledge of the unseen world now contained in the Quran and the Sunnah. But the source of the knowledge of a kahin is the jinn, a knowledge which he steals from heaven but mixes up with lies. Aisha puts it to Muhammad: Messenger of Allah! they [kahins] at times tell us things which we find true. Muhammad replies: That is a word pertaining to truth which a jinn snatches away and then cackles into the ear of his friend [the kahin] as the hen does. And then they [the jinns] mix in it more than one hundred lies. For pure and unadulterated knowledge of the occult world, the Quran and the Sunnah are the source. All other avenues of knowledge of the unseen world are limited and thus not fully authentic and reliable, the translator assures us.

Meteors

Muhammad did not believe in a star promising rain, but that does not make him a rationalist as we understand the word today. The two worlds-the world of Muhammad and that of the modern rationalist-are very different. There is an interesting hadIs on shooting stars which tells us what Muhammad believed about the world, nature, and the law of causality, and incidentally about how the jinns steal their knowledge of the heavens.

The pre-Muslim Arabs believed that meteors symbolized the death or birth of a great man, a belief found in the lore of many countries, including India. Muhammad corrected this belief and provided another explanation. His view is a little complicated but worth quoting. It seems that Muhammad believed in the hierarchy of angels. First in rank are the supporters of the Throne; next come the dwellers of the heaven; the third group lives in the heaven of the world. When these different orders communicate with each other, the jinn has his chance. Muhammad explains: Allah, the Exalted and the Glorious, issues Command when He decides to do a thing. Then the angels supporting the Throne sing His glory, then sing dwellers of the heaven who are near to them until this glory of God reaches them who are in this heaven of the world. Then those who are near the supporters of the Throne ask those supporters of the Throne: What has your Lord said And they accordingly inform them what He says. Then the dwellers of heaven of the world seek information from them until this information reaches the heaven of the world. In this process of transmission the jinn snatches what he manages to overhear and he carries it to his friends. And when the angels see the jinn they attack them with meteors. If they narrate which they manage to snatch that is correct, but they alloy it with lies and make additions to it.

The snatching of the heavenly news by the jinn is referred to in several places in the Quran. The interested reader may look up the Suras Hijr (:-), SAffAt (:-), Mulk, and Jinn (:-).

Winds and Clouds

The fact is that the world of Muhammad is as weird and full of imps and jinns as the world of the kahins and has little in common with the world as moderns understand it. As we have already seen in the chapter on salAt (see page) Muhammads approach even to phenomena so close to home as clouds and rain and wind was neither scientific nor even poetic but magical and superstitious. Their sight filled him with fear. Aisha tells us that when he saw dark clouds or wind, the signs of fear were depicted on his face. She asked him: I find people being happy when they see the dark cloud in the hope that it would bring rain, but I find that when you see that [the cloud] there is an anxiety on your face. He replied: Aisha, I am afraid that there may be a calamity in it, for it may be like the people of Ad who saw a cloud formation and thought It is a cloud which would give us rain, but were destroyed by it (Quran :; hadIs).

Snakes, Ants, Cats

Aisha reports that the Prophet commanded the killing of a snake having stripes over it, for it affects eyesight and miscarries pregnancy. Like snakes, dogs too cause miscarriage and affect the eyesight adversely. So they too should be killed.

Ants fared better, but this was due to the intervention of Allah Himself. An ant had bitten a prophet... he ordered that the colony of the ants should be burnt. And Allah revealed to him: Because of an ants bite you have burnt a community from amongst the communities which sing My praise. The book ends on a compassionate note. It is forbidden to kill a cat. It is also meritorious to supply water to thirsty animals.

Correct Words, Poetry, Visions

The next three books are very small. One relates to the use of correct words; another is on poetry (kitAb al-shir); and the third is on visions (kitab al-ruya).

At a place known as Arj, Muhammad once saw a poet reciting a poem. Catch the Satan, Muhammad commanded. Filling the belly of a person with pus is better than stuffing his brain with poetry, the Messenger of Allah added.

This is only a part of the story and does not represent the positive side of the Prophets attitude toward poets. True, he did not think highly of them. He himself was described by some as a poet but declined the honor because it detracted from the dignity of apostleship, the only status he cared to claim. This is the speech of an honoured Apostle; it is not the speech of a poet nor of a soothsayer, he vehemently insisted.

Muhammad took a utilitarian view of poets. The more inconvenient ones he had eliminated, even by the method of assassination, as in the cases of AsmA, the daughter of MarwAn, the centenarian poet Abu Afak, and Kab ibn Ashraf. This taught many of the others to behave better. Muhammad also employed and honored some of the more pliable poets, among them Kab ibn MAlik, HassAn ibn SAbit, and Kab ibn Zuhair. The last-mentioned was the son of a famous poet of his times. At first Kab ibn Zuhair put himself under the ban by writing poems unfavorable to the Muslims. When Mecca was conquered, his brother, who was already a convert, warned him of the fate suffered by many other opponents of Islam and advised him to either submit or seek asylum somewhere else. He wrote Kab that the Apostle had killed some of the men in Mecca who had satirized him and that the Quraish poets who were left, like Ibn al-ZibarA and Hubayra b. Abu Wahb, had already fled in all directions. If you have any use for your life then come quickly to the Apostle, for he does not kill anyone who comes to him in repentance. If you do not do that, then get to some safe place, he advised, according to Ibn IshAq.

Kab took his brothers advice and one day appeared before Muhammad without revealing his identity. O Apostle, Kab b. Zuhair has come to ask security from you as a repentant Muslim. Would you accept him as such if he came to you Kab inquired of the Prophet. Receiving an affirmative answer, he said, I am Kab, the son of Zuhair. Some of the people around Muhammad wanted his permission to kill him, but he was spared.

Then Kab sought the Prophets permission to recite a qasIda in his praise. The permission was readily given. He began reciting: He surpassed all the prophets in constitution and disposition, / Nor did any approach him either in knowledge or nobleness. But when he came to the lines, Indeed, the Prophet is a Light providing guidance to the world / And a drawn sword from the armoury of Allah [suyUf Allah], the Prophet was so delighted that he took off his mantle and bestowed it on Kab. The poem came to be known in the Muslim world as the Poem of the Mantle (QasIdat-ul-Burda). The mantle became a precious heirloom of the poets family and was bought from one of his descendants by a future KhalIfa, Muawiyah, for, dirhams. The khirqai-sharIf (holy mantle) became successively the property of the Ummayads and then of the Abbasides. Some say it was burned when Baghdad was sacked by the Tartars; others believe that it passed into the hands of the Ottoman caliphate. Whether real or fake, the Ottoman mantle is taken out as a national standard in times of great emergency.

Chess

Playing chess is also forbidden. He who played chess is like one who dyed his hand with the flesh and blood of a swine, says Muhammad.

Visions

The next book, again very small, is on visions and dreams. A bad dream is called hulm, an ordinary one manAm and al-rUyA is a heavenly vision.

Muhammad says that good dreams come from Allah and bad ones from Satan. If one has a bad dream (hulm), he should do two things: he should spit thrice on his left side and not disclose it to any one. But a good dream one may reveal to his beloved friends.

Muhammad says that the vision of a believer is the forty-sixth part of prophecy ; in other ahAdIs it becomes the seventieth part. The difference between the forty-sixth and the seventieth parts depends upon the difference in the standard of piety of the dreamer, as the translator explains.

Here too is some bad news for professional psychoanalysts. Do not narrate to the people the vain sporting of Satan with you in your sleep, Muhammad advises his followers.

Muhammad also makes a very self-satisfied statement: He who saw me in a dream in fact saw me, for the satan does not appear in my form.

MUHAMMADS DREAMS

Muhammad also narrates some of his own dreams and gives their interpretations. Once in a dream, he was made to wear two bangles on his hands.

At this he felt a sort of burden upon him (for a bangle is the ornament of women, the translator explains); Muhammad then was made to blow upon them and they both disappeared. I interpreted the two bangles as the two great liars who would appear after me and the one amongst them was AnasI the inhabitant of Sana and the other one was Musailima the inhabitant of YamAma, Muhammad says.

Both of these men lived at the time of the Prophet. Both claimed prophethood; Musailima al-KazzAb (the greater liar as he is called by Muslim theologians) even claimed a joint share in the prophethood of Muhammad. AnasI and Musailima both led revolts and were killed.

MUHAMMAD ON MUHAMMAD

The twenty-eighth book pertains to the Excellent Qualities of the Prophet (Kitab al-Fazail).

Self-estimation

The book opens with the Prophets own self-estimation. Verily Allah granted eminence to KinAn from amongst the descendants of IsmAil and He granted eminence to the Quraish amongst KinAns and He granted eminence to BanU HAshim amongst the Quraish and He granted me eminence from the tribe of Banu Hashim.

I recognize the stone in Mecca which used to pay me salutations before my advent as a Prophet and I recognize that even now. So it seems that a stone can pay but not receive salutations. Idolatry in reverse.

I shall be preeminent among the descendants of Adam on the Day of Resurrection and I will be the first intercessor and the first whose intercession will be accepted.

Muhammad uses an effective simile to show the difference between himself and the five or six Apostles that he recognized as having preceded him. The religion of the other apostles is like a building imposing and beautiful but for one brick. I am that final brick, he says. With his coming, the edifice of religion becomes perfect, and there is no room or use left for any future prophet. I have come to finalize the chain of Apostles, he says. With him the old religions are abrogated and the possibility of any new one is exhausted. So any new religion or revelation must be a mischievous innovation.

Muhammad uses another simile to characterize three types of people who receive his message, which itself is like rain falling upon the earth. The first are like a good piece of land which receives the rainfall eagerly and produces herbage and grass abundantly. These people absorb the message of the Prophet and develop understanding about it and become a source of benefit to others. The second ones are like a land hard and barren, which itself grows nothing but retains water for the benefit of others. These people have no deep understanding of the message but acquire knowledge of religion and impart it to others. The third type is like a barren land which neither absorbs nor retains the rainwater. These people do not accept the guidance of Allah with which I [Muhammad] have been sent. In yet another simile, Muhammad tells the believers that while he is trying to save them from the hellfire, they are rushing headlong into it. My example and your example is that of a person who lit the fire and insects and moths begin to fall in it and he would be making efforts to take them out, and I am going to hold you back from fire, but you are slipping from my hand.

The Names of Muhammad

A little further in the book, Muhammad says: I am Muhammad and I am Ahmad, and I am al-MAhI [the obliterator] by whom unbelief would be obliterated and I am HAshir [the gatherer] at whose feet mankind will be gathered, and I am Aqib [the last to come] after whom there will be no prophet. He is also MuqaffI (the last in succession), and also the Prophet of Repentance as well as the Prophet of Mercy.

The statement will have Vedantic echoes for some ears; and many Hindus, predisposed to find synthesis and not caring whether it is a false one, may seize on this hadIs to prove that Vedantism and Prophetism are the same. But in fact the two approaches are widely apart in spirit.

Muhammad at the Heavenly Cistern

We learn from thirty-three ahAdIs, on Muhammads own asSurance, that he will be at the Cistern in heaven waiting to receive his followers. I shall be there ahead of you at the Hauz Kausar, he tells them. The Hauz Kausar, or Cistern, is a great water reservoir in Paradise, requiring a months journey to go around it. All the followers of Muhammad will be presented to him here except those who disobeyed the Prophet and made innovations in his religion. According to some authorities quoted by the translator, these are the people who turned apostates after the death of the Holy Prophet and were killed by the army of Hazrat Abu Bakr.

A Prophets Double Role

When an ummah is safe from the wrath of God, He calls back his Messenger as a harbinger and recompense in the world to come. But when God intends to cause destruction to an ummah, He punishes it through His living Apostle. Allah destroys it [the Ummah] as the Apostle witnesses it and he cools his eyes by destruction as they had belied him and disobeyed his command.

Adulation

The book also tells us what Muhammads followers thought of him. It gives many ahAdIs on this subject, many of them by Anas, who was the Prophets servant for nine or ten years. He found Muhammad most valorous, most courageous, sublimest among people and the most generous amongst them and he was the bravest of men.

Aisha, however, tells us that whenever the Prophet had to choose between two things he adopted the easier one, provided it was no sin.

Muhammads Generosity

Muhammad gave freely from his war booty not only to his followers but also to other important chiefs to incline them to Islam. This was called his charitable disposition. Anas says that the Prophet never failed to give when asked for anything in the name of Islam. A person came and Muhammad gave him a large flock of sheep and goats. He went back to his people and said: My people, embrace Islam, for Muhammad gives so much charity as if he has no fear of want. Anas adds that this man embraced Islam for the sake of the world but later he became Muslim until Islam became dearer to him than the world.

Another hadIs tells us that after he was granted a victory at Hunain by Allah, the Prophet gave one hundred camels to SafwAn b. Ummaya. He then gave him another hundred and yet another hundred. The man was overwhelmed. He [Muhammad] was the most detested person amongst people in my eyes. But he continued giving to me until now he is the dearest of people to me, the recipient said.

Muhammads promises of booty were fulfilled even posthumously. He promised someone: In case we get wealth from Bahrain, I would give you so much. The Prophet died before the wealth arrived from Bahrain, but when it did, Abu Bakr gave the man a handful of coins. He asked me to count them. I counted them as five hundred dinars and he [Abu Bakr] said: Here is double of this for you, the beneficiary tells us.

Even prophets are not above using material inducements to win converts. Do not be angry, for I give property to the MUlfat QulUb, Muhammad tells his faithful followers, according to a tradition quoted in Mirkhonds Persian biography of the Prophet.

This is done in order to rivet their hearts to faith more securely. The mUlfat qulUb are nominal Muslims, or what Mahatma Gandhi calls in another context rice Christians; they are convinced by more palpable economic and political advantages. In their new mission work in India and other countries of Asia and Africa, the oil-rich sheikhs are following a holy and hoary tradition.

Rob Peter to pay Paul. In the prophetic theology both acts are meritorious. One is called jihAd, the other sadaqa, or charity.

The Prophets Bodily Characteristics: Fragrance

There are many ahAdIs about the Prophets bodily characteristics: his face, appearance, complexion, hair, eyes, and even heels.

The Prophets body was soft. Anas never touched brocade or silk and found it as soft as the body of Allahs Messenger. His perspiration shone like pearls. His body was also fragrant. Anas never smelt musk or ambergris and found its fragrance as sweet as the fragrance of Allahs Messenger. His mother collected the Prophets sweat in a bottle. She told Muhammad: That is your sweat which we mix in our perfume and it becomes the most fragrant perfume.

The Prophets Appearance

Al-BarA says that Muhammad was neither very tall nor shortstatured. He also found his face very handsome. He put on a red mantle over him, and never have I seen anyone more handsome than Allahs Apostle.

The Prophets Hair

There are many ahAdIs on the Prophets hair. The hair grew in the lobes of his ears. He used to part his hair. Ibn AbbAs says the following on the subject: The People of the Book [Jews and Christians] used to let their hair fall on their forehead and the polytheists used to part it on their heads, and Allahs Messenger liked to conform his behaviour to the People of the Book in matters in which he received no command from God; so Allahs Messenger let fall his hair upon his forehead, and then he began to part it after this.

That the Prophet reverted to the ways of the polytheists after following the Jewish practice shows, according to the translator, that a revelation was involved in the matter. Furthermore, to him the hadIs is a clear proof of the fact that Allahs Messenger received wahy [revelation] from the Lord, in addition to what is contained in the Quran, and he acted according to it.

Muhammad had some white hair but he did not dye it; Abu Bakr and Umar, younger than he, dyed their hair with pure henna.

His hair was collected. Anas reports that when the Prophet got his hair cut by the barber, his Companions came round him and they eagerly wanted that no hair should fall but in the hand of a person.

The Seal of Prophethood

His followers believed that Muhammad carried the seal of prophethood even physically as a protuberance on his back. Abdullah b. Sarjis says that he saw the seal of Prophethood between his shoulders on the left side of his shoulder having spots on it like moles. Another man, JAbir, also saw it on his back as if it were a pigeons egg.

Physical Changes Under the Influence of Wahy

According to Aisha, when a revelation descended upon Muhammad, his forehead perspired. According to UbAda, under its influence, the colour of his face underwent a change, and his head was lowered. Muhammad himself says that at times wahy comes to me like the ringing of a bell and that is most severe for me.... and at times an Angel in the form of a human being comes to me and speaks..... The reference is to Dihya KalbI, a young follower of his of striking beauty. In fact, Umm Salama, Muhammads wife, once saw Gabriel talking to Muhammad and mistook the angel for Dihya KalbI.

Muhammad was commissioned as a prophet by Allah when he was forty years old; and he died at the age of sixty-three. He stayed in Medina for ten years.

The Prophet had the Best Knowledge

The Prophet had the best knowledge, and therefore it was obligatory for the believers to follow him obediently. Sometimes, Muhammad did or said something that some of the Companions did not approve. When this reaction was conveyed to the Prophet, he stood up and delivered an address: What has happened to the people to whom there was conveyed on my behalf a matter for which I granted permission and they disapproved it and avoided it By Allah, I have the best knowledge amongst them.

The test of true faith in Allah is for the believer to submit willingly to every decision made by His Apostle. Once there was a dispute between Zubair and an ansAr. Muhammad gave his decision, but the ansAr openly said that it favored Zubair, who was the Prophets cousin-his fathers sisters son. The Prophets color changed and Allah sent him this verse: Nay, by the Lord, they will not really believe until they make thee a judge of what is in dispute among them, and find in this no dislike of what thou decidest and submit with full submission (Quran :; hadIs).

But there is one hadIs, rather unusual, in which the Prophet strikes a more modest note. Muhammad once passed by as some people were grafting date-palm trees, i.e., combining the male with the female tree for a larger yield. Muhammad said: I do not find it of any use. As a result, people no longer grafted their trees and the yield declined. When Muhammad, a practical man, learned this, he said: If there is any use of it, then they should do it, for it was just a personal opinion of mine, and do not go after my personal opinion; but when I say to you anything on behalf of Allah, then do accept it, for I do not attribute lie to Allah, the Exalted and Glorious. This is the only instance of its kind but a godsend for Muslim reformers who seek the emancipation of secular thought from the clutches of the ulemas. I do not think this approach can go very far, but Muslim reformers and innovators have to make the best of it.

MIRACLES

The book also reports many miracles, mostly patterned after those of Jesus. A small quantity of water was brought to Muhammad, but when he placed his hand in the vessel, everyone was enabled to perform ablution. I saw water spouting from his fingers and the people performing ablution until the last amongst them performed it, the irrepressible Anas tells us. But he has two options to offer about the number of people seeking ablution. In one place, he tells us that their number was between fifty and eighty, in another three hundred.

On another occasion, the Prophet gives someone half a wasq of barley. It sufficed him and his family and his guests till the curious one weighed it. Had you not weighed it, you would be eating out of it and it would have remained intact for you, JAbir heard Muhammad telling him.

On the battlefield, on the day of Uhud, Sad saw Gabriel and Michael on the right and left sides of the Prophet in white clothes.

Other Apostles

At the end of the book, there are ahAdIs on the merits of other apostles like Jesus, Abraham, and Moses.

Muhammads world was not very large. He knew his own people, the tribes allied with them, the Arab Bedouins, the neighboring Jews and Christians. To the Jews and Christians, he offered his leadership, and in making that bid adopted some of their beliefs and practices and also gave recognition to their apostles. But when he failed in his bid, he made another use of these apostles-he used them against their own followers. What he spoke was not merely the voice of Allah but also the voice of all the apostles that had come before him. Therefore, those who did not believe in him did not in fact believe in their own apostles; and therefore they were as good as apostates. Recognizing the other prophets, though on his own terms, served a still greater purpose. It provided him with an apostolic lineage. Speaking of himself and Jesus, Muhammad says: Prophets are brothers in faith, having different mothers. Their religion is, however, one and there is no apostle between us [between Jesus and himself]. Muhammad comes as the last of the apostles and abrogates all previous revelations.

Al-zimma (People of the Covenant or Obligation)

Some ahAdIs on the merits of Moses reveal an interesting fact: the zimmIs did not originate with Umar but were already there in the time of the Prophet. The Jews were already second-class citizens and were treated roughly by the believer-hoodlums in Muhammads own day. For example, a Jew was selling goods; when an ansAr offered a price that was not acceptable to him, a dispute rose. During the dispute, the Jew said: By Allah, Who chose Moses amongst mankind. The ansAr gave him a blow on the face, chiding him for invoking Moses when Allahs Messenger is living with us. The Jew went to Muhammad, narrated the whole story, and supplicated him, saying: Abul-QAsim, I am a Zimmi [thus need your protection] by a covenant. Muhammad chided the ansAr and told him: Dont make distinction amongst the Prophets of Allah.

This is the liberalism we have found from Muhammad at his rare best. But he could not arrive at the still larger truth which declares: Dont make a distinction between different ummahs, for they are all part of one human brotherhood; dont make a distinction between different gods, for they all express the same Truth; dont make a distinction between Allah and AllAt, for one is also the other. An exclusive concept of God leads to an exclusive concept of ummah. This is so with other religions of Semitic origin too, an attitude of either/or, seldom both.

6

The Prophets Companions

The twenty-ninth book is on the Merits of the Companions (KitAb FazAil Al-SahAbah) of the Prophet. It praises Muhammads Companions, his lieutenants and relatives like Abu Bakr, Umar, and UsmAn; members of his family like FAtima, AlI, Hasan, and Husain; his wives like KhadIja, Aisha, Salama, and Zainab; and some loyal ansArs and other men associated with events and occasions important in the eyes of the Muslims of the days of the Prophet, like the Battle of Badr and the Oath of Allegiance under the Tree (Bayat al-RizwAn) at Hodeibia in March A.D. (those who took this oath were promised by Muhammad that they would never enter the fire of hell).

All of these people are praised not because they had a larger vision or a deeper humanity or a wider sense of justice than others but solely on one basis: their loyalty and utility to Muhammads person and cause. In totalitarian ideologies and creeds, faith and loyalty to the leader are the supreme virtues. The followers need have no other. To be saved, it is enough to be subservient.

THE MERITS OF ABU BAKR SIDDIQ

The original name of Abu Bakr SiddIq was Abdul Kabah. Muhammad changed his name to Abdullah Ibn AbI QuhAfa, but he soon came to be known by another name, Abu Bakr, the father of the maiden, the maiden being Aisha, whom Muhammad betrothed when she was six and married when she was nine. Abu Bakr became Islams first KhalIfa after Muhammad.

Muhammad had a high regard for Abu Bakrs services. If I were to choose as my bosom friend I would have chosen the son of Abu QuhAfa as my bosom friend, Muhammad said. When Muhammad was asked whom he loved best, he answered: Aisha, Aisha's father, Abu Bakr, and Umar in that order.

There are ahAdIs justifying the succession of Abu Bakr that may have been manufactured by their authors, even half-believingly, during the conflict around the question of succession that arose after Muhammads death. A woman came to Muhammad during his last sickness and asked him whom she should go to when he was no longer there. To Abu Bakr, Muhammad answered. Aishas report is even more to the point: Allahs Messenger in his last illness asked me to call Abu Bakr, her father, and her brother too, so that he might write a document, for he feared that someone else might be desirous of succeeding him.

Abu Bakr came to power through a coup détat. As soon as Muhammad died, the struggle for power began in earnest. AlI and AbbAs, the Prophets cousin and uncle, respectively, made the most of his dead body; they kept it to themselves and allowed no one else to take a hand in preparing it for burial. They locked the room from inside and secretly buried the body during the night in the very room in which he had died. Even Aisha, his favorite wife, was kept in the dark about it-she was sleeping in another hut at this time.

Outside, the struggle raged between the ansArs and the Emigrants. The ansArs met in the hall of Banu SAida to choose Sad b. UbAda, one of their own tribesmen, as the chief. When Abu Bakr and Umar got wind of this, they hurried to the spot with their own supporters. Abu Bakr told the Medinans that the Quraish were the best of the Arabs in blood and country, and that the Arabs will recognize authority only in this clan of Quraish. He told them: We are the Ameers; and you are our Wazeers. When this drew a protest from the ansArs, it was proposed that each party should choose its own separate Ameer. But this was not acceptable to the Meccan party, and Abu Bakr was chosen as the Ameer of Islam. In doing this, we jumped on Sad b. UbAda and someone said that we killed him. I said,

God kill him, Umar reports according to Ibn IshAq. The story is repeated by TabarI.

The next day, Abu Bakr declared himself the KhalIfa of Islam.

The Excellent Qualities of Umar B. Khattab

Umar b. KhattAb and Abu Bakr were an inseparable pair. I came and there came too Abu Bakr and Umar; I entered and there entered too Abu Bakr and Umar; I went out and there went out too Abu Bakr and Umar, Muhammad observed.

Umar was loyal to Muhammad. Once, while asleep, Muhammad found himself in Paradise and a woman performing ablution by the side of a palace. When he inquired, he was told that it (it is not clear whether it stands for the woman or the palace or both) was for Umar. So Muhammad thought of Umars feelings and turned back and went away. Umar wept when he was told about it. Could I at all feel any jealousy about you he said to Muhammad.

Umar was fanatical, narrow-minded, and strong in his hatred. Once Muhammad was persuaded to offer a funeral prayer for someone whom the Muslims called a hypocrite. Umar caught hold of the clothes of Allahs Messenger and said: Allahs Messenger, are you going to offer prayer, whereas Allah has forbidden to offer prayer for him. But Muhammad persisted. And lo, as he prayed, Allah revealed the following verse: Nor do thou ever pray for one of them that dies, nor stand at his grave; for they rejected God and His Apostle, and died in a state of perverse rebellion. Islam carried its hatred of its enemies even beyond the grave.

In fact Allah vindicated Umar more than once. The Muslim doctors mention fifty cases in which Umars ideas became Quranic revelations. Umar, however, modestly mentions only three. My Lord concorded with my Judgments on three occasions. In case of the Station of IbrAhIm, in case of the observance of the veil, and in case of the prisoners of Bardr.

The first instance refers to the fact that Muhammad and his followers prayed facing Jerusalem, the place of the Jewish

Temple, during the first fifteen months of their stay in Medina. Later on, by a divine injunction, the direction was changed to Mecca, a course which Umar had advocated even earlier.

We have already recounted the incident about the veil in our discussion of the Book of Salutations and Greetings, and shown how the divine injunction merely corroborated what Umar already stood for.

The third incident refers to the Quraish prisoners, one of whom was the Prophets uncle, AbbAs. Bakr had advised that they be freed for ransom, and Umar that they be killed. Muhammad accepted Bakrs advice in this particular case, but Allah concorded with the general approach of Umar. In fact, Allah chided the Prophet and told him that greed for gain in the shape of ransom should have no part in his calculations, and that his first duty as a Prophet was to engage in slaughter in the land: It is not for a Prophet to have captives until he has made slaughter in the land.... Had it not been for a previous ordainment from Allah, a severe penalty would have reached you for the ransom you took.

Umar is highly honored in Islamic history for his role in the spread of Arab imperialism. True, its real founder was Muhammad himself, a founder par excellence, who provided it with a theory, an ideology, a continuing motive, and the necessary religious rhetoric, successfully working out a grand model for his successors to imitate. But after him, Umars contribution too was considerable. He forged new instrumentalities, provided a new taste for booty, a new incentive. He put every Arab, even including newborn babes, on the states payroll. An Arab, he made it clear, had no other function except to be a coloniser and a soldier of Islamic imperialism.

This role of Umars is brought out in several ahAdIs. In a dream Muhammad saw himself drawing water from a tank. Then Abu Bakr took hold of the leather bucket, but he drew only two buckets; there was also weakness in his drawing. Then Umar took over with real strength. I did not see a person stronger than he drawing water, said Muhammad. These ahAdIs, we are told, refer to Umars future role in the spread of Muslim hegemony. In the Muslim annals, we find that Umar needed no great provocation to flourish his sword but was no great warrior on the battlefield.

In the lists of the slayers of the polytheists in the Battles of Badr and Uhud, his name appears only once. But if a man was a captive or was otherwise in his power, then Umar was quite brave with his sword. He met Mabad ibn Wahb, a Meccan who was captured in the Battle of Badr, and said to him tauntingly, Well, you are beaten now. The man said, Nay, by LAt and Uzza. Is that the manner of speech for a captive infidel towards a Believer asked Umar as he cut off his head with his sword.

On another occasion, as we have already seen, Umar advised similar treatment for seventy other prisoners. Hand them over to us so that we may cut off their heads, he told Muhammad. Give Aqil [AlIs brother] to AlI that he may cut off his head, and hand over such and such relative to me that I may cut off his head, he said.

Killing captives in cold blood was cruel enough. But why should a man be made to slay his own kith and kin so pointedly This agreed with the requirements of the new creed, which weakened a mans old ties and strengthened his new ones as a means of increasing his ummah consciousness. This was also the most effective way of proving ones loyalty to the new creed and the new leader. If one killed a parent or a brother or a cousin for the sake of Allah, it was something to be proud of. It was a feather in ones ideological cap. The same psychology was at work when Umar, on another occasion, tried to persuade Abu Jandal, the son of Soheil, to kill his own father because the father was merely one of the idolators whose blood is equivalent to that of dogs. The story is quoted in full in Mirkhonds biography of the Prophet.

Umar was fortunate in this respect. The only man he was able to slay in the Battles of Badr and Uhud was his maternal uncle. You are under the impression that I killed your father, Umar said to SaId b. al-As. As a matter of fact I killed my maternal uncle al-As b. HashAm b. al-MughIra, he said, trying to correct SaIds mistaken impression.

It is difficult to accept this attitude, so contrary to human nature and custom. But there is nothing unusual about it. The same things have taken place in our own time under Communism. Only a few decades ago, in Russia and even in China, members of the Party were encouraged to denounce their parents and close relatives and inform on them. It was supposed to strengthen their class consciousness. Those who indulged in such unfilial behavior were honored as heroes. Similar ideologies and attitudes lead to similar values and usages.

The ethics of this practice was valid for the followers but not necessarily for the Prophet. And though he sent his parents and uncle to hellfire, he was more considerate toward his living kinsmen. He was kind to Abul As b. al-RabI, his son-in-law, who was taken prisoner in the Battle of Badr, releasing him without any ransom. In the same battle, Muhammad also ordered his followers not to kill any member of the BanU HAshim, the family to which he belonged, and also to spare his uncle, al-AbbAs. But one Muslim, Abu Huzayfa, who had participated in the slaying of his own father, did not like this. Are we to kill our fathers and sons and our brothers and our families and leave al-AbbAs By Allah, if I meet him I will flash my sword in him, he said aloud.

When this reached the ears of Muhammad, he was much troubled. O Abu Hafs, ought the face of the apostles uncle to be marked with the sword he said to Umar, who replied, Let me off with his head! By Allah, the man is a false Muslim. Abu Huzayfa used to say, I never felt safe after my words that day. I was always afraid unless martyrdom atoned for them. He was killed as a martyr in the Battle of al-YamAma. This story is narrated by Ibn Ishaq.

USMAN B. AFFAN

UsmAn b. AffAn converted to Islam because of his love for Ruqayya, one of the daughters of Muhammad, whom he married. After she died, Muhammad gave him another of his daughters, Umm Kulsum. According to Muslim tradition, UsmAn was somewhat of a dandy. When the Emigrants went to Medina and built their mosque with voluntary labor, it was complained that he shirked manual work while one AmmAr, a convert from the proletarian strata, was burdened with work that was too heavy. UsmAn became the third KhalIfa of Islam and died, in the tradition of many other Muslim KhalIfas, at the hands of his brethren in faith.

Aisha reports that the Prophet would receive Bakr and Umar while lying in bed with his thigh or his shank uncovered. But when UsmAn came, he arranged his clothes and covered his thigh and shank, saying, Should I not show modesty to one whom even the Angels show modesty.

From this hadIs, some Muslim doctors have derived a rule of decorum that when one is receiving a visitor, the thigh of a person is not that part of the body which should be necessarily covered. Other doctors of theology and law, with great ingenuity, did not agree with this conclusion. From the arguments advanced on both sides, one can get the feel of Islamic scholarship at work, the order of truth it deals with, and its way of arriving at truth. It can be subtle about nothing, and its concerns are mostly with trifles.

There is another interesting hadIs given under this head. Allahs Messenger was in one of the gardens of Medina [he had seven], reclining against a pillow-a person came asking for the gate to be opened, whereupon he said: Open it for him and give him glad tidings of Paradise and lo, it was Abu Bakr. Umar and UsmAn also visited the Prophet under the same circumstances and received the same tidings. Here we have in one hadIs the trinity of successive KhalIfas with the promise of Paradise in store for each.

ALI B. ABI TALIB

AlI b. AbI Talib was the cousin and son-in-law of Muhammad. There were several ahAdIs to support the claim that the supreme position in Islam rightfully belonged to him and his family by inheritance. Muhammad had once told AlĪ: You are in the same position with relation to me as Aaron [Harun] was in relation to Moses but with this explicit difference that there is no prophet after me.

Another hadIs tells us whom Muhammad regarded as his family and, therefore, as the rightful heirs of at least his secular powers. In a mubahala (trial by prayer and curses) with the Christians, Muhammad had said: Let us summon our children and your children. For his part the Prophet called AlI, FAtima, Hasan, and Husain. O Allah, they are my family, he said.

According to another hadIs, almost on his deathbed Muhammad told the believers: I am leaving behind you two weighty things:... the Book of Allah... [and] the members of my household. I remind you of your duties to the members of my family. The definition of the members of my family, or people of the house (ahlul-bait), is such that it excluded the Prophets wives but included those for whom zakAt was forbidden; i.e., AlI, Aqil, Jafar, and AbbAs and their offspring.

Another hadIs also proves AlIs claim. On the day of Khaibar, Muhammad said he would give the standard to a person who loves Allah and His Messenger and Allah and His Messenger love him too. Then he called AlI, whose eyes were inflamed, and applied his own saliva as a cure. Then the Prophet told him: Fight with them until they bear testimony to the fact that there is no god but Allah and Muhammad is his prophet. AlI accepted the responsibility and told the Prophet: I will fight them until they are like us (,).

Now in granting AlI the banner of victory, to the exclusion of Bakr and Umar, was not the Prophet symbolically granting him the future leadership of Islam, a leadership which Umar coveted in his heart Never did I cherish for leadership but on that day [the day of Khaibar], Umar says.

Allah is partial. The fact that He and His Messenger loved AlI made many things different for him. Acts of omission and commission which were punished in others were overlooked in AlI. After a battle fought under his general command, he took a slave-girl for himself even before the holy one-fifth had been made over to the Apostles exchequer, a serious lapse inviting secular as well as divine punishment. KhAlid b. WalId, the second-in-command, complained to Muhammad. The Prophet was furious, his face becoming red with anger, at the complaint.

He would not even entertain such an accusation against AlI, for AlI loves Allah and His Messenger, and Allah and His Messenger love AlI (TirmizI, vol. II, hadIs). What would you say of the state of justice when the authorities refuse even to record the first report

In a battle, AlI was both brave and cunning. During the Battle of the Ditch, Amr b. Abdu Wudd, a man of ninety years, and AlI agreed to meet in single combat. At one point in the contest, AlI said to Amr: Have we not agreed that no one should come to my or to thy aid. Amr asked: Then what has happened AlI replied: See, thy brother is coming behind thee. As Amr looked to his rear, AlI snatched an opportunity to strike that accursed man. Amr exclaimed: Boy, thou hast deceived me. But the lord and receptacle of victory exclaimed: War is a deception. The story is given by Mirkhond.

AlI was not only Muhammads best general, he was also his executioner. While Muhammad awarded the punishments, AlI was often chosen to execute them. He was asked to flog people found guilty of drinking or of fornication ; he also beheaded people on the orders of the Apostle. But the most gruesome case was that of the captives of the BanU Quraiza, eight hundred strong, who were all beheaded in a single day in the market of Medina by AlI and Zubair (see above p.). The apostle of God ordered a trench to be dug in a suitable place, and as they [the prisoners] were brought out in squads... AlI and Zubair set about striking off their heads, by order of his lordship the apostle.... On that day AlI and Zubair were till the evening engaged in slaying the BanI Quraiz, and when the night set in, the lamp of life of those who yet remained [to be executed] was extinguished by torchlight, Mirkhond records in his Persian biography of the Prophet.

SAD B. ABI WAQQAS

Sad b. AbI WaqqAs joined Muhammad when he was only thirteen and accompanied him on almost all his campaigns. He was one of those ten men who had been promised Paradise during their own lifetime by Muhammad. He worked as a doorman or sentinel for Muhammad during the night. After he was appointed to this responsibility, Aisha tells us, Allahs Messenger slept such a sound sleep that I heard the noise of his snoring.

Sad was also the impetus for several Quranic verses. We give one example. His mother took an oath that she would never talk with him until he abandoned his faith, and she neither ate nor drank and said: Allah has commanded you to treat well your parents and I am your mother and I command you to do this. This, however, was the old polytheistic morality. But Allah now taught a new code and revealed the following verse of the Quran: We have enjoined on man kindness to parents: but if they strive to force thee to join with Me anything of which thou hast no knowledge, obey them not (:; hadIs).

THE MERITS OF ZAID B. HARIS

Zaid b. Haris was the adopted son of Muhammad and participated in most of his expeditions. Muhammad saw Zaids wife half-uncovered and felt a great attraction for her. Though the whole matter caused a great scandal, he got Zaid to divorce her and married her. This was facilitated by the descent of a revelation from the High Heaven. Until now, following the old Arab custom, Zaid was socially known as the son of Muhammad; but after this marriage, he again began to be called by the name of his natural father. This too was dictated by a revelation from Allah: Call them by the name of their fathers. This is more equitable with Allah (Quran :; hadIs).

THE MERITS OF KHADIJA

In the list of merits, only four wives of the Prophet are mentioned: KhadIja, Aisha, Salama, and Zainab. KhadIja was Muhammads first employer and, though senior to him in age by fifteen years, his first wife; she was also the first to encourage him in his apostolic mission. According to Muhammad, KhadIja was the best of the women of her time, just as Mary, the daughter of Imran, was the best of the women of her time.

Aisha says: Never did I feel jealous of any woman as I was jealous of KhadIja. She had died three years before he [Muhammad] married me. I often heard him praise her, and his Lord... had commanded him to give her the glad tidings of a palace of Jewels in Paradise, and whenever he slaughtered a sheep he presented its meat to her female companions. Once, in a fit of jealousy, Aisha told Muhammad: Why do you remember one of those old women of the Quraish with gums red and who is so long dead-while Allah has given you a better one in her stead.

THE MERITS OF AISHA

The chapter on Aisha is the longest. A daughter of Abu Bakr, she was betrothed to Muhammad when she was six years old and he was fifty. The marriage was consummated when she was nine. Muhammad had a very soft spot for her. The excellence of Aisha as compared to women is that of TharId [a dish of very thin bread soaked in a broth of meat and sometimes vegetables which Muhammad very much relished] over all other food, Muhammad said.

He told her sentimentally: I saw you in a dream for three nights when an angel brought you to me in a silk cloth and he said: Here is your wife. On another occasion, he told her: I can well discern when you are pleased with me and when you are annoyed with me.... When you are pleased with me you say: No, by the Lord of Muhammad, and when you are annoyed with me, you say: No, by the Lord of IbrAhIm.

According to a hadIs on Aishas own authority, People sent their gifts when it was the turn of Aisha seeking thereby the pleasure of Allahs Messenger. A time-honored practice. When people want to please an official or any person in authority, they try to please his son or his wife or even his butler, though a strict code might call this bribery.

Aisha also narrates what modern newsmen would call a human-interest story. The other wives of Muhammad sent FatIma, his daughter, to him. Muhammad saw her when he was lying with me in my mantle, Aisha narrates. FatIma told Muhammad: Allahs Messenger, verily, your wives have sent me to you in order to ask you to observe equity in case of the daughter of Abu QuhAfa. O daughter, dont you love whom I love Muhammad replied with a counterquestion. She said yes;

and having been thus silenced, she went back. The wives wanted her to go again but she said: By Allah, I will never talk to him about this matter.

Then they chose Zainab to represent them. Zainab too was a favorite wife of Muhammad, someone who was somewhat equal in rank with me in the eyes of Allahs Messenger, as Aisha puts it. Muhammad received her in the same very state when FatIma entered. She too told him that the other wives had sent her to seek "equity in the case of the daughter of Abu QuhAfa. Muhammad made no answer. But, in the words of Aisha, she [Zainab] then came to me and showed harshness to me and I was seeing the eyes of Allah's Messenger whether he would permit me. Zainab went on until I came to know that Allahs Messenger would not disapprove if I retorted. Then I exchanged hot words until I made her quiet. Thereupon Allahs Messenger smiled and said: She is the daughter of Abu Bakr.

Another hadIs throws some more light on Muhammads conjugal life and also on the life of the women around him. Aisha reports that when Allahs Messenger set out on a journey, he used to cast lots amongst his wives to determine which of them would accompany him. Once, as luck would have it, Hafsa and Aisha were selected. When it was night Allahs Messenger used to travel on camel with Aisha. But Hafsa asked Aisha if she would agree to change seats with her, for then you would see what you do not generally see and I would see what I do not generally see. Aisha generously agreed, but when she saw Hafsa and the Prophet together she fell into a tantrum. The translator explains that though Aishas position was eminent and exalted, she was yet a woman and thus could not be absolutely free from envy. About Muhammads own behavior, he says that in journey it is not compulsory to observe perfect equity amongst women in all respects. A rule within a rule, but all very convenient.

Even during his last illness, Muhammad was thinking of Aisha. Where I would be tomorrow, where I would be tomorrow he inquired, thinking that the turn of Aisha was not near. And when it was my turn, Allah called him to his heavenly home and his head was between my neck and chest, Aisha tells us.

Once Muhammad told her: Aisha, here is Gabriel offering you greetings. She replied: Let there be peace and blessing of Allah upon him, and added: He sees what I do not see. One may wonder whether she always believed in Muhammads angels, but certainly she enjoyed her role as the Prophets favorite wife.

In fact, Aisha knew her Prophet a little too well. There is an interesting story narrated by Ibn IshAq. During his last illness, just a few days before his death, Muhammad found Aisha crying with headache. Muhammad said to her: Would it distress you if you were to die before me so that I might wrap you in your shroud and pray over you and bury you Aisha replied: Methink I see you if you had done that returning to my house and spending a bridal night therein with one of your wives. The Apostle smiled and then his pain overcame him as he was going the round of his wives, until he was overpowered in the house of MaimUna. He then called his wives and asked their permission to be nursed in my house, and they agreed, Aisha adds. And there Muhammad died in her bosom.

THE MERITS OF FATIMA

Fatima was Muhammads daughter by his first wife, Khadija. She was married to AlI, his cousin. She had two surviving sons, Hasan and Husain, from whom are descended the posterity of Muhammad, known as the Saiyids, meaning masters.

Stating the position of Muslim theology, the translator assures us that FatIma is undoubtedly the chief of the ladies of Paradise and her two sons ImAm Hasan and Husain are the chiefs of the young people of Paradise. Muhammad himself called her al-batUl, the virgin.

The ahAdIs on FatIma tell us an interesting story. After Mecca was conquered, AlI sent a proposal of marriage to the daughter of the late Abu Jahl, an adversary of Muhammad and important chief of the BanU MakhzUm. FatIma, his wife, complained about it to Muhammad. Muhammad put his foot down on the proposal and declared from the pulpit: I would not allow them; I would not allow them; the only alternative is that

AlI should divorce my daughter [and then marry their daughter], for my daughter is part of me. He who disturbs her disturbs me and he who offends her offends me.

So it seems that if the father of a woman had sufficiently strong influence, her husband could not marry another woman in spite of the custom of polygamy. In the case of KhadIja, she had the influence in her own right and as an employer held all the strings in her hands. Therefore, even though she was very much older than Muhammad, she was his only wife while she lived. It was only after her death that Muhammad started on his practice of polygamy.

THE MERITS OF ZUBAIR AND TALHA

Zubair embraced Islam when he was fifteen or sixteen. He was Muhammads cousin and Abu Bakrs son-in-law. Thanks to his political connections, he later became the richest person in Arabia. He was the proud owner of a thousand slaves-a number unknown in pre-Muslim Arabia. Slavery in earnest and on such a large scale began with the advent of Islam.

About Zubair Muhammad said: For every prophet there is a helper and my helper is Zubair. In the battle over the succession that raged later on, Zubair fought against AlI with the help of Aisha and was killed at the age of sixty-four by one of the partisans of Ali.

During the Battle of Uhud, Talha saved the life of Muhammad, and subsequently he took part in all the campaigns led by Muhammad. On the day of the Battle of Camel (in which Aisha, sitting on a camel, led rebel forces against AlI), Talha was murdered by one MarwAn b. Hakam in revenge; for it was alleged that he had a hand in the murder of UsmAn, the third KhalIfa.

THE MERITS OF SAD B. MUAZ

When Sad b. Muaz died as a result of wounds received at the Battle of Badr, Muhammad said that the Throne of the most Gracious shook at his death. Most Muslim traditionalists take this literally, but some regard it as a metaphor denoting Allahs joy at receiving a beloved friend in His heavenly home.

There are other traditions about him, some of them recorded by Ibn IshAq. Sad was a fat man, but his bier was very light to carry. Muhammad said that unseen angels were giving him their shoulder. On the same occasion he also said: Every wailing woman lies except the one who wept Sad b. Muaz. Sad was a chief of the BanU Aus, who embraced Islam at Medina after the first pledge at Al-Aqaba. Seen through less-believing eyes, he was treacherous and a fanatical sadist. On the day of the Battle of Badr, he was guarding Muhammads hut along with some other ansArs. He watched with displeasure as the Muslim soldiers laid their hands on the prisoners. You seem to dislike what the people are doing, Muhammad said to him. Yes, he replied. By God, it is the first defeat that God brought on the infidel and I would rather see them slaughtered than left alive, he added, according to a tradition quoted by Ibn Ishdq.

The conspiracy to murder Kab ibn Ashraf, the poet, was worked out in consultation with Sad b. Muaz. He also played a prominent part in causing the slaughter of eight hundred men of the Bang Quraiza, the erstwhile allies of his own tribe, the Aus.

BILAL

One night Muhammad heard the sound of BilAls steps before him in Paradise. The next day, he asked him to narrate the act by which he hoped to receive such a good reward. BilAl replied that he had done nothing so deserving except that I perform complete ablution during the night or day I observe prayer with that purification what Allah ordained for me to pray.

Consistent with his lowly position, this is all the notice BilAl receives in the Book of the Companions (in fact it is the shortest notice in the whole book). We would have skipped over him altogether but for the fact that he exemplifies a certain moral. He was an Abyssinian slave who was persecuted by his master, Umayya b. Khalaf, in Mecca. Since the Arab custom allowed manumission, he was ransomed by Abu Bakr and then converted to Islam. We are glad that BilAl escaped his alleged persecution, but what does this conversion to Islam mean Did he become a better man Did he became more forgiving, more kind and compassionate, less of a persecutor in his own turn The brief references we have to him in the annals of early Islam hardly give us that impression.

Abdul-RahmAn, an important Companion, tells us a story which is narrated by Ibn IshAq and repeated by TabarI. On the day of the Battle of Badr, Abdul-RahmAn was carrying coats of mail which, he said, he had looted. Just at that time he encountered his old friend Umayya b. Khalaf and his son. Umayya, who belonged to the routed army of the Quraish, saw that he might have a chance of saving his life if he fell into the hands of Abdul-RahmAn as a prisoner, a state which would give him protection and from which he could be redeemed by paying an appropriate ransom. O Abdul-RahmAn, he said, wont you take me a prisoner, for I am more valuable than the coats of mail which you have. Abdul-RahmAn in turn replied, By God, I will. Then he threw away the coats of mail and took his friend and his friends son, now his prisoners, by their hands.

Just then, BilAl saw his old persecutor and began to shout: The arch-infidel, Umayya b. Khalaf! May I not live if he lives. The Muslims gathered. In vain did Abdul-RahmAn claim immunity for his prisoners. BilAl kept shouting, and the Muslims hewed them to pieces with their swords until they were dead. In later days, Abdul-RahmAn used to say, God have mercy on BilAl. I lost my coats of mail and he deprived me of my prisoners.

There is another instance of the same kind denoting a sadistic pleasure in cruelty for its own sake. At the Battle of Khaibar, after the great carnage of the day, Muhammad ordered BilAl to bring to him SafIyya, the young wife of the chief of the vanquished tribe, whose husband, father, and brother had just been murdered. BilAl brought her and her cousin across the battlefield, which was littered with the corpses of their kith and kin. They cried in pain and horror. BilAl explained that he did it on purpose; he wished to see their grief and anger stirred up.

Most conversions carried out by the soldiers and priests of proselytizing religions are of this nature. They bring no change in the individual. In fact, often they make him worse. But organized conversions are now, as they have always been, part of an aggressive politics.

THE MERITS OF ABU DUJANA

Anas reports: Allahs Messenger took hold of his sword on the Day of Uhud and said: Who would take it from me Everyone present stretched his hand saying: I would do it. He [Allahs Apostle] said: Who would take it in order to fulfil its rights Then the people withdrew their hands. SimAk b. Kharasha Abu DujAna said: I am here to take it and fulfil its rights. He took it and struck the heads of the polytheists.

The Two Abdullahs

The names of two Abdullahs also appear on the merit list. One of them was the son of Umar; the other was the son of Zubair by Asma, the daughter of Bakr. Both were killed by the Umayyad general HajjAj. The general even led the funeral prayer for Abdullah b. Umar after contriving to murder him. The body of Abdullah ibn Zubair was found hanging outside Medina on the road to Mecca. He died when he was seventy-two after having been a Khalifa of a sort for nine years.

THE MERITS OF ANAS AND HURAIRA

On the list of merits also appear the names of Anas, Muhammads servant and bodyguard for ten years, and Huraira, to whom we owe a disproportionately large number of traditions. Huraira in his own lifetime was known as Huraira the liar. He explains: You are under the impression that Abu Huraira transmits so many ahAdIs from Allahs Messenger.... I was a poor man and I served Allahs Messenger... whereas the immigrants remained busy with transactions in the bazaar.... I never forgot anything that I heard from him [Muhammad].

THE MERITS OF HASSAN B. SABIT

An interesting person on the merit list is HassAn b. SAbit, a poet whom Muhammed employed for replying to the lampoons against him by unbeliever poets. Muhammad said to him:

Write satire against the unbelievers; Gabriel is with you. On another occasion, Muhammad told him: HassAn, give a reply on behalf of the Messenger of Allah. And to Allah Himself, he petitioned: O Allah, help him with RUh-ul-Qudus [the holy spirit].

Aisha gives us a fuller version of the story. According to her, Muhammad had said: Satirise against the Quraish, for the satire is more grievous to them than the hurt from an arrow. With that end in view, Muhammad sent for two poets, Ibn RawAha and Kab b. MAlik, and commissioned them to write satires. Unsatisfied with their compositions, the Prophet next sent for HassAn b. Sabit, who told him: Now you have called for this lion who strikes the enemies with his tail.... I shall tear them with my tongue as the leather is torn. He then declared his intention to satirize Abu SufyAn. Permit me to write satire against Abu SufyAn, he said to Muhammad. But there was a difficulty: how could it be done successfully without involving the Prophet, for Muhammad and Abu SufyAn shared the same lineage Abu Bakr was appointed to help HassAn with the lineage of the Quraish, which he knew very well. Understanding the intricacies, HassAn then went to Muhammad and assured him: By Him Who has sent you with Truth, I shall draw out from them your name as hair is drawn out from the flour.

HassAn gave Muhammad complete satisfaction. I heard Allahs Messenger saying: HassAn satirised against them and gave satisfaction to the Muslims and disquieted the non-Muslims, says Aisha (,).

Muhammad was grateful to HassAn, who was not altogether cut when he later took an active part in the scandal against Aisha, though all the participants were flogged. Aisha was the first to excuse HassAn. Leave him for he defended Allahs Messenger, she said. Muhammad was opposed to poets and poetry, but when they were in his service, it was a different matter.

MUHAMMAD AT THE CENTER

Muhammad is at the center of everything. He tells his followers: I am a source of safety and security to my

Companions.... and my Companions are a source of security for the Ummah.

As things converge toward Muhammad, they become better, but as they proceed further away from him, they decline in status as well as in quality and authenticity. The best of my Ummah would be those of the generation nearest to mine. Then those nearest to them, then those nearest to them. In this ranking and ordering, the Prophet comes first; then come his Companions; then come the successors of the Companions (tAbiUn). Muslim divines have not been idle, and they have worked out the exact period of each era. According to one important opinion, the first period is coextensive with the life of the Companions (i.e., years, as the last Companion died in A.H.); the second period extends till the life of the successors of the Companions (UP to A.H.); and the third is coextensive with the life of those who followed the successors (till A.H.).

At the end of the book, the Prophet warns the coming generations of Muslims: Do not revile my Companions, do not revile my Companions.

VIRTUE, DESTINY, KNOWLEDGE, REMEMBRANCE OF GOD

The thirtieth book is on Virtue, Good Manners, and the Joining of the Ties of Relationship.

Many of the principles enunciated in this book are good except that they have a sectarian orientation. While the Muslim has a permanent quarrel with polytheists, he must not feel enmity toward a fellow Muslim. It is not lawful for a Muslim that he should keep his relations estranged with his brother beyond three days.

A Muslim is the brother of a Muslim. He neither oppresses him nor humiliates him nor looks down upon him.... All things of a Muslim are inviolable for his brother in faith: his blood, his wealth and his honour.

A Muslim should visit his sick brother. When a Muslim visits his brother in Islam he is supposed to remain in the fruit garden of Paradise until he returns. And, of course, the sickness of a Muslim is no sickness; it is a reward. When a Muslim falls ill, his compensation is that his minor sins are obliterated. If he suffers pain, even to the extent of stepping on a thorn, Allah elevates him in rank or effaces his sins because of that. This idea runs through many ahAdIs

Believers should not nurse mutual rancor. The gates of Paradise are not opened but on two days, Monday and Thursday, and then every servant of Allah is granted pardon who does not associate anything with Allah except the person in whose heart there is rancour against his brother.

In short, all Muslims should help each other, stand by each other, and feel for each other. A believer is like a brick for another believer, the one supporting the other. All Muslims are one body. The believers are like one person; if his head aches, the whole body aches with fever and sleeplessness.

Other Virtuies

Charity and forgiveness are recommended. Abuse and backbiting and tale-carrying are censured (,, and). It is meritorious to speak the truth, for truth leads one to Paradise. But lying is permissible in three cases: In battle, for bringing reconciliation amongst persons and the narration of the words of the husband to his wife, and the narration of the words of a wife to her husband.

Nonviolence

Nonviolence of a sort is also preached. When any one of you fights with his brother, he should spare his face. The face should be avoided because, as the Prophet himself explains, Allah created Adam in His own image.

Similarly, if a man goes to a bazaar or a mosque with arrows, he should take care of their pointed heads so that these might not do any harm to a Muslim.

Retribution

If we could forget Allahs partiality for Muslims, the following could be considered an eloquent rendering of the law of retribution: The claimants would get their claims on the Day of Resurrection so much so that the hornless sheep would get its claim from the horned sheep. Therefore a Muslim should not oppress another Muslim and, in fact, should help him. A Muslim is the brother of a fellow-Muslim. He should neither commit oppression upon him nor ruin him, and he who meets the need of a brother, Allah would meet his needs, and he who relieves a Muslim from hardship, Allah would relieve him from hardships to which he would be put on the Day of Resurrection, and he who did not expose the follies of a Muslim, Allah would conceal his follies on the Day of Resurrection.

Subject People

Such benevolence as is compatible with jizyA, spoils, and holy war was allowed by some believers toward the nonbelievers too. When HishAm saw the farmers of Syria, who had been made to stand in the sun... [and] detained for JizyA, he was reminded of the Prophets words: Allah would torment those who torment people in the world. Obviously, HishAm extended the definition of people to include men other than Muslims.

THE PROPHETS COVENANT WITH ALLAH

Muhammad was somewhat more indulgent toward his own lapses. If he ill-treated his followers, that brought him no blame, secular or divine, and, in fact, turned into a blessing for the sufferers. O Allah, I make a covenant with Thee against which Thou wouldst never go. I am a human being and thus for a Muslim whom I give any harm or whom I scold or upon whom I invoke curse or whom I beat, make this a source of blessing, purification and nearness to Thee on the Day of Resurrection. One would think that to err is human, not apostolic; at least, not in such grave matters.

The Book of Piety and Softening of Hearts

The subject of virtue is also discussed in the fortieth book, pertaining to Piety and Softening of Hearts (al-zuhd wa al-raqAiq).

Here are mentioned certain acts which are considered pious and meritorious. Widows, orphans, and the poor should be treated benevolently. Charity should be given to the poor and the wayfarer. The merit of building mosques is stressed. He who builds a mosque for Allah, Allah would build for him a house in Paradise.

Any ostentatious display of ones deeds is deplored. If anyone makes a hypocritical display, Allah will make a display of him. Therefore, one should not publicize ones lapses and omissions. All the people of my Ummah would get pardon for their sins except those who publicize them.

The great theological sin of polytheism does not go unmentioned. Allah the Most High and Exalted states: I am the One, One who does not stand in need of a partner. If anyone does anything in which he associates anyone else with Me, I shall abandon him with one with whom he associates Allah. This is the first time that Allah lets a man off so lightly and does not seize him and roast him in hellfire for the great sin of polytheism.

Muhammad also disapproved of sneezing and yawning. The yawning is from the devil, he said.

The Vanity of Worldly Riches

Several ahAdIs at the very beginning of the book show the vanity of worldly possessions, and how worldly wealth perishes and only good deeds remain. Muhammad sent Abu Ubaida to collect jizyA from the tribes of Bahrain. As soon as the news of his return came, the ansArs gathered round Muhammad. Muhammad smiled and said: I think you have heard about the arrival of Abu Ubaida with goods from Bahrain. They said: Yes. Muhammad now did some thinking out loud and said that the new riches might corrupt them. By Allah, it is not the poverty about which I fear in regard to you but I am afraid in your case that the worldly riches may be given to you as were given to those who had gone before you and you begin to vie with one another for them as they vied for them, and these may destroy you as these destroyed them.

This sentiment was duplicated by Umar while distributing the holy one-fifth amongst the Medinans, part of a booty valued at thirty million dirhams (besides many maidens and a vast number of fine Persian horses, nine falling to the lot of every combatant) won at the Battle of Jalola under the generalship of Sad, from an outlying province of Persia. The sentiment sounded pious and it still does. It has come down the corridor of history proving the great piety of Umar. But the basic question about the whole business of holy war, burning, pillage, booty, jizyA, and how these can become legitimate and moral has really never bothered Muslim theologians and scholars or even the Sufis. They can strain at a gnat but are ready to swallow a camel.

Several ahAdIs show that the holy war against the infidels was not only a pious act but a profitable business. Utba b. GhazwAn tells us: I was the seventh amongst seven who had been with Allahs Messenger and we had nothing to eat but the leaves of the tree.... We found a sheet which we tore in two and divided between myself and Sad b. Malik. I made the lower garment with half of it and so did Sad.... and today there is none amongst us who has not become the governor of a city.

Theology Dominates Morality

The Prophets moral teaching is dominated by theology. For example, the Book of Virtue and Good Manners opens with ahAdIs which enjoin the believers to accord benevolent treatment to their parents and to obey them. Who among the people is most deserving of good treatment Your mother, again your mother, again your mother, then your father, then your nearest relatives according to the order of nearness, replies Muhammad.

But if morality conflicts with Muslim theology, the latter prevails. We have already seen how Allah Himself ordered Sad b. AbI WaqqAs not to obey his parents if they stood for polytheism (Quran :, :).

Not merely to disobey them, but if necessary to oppose them in more active ways. The son of Abdullah ibn Ubayy, an ansAr, tells Muhammad: If you really want him [his father] killed, command me to do it and I will bring you his head... [but] if you order another to kill him, I shall not afterwards be able to bear the sight of his murderer.... I shall kill him-and then

I shall have killed one of the faithful for an infidel, and I shall go to hell. What a combination of piety and filial duty!

Similarly, there are several traditions which boast how Abu Hozayfa, an Emigrant, helped Hamza to kill his own father by giving him a cut with his sword at the Battle of Badr.

Muhammad is praised in Islamic lore for joining of the ties of relationship. But the fact is that the believers were encouraged to rebel against these very ties in order to disorient them altogether from the old life and to strengthen their exclusive loyalty to the new leader and the new ummah. For the assassination of a poetess of Medina, Asma hint MarwAn, one Umayr ibn Adi, a man of her own clan, was chosen. That helped him to prove his zeal and loyalty to the cause of Islam. After driving his sword through the sleeping woman with one of her children still at her breast, he came to Muhammad to inform him. You have done a service to Allah and His Messenger, the Prophet told him gratefully.

Muhammads Mother in Hell

For the same theological reason, Muhammad was ready to consign his father, his noble-hearted uncle Abu TAlib, and even his mother to the flames of hellfire.

In this respect, the polytheists, who were not theological, were better than the Muslims. After the conquest of Mecca, when Muhammad became supreme in Arabia, and the smaller tribes had to pay homage to his power and prophethood, two brothers, chiefs of a tribe inhabiting Yemen, came to Muhammad and showed their willingness to embrace Islam. They were converted. They hated to eat the heart of an animal but were made to do so in order to prove that their break with their old polytheism was genuine. Later on, during a conversation with Muhammad, their late mother came in for a mention, and Muhammad told them that she was in hell. Both turned away from him in anger. Come back, my own mother too is there with yours, Muhammad cried in an unsuccessful effort to entice them back. As they departed the two brothers said: This man has not only made us eat the heart of the animals, but said that our mother is in hell: who would follow him

Lack of Universality

Another feature of the Prophets teaching on morals, inevitably flowing from its predominantly theological nature, is its lack of universality. Faith, equity, justice are only for the Muslims in their mutual relationships. To the infidels and unbelievers another code, another set of rules, is applied. The lives of their males are forfeit; their women are legitimate objects of concubinage and bondage; their children are meant for slavery; and their wealth and property for pillage and booty.

A sectarian attitude informs all matters large or small. When two Muslims meet, they are to greet each other. The better of the two is one who is the first to give a greeting. But Muhammad advises his followers not to greet Jews and Christians first. Similarly, if you meet a Muslim on the road, you are to be courteous and step aside to give him the way, but if you meet a Jew or a Christian, you are to push him aside.

When a Muslim dies, fellow Muslims should follow his bier. in fact, this is one of the five or six rights of a Muslim over another Muslim. And in the same vein, a Muslim should offer a prayer of mercy for a fellow Muslim. But Allah forbids this courtesy toward non-Muslims. It is another matter that some Muslims do not live up to the Prophets teachings. But Muhammad himself was very particular about keeping away from the funerals of non-Muslims. According to Muslim tradition, one MukhayrIq, a learned Jewish priest, recognized Muhammad as the promised prophet and even bestowed seven gardens on him (according to some traditions, they were part of the war booty seized from the Jews of Medina). He also fought alongside Muhammad on the day of Uhud, though it was a Sabbath, and died in the battle. But though his corpse was allowed to be buried near the Muslims, Muhammad did not attend his funeral or pray for him. MukhayrIq was the best of the Jews, as Muhammad called him, but he was still not entitled to a Muslim funeral prayer.

Lack of Inwardness

Muhammads moral teaching also lacks inwardness. It does not seem to know that mans acts emanate from his thoughts and desires, which in turn are rooted in the separative ego and in nescience. True, Muhammad could not have heard of Indian Yoga, though the Buddhist influence had been penetrating the Middle East for many centuries; but this idea was not entirely unknown to Semitic traditions which he knew and in some ways had made his own. Jesus had preached that out of the heart proceed evil thoughts, murders, adulteries, fornications, theft, false witness, blasphemies. But Muhammad failed to benefit from this source. The fact is that he founded a very outward religion.

Without inner purification, there can be no higher ethical life. Even piety is no substitute for purity and for inner self-understanding and inner self-culture and aspiration. An unpurified heart merely rationalizes mans lusts, violence, and prurience; garbing itself in pious clothing, it gives the theology of a Moloch-Allah demanding the blood of the infidels; it gives an ethics of jihAd, war booty, and tribute.

The lack of a philosophy and praxis of inner culture fails to bring about any real sublimation; it imposes only an outer code, leading to a reluctant and even rebellious conformity. For example, Muhammad customarily visited his wives in rotation. But, as might be expected, he found it burdensome to observe this practice. This I have power to do; but thou, O Lord, are the master over that of which I have no power [love for each], he said. So Allah had to intervene with more accommodating revelations.

Destiny

The thirty-first book, the Book of Destiny (Qadr), contains only fifty-one ahadis.

Muhammad believes that everything is predetermined. Evil one is he who is evil in his mothers womb. Each person passes through a series of stages. The constituents of one of you are collected for forty days in his mothers womb in the form of blood, after which it becomes a lump of flesh and forty days later Allah sends His angel to it with instructions concerning four things... his livelihood, his death, his deeds, his fortune and misfortune. As a result, it may even happen that a very good man who deserves Paradise and is only a cubit away from Paradise will suddenly be overcome by what destiny has written and begin to act like a denizen of hell. And, of course, the reverse may also happen.

The Prophet assures us that Allah has fixed the very portion of adultery which a man will indulge in.

This brings in the usual riddle: how to reconcile destiny with freedom of action. One day, Muhammad told his followers that there is not one amongst you who has not been allotted his seat in Paradise or Hell. They logically asked: Why then should we perform good deeds, why not depend upon our destiny Muhammad replied: No, do perform good deeds, for everyone is facilitated in that for which he is created.

Here is another theological riddle and another answer. If everything of men is decreed in advance, then would it not be an injustice to punish them Muhammad replies: Everything is created by Allah and lies in His power. He would not be questioned as to what He does, but they [His creatures] would be questioned.

Knowledge

The thirty-second book, even smaller than the previous one, is the Book of Knowledge (Ilm).

The word knowledge here has a special connotation. It means the knowledge that we find in the Quran. Recite the Quran, and do not dispute about it-that is knowledge. Verily, the peoples before you were ruined because of their disputation in the Book, the Prophet warns the believers.

Muhammad also warns against people who believe that certain portions of the Quran are mere allegories and try to read their own meanings into them. Those who have a yearning for error go after the allegorical verses seeking to cause dissension, by seeking to explain them. On the other hand, those who are sound in knowledge say: We affirm our faith in everything which is from our Lord.

He also warns against hair-splitting. Ruined are those who indulged in hair-splitting, he says.

But in spite of these warnings, Muhammad is still apprehensive about his followers and feels that they will take to the path of the Jews and the Christians. You would tread the same path as was trodden by those before you inch by inch and step by step so much so that if they had entered into the hole of the lizard, you would follow them in this also, he remonstrates with the believers.

The book also includes a flattering reference to scholars. Verily, Allah does not take away knowledge by snatching it from the people but he takes away thc knowledge by taking away the scholars.

REMEMBRANCE OF ALLAH

The thirty-third book is on Remembrance of Allah (KitAb al-Zikr).

The believers are exhorted to remember Allah. Though Muhammad rebelled against the idea that Allah had visible forms, he retained His audible names. There are ninety-nine names of Allah; he who commits them to memory would get into Paradise, Muhammad tells us.

Why ninety-nine God is odd [witr] and He loves odd number, Muhammad explains.

Allah tells us that if a believer draws near Me by the span of a palm, I draw near him by the cubit. And if he walks towards Me, I rush towards him.

The statement is taken from the mystic lore, where it has a meaning very different from the one given to it in certain prophetic traditions. In the mystic tradition, walking toward Me means walking in truth, in conciliation, in compassion, in brotherliness, in purity, in wisdom; it means walking toward the Light within. In the prophetic tradition, the phrase means walking in enmity toward the polytheists, the infidels, in conformity to the commands conveyed by Allah through revelation to some favored fellow. Our own role is compliance and conformity and obedience to a revelation which is not ours. In this holy war which we are asked to wage with zeal, faith, and earnestness, our reward is booty, slaves, and empire if we succeed, and Paradise if we fall. Muhammads god, like his moral teaching, is sectarian and lacks both universality and true inwardness. Muhammads Allah is a tribal god trying to be universal through jihAd, conquest, and forced conversions. There is no God but Allah and Muhammad is the prophet of this godling is the true import of the Muhammadan kalimah (creed).

Some theologians exalt God but denigrate man; they are tearful about God but are quite dry-eyed and even cruel-hearted toward their fellow mortals, whom they give all kinds of names: heathen, infidel, polytheist, and so on. We should be wary of such theologians and their theologies.

Reciting Allahs Name Before Going to Sleep

AlI tells us that FAtima, his wife and the Prophets daughter, had a corn in her hand because of working at the hand-mill. They heard that there had fallen to the lot of Allahs Apostle some prisoners of war. So FAtima came to the Holy Prophet in the expectation of acquiring a slave for herself. But Muhammad had none to spare at the time, so he told FAtima: May I not direct you to something better than what you have asked for When you go to your bed, you should recite TakbIr [Allah-o-Akbar] thirty-four times and TasbIh [SubhAn Allah] thirty-three times and TahmId [al-Hamdu li-Allah] thirty-three times and that is better than the servant for you.

Allahs name did not always suffice as a substitute for a servant. The Prophet was in the habit of giving prisoners of war to his favorite believers as slaves and concubines. For example, he gave AlI a captured girl named Rayta, the daughter of HilAl, as a gift. She was part of the war booty won from the BanU Hawzin, the tribe of Muhammads foster mother. Two other girls from the same booty were given as gifts, one to UsmAn, Muhammads other son-in-law, and the second to Umar, who in turn gave her to his son Abdullah.

Supplicate Allah and Flee From Satan in the Morning

We may quote one more hadIs apropos: When you listen to the crowing of the cock, ask Allah for His favour as it sees

Angels and when you listen to the braying of the donkey, seek refuge in Allah from the Satan for it sees Satan, Muhammad tells the believers. Demonology is the other side of theology.

Paradise, Hell, Their Inmates, the Last Day

The next four books tell us something about Paradise and Hell and their respective inhabitants; they also tell us about the Day of Judgment, and the Turmoils and Portents of the Last Hour.

In book thirty-four, called the Book of Heart-Melting Traditions (al-RiqAq), Muhammad tells us that he stood upon the door of Fire [Hell] and the majority amongst them who entered there was that of women. On the other hand, amongst the inmates of Paradise, women will form a minority.

Muhammad says that he has solved all the problems of the believers except the problems created by women. I have not left after me turmoil for the people but the harm done to men by women.

According to another tradition, he tells his ummah: The world is sweet and green [alluring] and verily Allah is going to install you as Viceregent in it in order to see how you act. So avoid the allurement of women: verily, the first trial for the people of Israel was caused by women.

The Poor

The poor fare better at Muhammads hand. I had a chance to look into Paradise and I found that majority of the people was poor. If they so wish, the Communists can claim Muhammad as their own, though Paradise may be no more than an opiate of the poor.

The Day of Judgment

In book thirty-seven (Al-QiyAma wal Janna wan-NAr), giving a description of the Day of Judgment, and of Paradise and Hell, Muhammad tells us that on the Last Day Allah, the Exalted and Glorious, will take in His grip the earth... and roll up the sky in His right hand and would say: I am the Lord; where are the sovereigns of the world.

The Creation

Muhammad tells us that Allah created the clay on Saturday and He created the mountains on Sunday and He created the trees on Monday and created the things entailing labour on Tuesday and created light on Wednesday and He created the animals to spread on Thursday and created Adam after Asr [the afternoon prayer] on Friday; the last creation at the last hour of the hours of Friday, i.e., between afternoon and night.

The Destruction

The Last Day-the day of the destruction of the world-is also described. On this day, Muhammad said, the earth would turn to be one single bread... and the Almighty would turn it in His hand as one of you turns a loaf while on a journey. It would be a feast in honour of the people of Paradise. Then he laughed until his molar teeth became visible; then he asked his audience whether they would also like to be informed about that with which they would season it [bread]. With bAlAm and fish, he told them. BAlAm is ox and fish from whose excessive livers seventy thousand people would be able to eat.

Nonbelievers

On the Day of Resurrection, while the inmates of Paradise are feasting on the fare described above, the nonbelievers would be made to assemble by crawling on their faces.

The believer will be doubly blessed. Allah would confer upon him His blessings in this world and would give him reward in the Hereafter. But the next hadIs suggests a more balanced distribution of Allahs blessings. Allah rewards the nonbeliever in this world and the believer in the hereafter. Thanks to his reward in this world, the nonbeliever finds no virtue for which he should be rewarded in the Hereafter.

Either way, it is still not a fair deal. In fact, it is cheating. What is this world compared to the hereafter Not even a gnat. What are all the pleasures of the earth compared to even one distant feel of the hellfire Nothing. But what can Allah do The nonbeliever is a bad cost accountant, and heedless. On the Day of Resurrection, Allah will ask the nonbeliever, even the one least tormented, whether, if he possessed all the gold of the earth, he would like to secure his freedom from the awaiting fire by paying all that gold. The nonbeliever will answer yes, but it would be said to him: You have told a lie; what had been demanded from you was quite easier than this [the belief in the Oneness of Allah] but you paid no heed to it.

Allahs Patience

Allah is long-suffering. He shows patience at listening to the most irksome things.... Partnership is associated to Him [polytheism], and fatherhood of a child is attributed to Him [Christianity], but in spite of this He protects them [people) and provides them sustenance.

Muhammads Curses

Allah may be patient but not His Prophet. Muhammad simply could not stand the nonbelievers. When Allahs Messenger saw people turning back from religion he said: O Allah, afflict them with seven famines as was done in the case of Yusuf, so they were afflicted with famine by which they were forced to eat everything until they were obliged to eat the hides and the dead bodies because of hunger.

The Splitting of the Moon

Besides the power to curse, Muhammad had other miraculous powers at his command. For example, the moon was split into two, one part of it behind the mountain and the other part on this side of the mountain. Muhammad told his companions: Bear witness to this.

The Jewish Scholars

While Muhammad had power over nature, this power failed him when it came to persuading the Jewish scholars. If ten scholars of the Jews would follow me, no Jew would be left upon the surface of the earth who would not embrace Islam, Muhammad declared.

Satan and the Prophet

Muhammad robbed Satan of his divinity but evidently not of his power for mischief, particularly in the matter of sowing dissension among the believers. Verily, the Satan has lost all hopes that the worshippers would worship him in the peninsula of Arabia, but he is hopeful that he would sow the seed of dissension amongst them, Muhammad declared.

Everyone Has His Own Devil: Qarin

Muhammad did not believe that everyone has his own god but he did believe that everyone has his own devil. There is none amongst you with whom is not an attache from amongst the jinn [devil]. The Companions said: Allahs Messenger, with you too Thereupon he said: Yes, but Allah helps me against him and so I am safe from his hand and he does not command me but for good.

This concept is known as qarIn in Islamic theology. Literally, the word means the one united (pl. QuranA), and it refers to the demon that is joined inseparably to every man. The concept is mentioned in the Quran (We assign unto him a devil who would be his mate, :; also see :), but it finds its full development in the Sunnah. In the Quran, the demons are only attached to infidels; in the Sunnah, they are intimately joined to Muslims also.

A Gnostic theology sees a secret Godhead in man; a prophetic one, a devil. The former is pantheistic in approach and temper; the latter is pandaimonic or, more precisely, pandemonic.

Moderation in Giving Sermons

Abdullah b. MasUd tells us that Allahs Messenger did not deliver us sermons on certain days fearing that it might prove to be boring for us. A practice worthy of emulation by most sermonizers.

PARADISE (AL-JANNA - THE GARDEN)

The thirty-eighth book is called The Book of Paradise; Its Description, Its Bounties, and Its Inmates; but two-thirds of it really is on Hell and its inmates. In the Prophets eschatology, Paradise and Hell go together. In the Quran, the word Paradise (jannat) appears times, less than the word Hell (jahnam), which appears times. An-NAr, the Fire, the Qurans pet name for Hell, appears with still greater frequency- times. In Paradise, there is a tree under the shadow of which a rider of a fine and swift-footed horse would travel for a hundred years without covering the distance completely. The inhabitants of Paradise show their happiness by telling Allah: Why should we not be pleased, Lord, when Thou hast given us what Thou hast not given to any of Thy creatures. The pleasure of seeing others denied Paradise is in fact greater than the pleasure of seeing even ones own self rewarded. Paradise has its own version of a beauty salon, a street to which the inhabitants would come every Friday. The north wind will blow and would scatter fragrance on their faces and on their clothes and would add to their beauty and loveliness. A constant Bower of Bliss.

Hierarchy

Paradise is not without its hierarchy, with rather exclusive quarters for the apostles. The inhabitants of the lower regions of Paradise will look to the upper apartment of Paradise as you see the planets in the sky. The ranking in Paradise will follow the ranking on earth. The first group of my Ummah to get into paradise would be like a full moon in the night. Then those who would be next to them; they would be like the most significantly glittering stars... then after them others in ranks.

Calvinism

In religions where theology is supreme, moral action occupies a secondary place. A man is justified by faith; he is already one of Gods elect or damned long before he is even born. Muhammad anticipates Luther and Calvin by a thousand years, None amongst you would attain salvation purely because of his deeds, Muhammad says. Observe moderation in your doings, he advises; but if you fail, try to do as much as you can do and be happy for none would be able to get into paradise because of his deeds alone. It is not Gods grace that wins salvation but either the atoning death of His only son or the intercessory power of His last Prophet.

Gods Height

Muhammad tells us the height of the inhabitants of Paradise and, incidentally, the height of Adam and even of God. The immeaSurable is measured. Allah, the Exalted and Glorious, created Adam in His own image with His length of sixty cubits.... So he who would get into Paradise would get in the form of Adam, his length being sixty cubits. Muhammad adds that the people who came after Adam continued to diminish in size up to this day.

Habitation, Lavation

For his habitation in Paradise, the believer will have a tent of a single hollowed pearl, the breadth of which would be sixty miles from all sides.

The inhabitants of Paradise will cat and drink but they will neither pass water, nor void excrement, nor will they suffer from catarrh, nor will they spit. Then what will happen to the food they cat The whole catabolic process will change. They will belch and sweat (and it would be over with their food), and their sweat would be that of musk. Their combs would be made of gold and the fuel of their braziers would be aloes and their sweat would be musk and their form would be the form of one single person according to the length of their father sixty cubits tall.

Spouses

The SahIh Muslim allows the believers only two spouses each in Paradise, less than on earth; but they will be so beautiful that the marrow of their shanks would be visible through the flesh.

THE QURANIC PARADISE

The SahIh Muslim is rather niggardly in its description and promise. Let us therefore add a few more details to the scanty picture of Paradise by referring to the Quran and some other traditions and commentaries.

The Quran promises the believers and mujAhids rivers of water incorruptible; rivers of milk whose taste does not change;

rivers of wine, a joy to those who drink; rivers of honey pure and clear. For food, they will have fruits, any that they may desire (:-). They will be reclining on raised thrones; and the shades of the Garden will come low over them; the bunches of fruits will hang low. And amongst them will be passed round vessels of silver and goblets of crystal; they will drink of a cup of wine mixed with ZanjabIl [ginger], and there would be a fountain called SalsbIl. And around them will be youths of perpetual freshness [viludAnum mukhaladUn], youths of such beauty that you would think them scattered pearls; upon them will be green garments of fine silk and heavy brocade, and they will be adorned with bracelets of silver (:-). Young slaves (ghilmAn) like hidden pearls will wait on them.

Houris

Houris are promised, houris with swelling bosoms, retiring glances; houris unfailing and unforbidden, on lofty sofas and of a rare creation, for ever virgins, beloved and equal in age.

What is denied on earth is promised in Paradise: silk dresses, wine, golden vessels. One would have thought that the believers provision of women in this world was pretty generous, but apparently any restrictions in the matter were irksome, so he will have women galore in Paradise.

We can only mention the subject here, but for a fuller account the reader can refer to the following verses in the Quran, and others.

Other Traditions

Other traditions, quoted in commentaries like the Tafseer MazaharI, the Tafseer QAdarI, and the Tafseer HaqqAnI, and reproduced in the Quran Parichaya, describe the sensual delights of the celestial region with greater abandon. For example, in every corner of the believers tent of a single hollowed pearl, which we have already mentioned, will dwell his wives, with whom he will make love successively. According to Abdullah b. Umar, Paradise will have a bazaar for the exclusive sale and purchase of beauty and beautiful faces. A man will be able to procure any beautiful woman he desires from that market. The believers will recline on lofty couches (according to some commentators, couches means women).

Number of Slaves

According to a tradition narrated by the same authority, even the least of the inhabitants of Paradise will have one thousand slaves waiting on him. According to Anas, the number of slaves is ten thousand. According to Abu SaId, the least amongst the people of Paradise shall have eighty thousand slaves, and seventy-two women.

Number of Houris

Anas stinted on women. According to Abdullah b. Umar, every inhabitant of Paradise will have at his disposal five hundred houris, four thousand virgins, and eight thousand women who have known men. He will have the strength to have, intercourse with them all.

Abu Huraira increases the number, though rather mathematically expressed, still further. According to him, every Muslim will own a mansion of pearls; every mansion will have seventy houses of rubies; every house will have seventy rooms of emeralds; every room will have seventy couches; and every couch will be covered with seventy carpets of every color, and a houri will be sitting on each carpet; every room will also have seventy tables laid out; and on every table there will be seventy dishes of seventy colors; every room will also have seventy maid-slaves. Every believer will have the capability of copulating with each of these houris and maids.

See-through Garments

According to Abu SaId, these women will put on see-through dresses. Each houri will have seventy garments, but her lover will be able to look through all of them and see the marrow of the bones of her legs, and she will have a crown on her head, the meanest pearl of which would give light between the east and the west. According to another tradition, when a believer embraces any such houri, each of them will have seventy thousand boys waiting on her, holding the train of her robe. According to a tradition mentioned by Aldous Huxley, in the Muslim Paradise, every orgasm will last for six hundred years.

No Similar Rewards for Women

It has been observed that faithful Muslim females are denied the analogous reward. Gibbon says that Muhammad did not give any specifics about the male companions of the female elect because he did not want to arouse the jealousy of the husbands or to disturb their felicity by inducing them to have suspicions about everlasting marriages in Paradise.

Sir William Muir makes the psychologically significant observation that Muhammads more voluptuous accounts of heaven derive from the period when he was living in a monogamic relationship with KhadIja, a woman of threescore years and also fifteen years his senior. But as his harem swelled, the sexual delights and orgies became subdued. In the Suras from this period, the houris of old are replaced by pure wives (Quran :, :).

HELL

Muhammads accounts of Hell are equally intimate. In caloric heat, the fire we know here on earth is only one-seventieth part of the Fire of Hell. There would be among them those to whom Fire will reach up to their ankles, to some up to their knees, to some up to their waists, and to some up to their collar-bones.

Stones will hurtle down on the inmates of Hell with great force. Abu Harair reports: We were in the company of Allahs Messenger when we heard a terrible sound. Thereupon Allahs Apostle said: Do you know what is this We said: Allah and His Messenger know best. Thereupon he said: This is a stone which was thrown seventy years before in Hell and it has been constantly slipping down and now it has reached its base.

The hunger of Hell is inexhaustible. The sinners would be thrown therein and it would continue to say: Is there anything more. In Hell, the molar teeth of an unbeliever will be like Uhud [a hill just outside Medina] and the thickness of his skin a three nights journey. The idea of investing the unbeliever with such a thick skin is that he should be able to suffer the torment of the Hell-Fire for a long time, as the translator explains.

Those who tampered with the pure religion of Ishmael, the son of Abraham, the legendary progenitor of the Arabs, are severely punished. I saw Amr b. Luhayy b. Cama b. Khinzif, brother of BanU Kab, dragging his intestines in Fire, Muhammad tells Abu Huraira. According to Muslim thinking, Amr was the first Khozaite king (A.D.) who set up idols brought from Syria.

Similarly, Muhammad also saw Amr b. Amir al-KhuzAi dragging his intestines in Fire. He was the first to dedicate animals to deity. There are two kinds of the animals to be dedicated: al-bahIra, animals which are left unmilked except for the idols; and as-sAiba, animals which are not loaded and are let loose for the deities.

Eternal Damnation

After the believers and the unbelievers are sifted and sent to their respective abodes, the chapter is closed forever. Allah would admit the inmates of Paradise into Paradise and the inmates of Hell into Hell. Then the Announcer would stand between them and say: O inmates of Paradise, there is no death for you. O inmates of Hell, there is no death for you. You would live forever therein.

The Polyeists

The punishment of the unbelievers does not wait till the day of Resurrection. It begins immediately after their death. The Prophet and his Companions sighted five or six graves during a journey. Muhammad asked if anyone knew in what state their occupants had died. As polytheists, somebody replied. These people are passing through the ordeal in the graves, Muhammad revealed.

Muhammad let the dead bodies of the unbelievers who fought and died at Badr lie unburied for three days. Then he sat by the side of the bodies, and addressing each of them by name, said: Have you not found what your Lord had promised you to be correct The bodies had decayed, and Umar wondered how the Prophet could hold a discourse with them. By Him in Whose Hand is my life, what I am saying to them, even you cannot hear more distinctly than they, but they lack the power to reply, Muhammad told him. Then he had the bodies (twenty-four in number) of the non-believers of Quraish... thrown into the well of Badr.

MUHAMMADS MISSION

While delivering a sermon one day, Muhammad said: Behold, my Lord commanded me that I should teach you which you do not know and which He has taught me today.... Allah looked towards the people of the world and He showed hatred for the Arabs and the non-Arabs, but with the exception of some remnants from the People of the Book. And He said: I have sent thee [Muhammad] in order to put you to test and put those to test through you. And I sent the Book to you.... Verily, Allah commanded me to burn [kill] the Quraish. I said: My Lord, they would break my head... and Allah said: you turn them out as they turned you out, you fight against them and We shall help you in this.... You send an army and I would send an army five times greater than that. Fight against those who disobey you along with those who obey you.

Voyeurism

There is a hadIs, narrated by Aisha, that should be of interest to Freudians. The Prophet revealed: The people would be assembled on the Day of Resurrection barefooted, naked and uncircumcised. Aisha asked in alarm, or perhaps in mischief: Allahs Messenger, will the male and the female be together on the Day and would be looking at one another The Prophet sagaciously replied: Aisha, the matter would be too serious for them to look to one another.

The Reckoning on the Day of Judgment

On the Day of Resurrection, there will be two kinds of reckoning: an easy one and a thorough one. The easy reckoning is merely formal and is for the believers, whose faults Allah wants to overlook. But woe unto the unbeliever, for his accounts will be closely scrutinized. He who is examined thoroughly in reckoning is undone.

The Quranic Hell

As was also noted in regard to Paradise, the treatment of Hell is more detailed in the Quran than in the SahIh Muslim, and similarly the Quranic Hell is more sizzling than the Hell of the HAdIs.

Though Muhammad does not refrain from holding out the threat of hellfire to his followers, hell is essentially a place reserved for the unbelievers, i.e., those who disbelieve in his apostleship and mission.

Hell has many names, and the Prophet dwells on them lovingly. The name he most loved to call it by is An-NAr, the Fire. Seven other names are also frequently mentioned, and the scholars of the Quran turned them into seven separate regions of Hell, each with its own potency, thermodegree, and inmates. Though the least of these hells would burn any man a thousand times over, that is not considered good enough punishment for many degrees of infidelity and unbelief. So hells increasingly more smoky, more blazing, and more scorching are conceived.

The Seven Regions

Curiously enough, even Muslims must go to Hell. Not one of you but must enter it [Hell]; this is Lords decree that must be accomplished, reveals the Quran. In order to fulfill the letter, if not the spirit, of Allahs command, a region in Hell is conceived which is least oppressive. It is called Jahanam. It is Hell only in name and is in fact a purgatory for Muslims, even a passage or bridge (sirAt) to heaven. Muslim theologians assure us that it will be pretty cool and pleasant for Muslims unless they have committed some great sins.

The real regions of Hell and their real torments are reserved for unbelievers, infidels, and polytheists of different hues and degrees. The blazing fire of LazA, which leaves nothing unconsumed, is for the Christians; the still more intense fire of Hutamah is for the Jews. Similarly, there is SaIr for the Sabians, Saqar for the Magi, JahIm for idolaters, and HAwiyah for the hypocrites. The last are those who saw through Muhammad and no longer believed in his mission but were afraid to admit it openly. They paid him only the prudential homage due to one who is powerful.

Muhammad is very ready to send unbelievers to hellfire, fire which permits nothing to endure, nor leaves anything alone. In the Sura GhAshiya (The Overwhelming Event, i.e., the Day of Judgment), Muhammad promises a sorry plight indeed for unbelievers of all shades: Jews, Christians, polytheists, idolaters, hypocrites. Has the tidings reached thee of the Overwhelming Event Some faces that Day will be humiliated, toiling, weary.... No food will there be for them but a bitter zarI which will neither nourish nor satisfy hunger (:-).

ZarI is a bitter and thorny plant, loathsome in smell. In other Suras (e.g., :, :, :-), another terrible food, the Tree of ZaqqUm, is mentioned; in the language of the last Sura, it will boil in their [eaters] inside like molten brass, like the boiling of scalding water.

There are other traditions in the same vein. If the infidels complain of thirst, they shall be given water like molten copper... which shall burst their bowels... which shall dissolve everything in their bellies. According to some commentators, the water is so hot that even a drop of it is capable of melting away all the mountains of the world.

The fire in Hell knows no rival in fierceness. It burnt a thousand years so that it became red, and burnt another thousand years till it became black and dark, and never has any light. This hadIs derives from Abu Huraira and is quoted in the Tafseer MazaharI. According to the same commentary, the infidels will be surrounded by a wall of fire so wide that it would take forty years to traverse the distance.

The Quran asks you to fear the Fire whose fuel is Men and Stones, and which is prepared for those who reject Faith. Some commentators have explained that the men and stones referred to in the verse are none other than the polytheists and the idols they worship.

Another tradition tells us that Hell will have seventy thousand jungles, each tree there having seventy thousand branches; every branch will house seventy thousand serpents and an equal number of scorpions. All these are the tormentors of the infidels and the hypocrites. The swelling of one bite of a scorpion will last for forty years.

Hell is an important limb of Islamic theology, referred to throughout the Quran and other Islamic canonical literature. In these texts the misanthropy and hatred of Muslim theology for mankind has found a free scope.

The Last Hour

The thirty-ninth book pertains to the Turmoils and Portents of the Last Hour (Al-Fitan wa AshrAt as-SAah). The subject is closely related to Paradise and Hell.

One is not sure whether by the Last Hour the Prophet means the last hour of Arabia or of the ummah or of the whole world. In some ahAdIs, he prophesies the destruction of Arabia. There is destruction in store for Arabia because of turmoil which is at hand, he said. He climbed up a battlement and told the Medinans: You do not see what I am seeing and I am seeing the places of turmoil between your houses as the places of rainfall. Rainfall here means catastrophe. He prophesied for them a period in which the one who sits will be better than one who stands and the one who stands will be better than the one who walks and the one who walks will be better than the one who runs.

The Destruction of the Ummah

Muhammad tells us: Allah drew the ends of the world near one another for my sake. And I have seen its eastern and western ends. After this apocalyptical vision Muhammad asked Allah three things and, He granted me two.... I begged my Lord that my Ummah should not be destroyed because of famine and He granted me this. And I begged my Lord that my Ummah should not be destroyed by drowning [deluge] and He granted me this. And I begged my Lord that there should be no bloodshed among the people of my Ummah, but He did not grant it (,).

While killing unbelievers is meritorious and wins Paradise for the believers, killing another believer is heinous and earns the punishment of hellfire. When two Muslims confront each other with their swords, both the slayer and slain are doomed to Hell-Fire. But this does not apply to the early Muslim heroes who engaged in internecine wars. The translator assures us: This rule does not apply in case of the confrontation between Hazrat AlI and his opponents. Both the slayer and the slain are doomed to Hell-Fire only when the enmity is based on personal grudges and material interests, but in the case of Hazrat AlI and his opponents it was the higher ideal which actuated most of them to come into conflict with one another.

Some Signs of the Last Hour

The great turmoil which would emerge like the mounting waves of the ocean will be preceded by many signs. The Last Hour would not come unless the Euphrates would uncover a treasure of gold. It will not come until fire emits from the earth of HijAz which would illuminate the necks of the camels of Busra. It will not come until the people have [again] taken to the worship of LAt and Uzza.

Before the Last Hour comes, the Kaba would be destroyed by an Abyssinian having two small shanks. According to the translator, this refers to either the Christians or the polytheists of Abyssinia. Before this Hour jizyA will stop coming and the people of Iraq will not send their qafIz and dirhims [their measures of foodstuffs and their money].

The last hour would not come unless the Muslims will fight against the Jews and the Muslims would kill them and until the Jews would hide themselves behind a stone or a tree and a stone or a tree would say: Muslim, or the servant of Allah, there is a Jew behind me; come and kill him. Only a very thorny tree known as the gharqad, which is painful to touch, will be loyal to the Jews and not reveal their identity, for it is the tree of the Jew. Another sign of the approaching Hour will be that the sun would rise from the West.

Dajjal

Muhammad prepares Muslims for the coming Hour. Hasten to do good deeds before six things happen: the rising of the sun from the West, the smoke, the DajjAl.... DajjAl is mentioned in many ahAdIs. He is a kind of Antichrist, blind in the left eye and red in complexion, with the word kAfir inscribed on his forehead. He would be followed by seventy thousand Jews of IsfahAn wearing Persian Shawls.

Ibn Sayyad

A very interesting story is told about one Ibn SayyAd, who was believed to be DajjAl by the Companions of Muhammad. He disputed Muhammads apostleship. Dont you bear witness that I am the Messenger of Allah Muhammad demanded of him. But he replied: I bear witness to the fact that you are the Messenger of the unlettered. Then there was a competition between the two. SayyAd had to guess what was in Muhammads mind. SayyAd could only say dhukh when the word in Muhammads mind was really dukhAn (smoke). He only chanted dhukh, dukh, and the hollowness of his claim stood exposed, the translator tells us. According to another story, Muhammad and his Companions met SayyAd sitting in the company of some children. The children stood up but not SayyAd. Muhammad did not like it, and he said to him: May your nose be besmeared with dust, dont you bear testimony to the fact that I am the Messenger of Allah SayyAd denied this and, in fact, made the very same claim for himself, asking Muhammad to bear witness to his status. Thereupon Umar b. KhattAb said: Allahs Messenger, permit me that I should kill him. Muhammad replied: If he is that person who is in your mind [DajjAl], you will not be able to kill him. Muhammad had many toughs at his beck and call, ready to do his bidding. That gave point to his claim.

Like the early Christians, Muhammad expected the Last Hour to come at any time. Pointing to a young boy, he told his followers: If this young boy lives, he would not grow very old till the Last Hour would come to you.

7

The Repentance

We now take up the thirty-fifth book, pertaining to Repentance and Exhortation to Repentance (Kitab al-Tauba).

Allah loves repentance in a believer. He is more pleased with the repentance of His servant than an Arab who found his lost camel in the waterless desert.

In fact, Allah loves to see the believer repent more than He hates to see him sin. If you were not to commit sins, Allah would have swept you out of existence and would have replaced you by another people who have committed sin, and then asked forgiveness from Allah, the Prophet told his ummah. Psychologists tell us that the joys of sinning are great but the joys of repentance are even greater.

SIN IS DOUBLY REWARDING

A mans sinning is doubly rewarding. It helps him as well as his Maker. It helps the believer to realize that he is a creature and provides an opportunity for Allah to exercise His mercy. According to Muhammad, Allah said: A servant committed a sin and he said: Allah, forgive me my sin, and Allah said: My servant committed a sin and then he came to realize that he has a Lord who forgives the sins.... He again committed a sin and said: My Lord, forgive me my sin, and Allah, the Exalted and High, said: My servant committed a sin and then came to realize that he has a Lord who forgives his sin. The servant committed yet a third sin, and Allah responded in the same way, but now He added: O servant, do what you like. I have granted you forgiveness. Sin is doubly blessed. It blesses him who sins and Him Who forgives. It helps man to realize his creaturely nature and Allah to realize His lordly and merciful essence. It is not an accident that theologies of mans sinful nature have also sought a God of mercy.

Allahs Wrath and Mercy

Allah says: My mercy predominates my wrath. Of this mercy, He bestows a one-hundredth part upon the Jinn and human beings and the insects, the part with which they love one another; but He has reserved ninety-nine parts for His servant on the Day of Resurrection. This reserve of mercy will be handy on this Day for saving the Muslims from the fire of hell, which is also needed for dealing with the infidels, or kAfirs. Gods wrath is an important concept in Semitic religions.

Good Deeds Take Away Bad Ones

A Muslim came to Muhammad and said: Allahs Messenger, I sported with a woman in the outskirts of Medina... [and] committed an offence short of fornication.... Kindly deliver verdict about me. The man wanted Muhammad to impose the penalty of hadd (a category of punishments defined in the Quran or in the HadIs) on him. Abu Bakr and Umar felt that the man had committed a serious offense, but according to some traditions, Umar gave him the oft-repeated advice of the Prophet, which is both worldly-wise as well as pious: Allah concealed your fault. You had better conceal it yourself also. Meanwhile, Muhammad had a revelation: And observe prayer at the ends of the day and in the first hours of the night. Surely good deeds take away evil deeds. Following this he dismissed the man, telling him: Allah has exempted you from the imposition of hadd, or from your sin. Someone who was present at the time asked Muhammad whether the promise of pardon related only to that individual alone. No, but the people at large, Muhammad said reassuringly to all the believers. The two prayers mentioned are the morning and evening prayers. The one destroys the sins of the night, and the other the sins of the day. And, presumably, after reciting them the believer is refreshed and ready for his next bout of sin. Such is human nature.

Nonbelievers as Replacements for Believers in Hell

The next five ahAdIs are very interesting. Allah does not exactly forgive the sins of the believers but visits them on the unbelievers. He punishes the unbelievers for the sins of the believers. In this way, both His wrath and His mercy are established. When it will be the Day of Resurrection Allah would deliver to every Muslim a Jew or a Christian and say: That is your rescue from Hell-Fire, Muhammad tells his followers. Allahs sense of fairness and justice is no better than that of the believers. Thus the believers create Allah in their own image.

Muhammad also promises his followers that on the Day of Reckoning, Allah will tell the Muslims: I concealed them [your sins] for you in the world. And today I forgive them. But as for the nonbelievers, their sins will be exposed before the whole world and there would be general announcement about them before all creation, and it will be advertised that they told lies about Allah.

The Necklace Affair

The book contains a long hadIs which relates to a scandal involving Aisha, the girl-wife of the Prophet. It happened in the fifth year of the Hijra (December A.D.), when Muhammad was returning to Medina after defeating the tribe of BanU l-Mustaliq in a surprise attack and taking many prisoners, including JuwairIyya. Aisha, who was thirteen years old at the time, had accompanied the Prophet on the expedition, together with another co-wife, Umm Salama.

Aisha reports: Whenever Allahs Messenger intended to set out on a journey he cast lots amongst his wives and took one with him in whose favour the lot was cast. Luck favored her (as it did suspiciously too often), and she accompanied the Prophet on the expedition. During the last, leg of the return journey, Aisha was left behind. In the early morning, she had gone out into the fields to relieve herself. Returning to the camp, she discovered that she had dropped her necklace, so she went back to recover it. While she was away, the caravan started for Medina. Apparently no one realized that she had been left behind because the camel carrying her haudaj was with the caravan. The bearers, thinking she was inside it, had placed the haudaj on the camel. The women in those days were light of weight and they did not wear much flesh, as they ate less food; so they did not perceive the weight of my haudaj as they placed it on the camel, Aisha explains.

When Aisha returned to the camp after finding her necklace, she discovered that the caravan had left. So she waited and even slept at the same spot, calculating that they would come to fetch her once the mistake was discovered. I was overpowered by sleep and slept, she says. Then a young soldier, SafwAn b. Muattal SulamI ZakwAnI, who had also lagged behind for some reason, saw her, recognized her, and gave her a ride back. By Allah, he did not speak to me a word and I did not hear a word from him except Inna lillAhi [InnalillAhi wainna ilaihi rAjiUn, we are for Allah and to Him we have to return] and I covered my head with my headdress. He made his camel kneel down and I mounted the camel... and he moved on leading the camel by the nosestring on which I was riding, Aisha says.

Under everyones gaze, Aisha and SafwAn returned together. This started gossip, which soon developed into a scandal. The participants in the gossip were not merely people who were lukewarm toward Muhammad, such as Abdullah ibn Ubayy, a member of the KhAzrajite clan of Awf and a leading citizen of Medina, who had come to distrust Muhammad; they also included supporters of the Prophet, such as the poet HassAn, Hamna, the daughter of Jahsh and sister of the Prophets wife Zainab, and Mistah, a relative and dependent of Abu Bakr, the father of Aisha.

Muhammad was much disturbed and perhaps had his own suspicions. He turned cold toward Aisha, so much so that she sought his permission to go to her fathers house. The permission was given. Aishas mother tried to console her, saying: By Allah, if there is a handsome woman who is loved by her husband and he has co-wives also they talk many a thing about her.

Muhammad consulted his close relatives, particularly AlI and UsAma b. Zaid. UsAma said: Allahs Messenger, they are your wives and we know nothing else about them but goodness. AlI advised Muhammad to divorce Aisha: Allah has not put any unnecessary burden upon you in regard to your wives. There are a number of women besides her. AlI also suggested that Aishas maid be questioned. BarIra, the maid, was sent for. AlI struck her (showing that the manners of the Prophets family were quite feudal and no better than those of the unbelievers), and warned her to speak the truth. BarIra could throw no light on the incident in question but said that she had never found any wrong in Aisha except that she goes to sleep while kneading the flour and the lamb eats that.

Thus a month passed. Now Muhammad went to the pulpit and reprimanded his followers for their scandalmongering. Who would exonerate me from imputations of that person [was the reference to Abdullah ibn Ubayy or to Hassn the poet, another KhAzrajite] who has troubled me in regard to my family By Allah, I find nothing in my wife but goodness, he appealed. This touched a loyal chord in the hearts of Sad b. Muaz and Usaid b. Huzair. They stood up and promised to punish any delinquent, if the Prophet so wanted it. I defend your honour.... If he [the delinquent] belongs to the tribe of our brother Khazraj and you order us we would comply with your order, Sad b. Muaz, the chief of the Aus, told Muhammad. A quarrel now broke out between him and the chief of Khazraj, Sad b. UbAda, but Muhammad pacified them for the time being.

Next Muhammad went to Abu Bakrs house, determined to put an end to the matter. He again asked Aisha to confess if she had done anything wrong. Aisha, this is what has reached me about you and if you are innocent, Allah would Himself vindicate your honour, and if accidently there has been a lapse on your part seek forgiveness of Allah, Muhammad told her. But Aisha maintained her innocence.

And Lo! Then and there a revelation descended on Muhammad establishing Aishas innocence, even to her own great astonishment. I was innocent but I did not expect that Allah would descend wahy matlu [a Quranic revelation] in my case as I did not think myself so much important.... I only hoped that Allah would in vision give an indication of my innocence to Allahs Messenger, Aisha says.

Coming out of his prophetic fit or trance, Muhammad announced the news: Aisha, there is glad tiding for you. Verily Allah has vindicated your honour. Everybody was happy. Aishas mother wanted her to get up and thank the Prophet. But she refused: I shall not thank him and laud him but Allah who has descended revelation vindicating my honour.

God in this revelation not only vindicated Aishas innocence but ordered punishment for those who spread unproved calumnies against chaste women. And those who launch charges against chaste women, and produce not four witnesses to support their allegation, flog them with eighty stripes and reject their evidence ever after, for such men are wicked transgressors. And the revelation also took to task those Muslims who had given ear to the scandal. And why did not the believers, men and women, when ye first heard of the affair, put the best construction on it in their own minds and say, This charge is an obvious lie And why did they not bring four witnesses to prove it When they had not brought the witnesses, such men, in the sight of Allah, stand forth themselves as liars (Quran :-; also see :).

In obedience to Allahs injunction, all the calumniators, including the poet HassAn, Abu Bakrs relative Mistah, and even Hamna, the sister of Muhammads favorite wife, Zainab, received eighty stripes each. Zainab had not joined her sister in calumniating Aisha, though Aisha says that she was the only lady who amongst the wives of Allahs Messenger used to vie with me [i.e., Aisha].

But it was not all punishment. Perhaps to buy their silence, the punishments were judiciously mixed with rewards. A valuable castle called BIr HA, in the vicinity of Medina, was bestowed on HassAn the poet. Muhammad even gave HassAn a slave-girl named ShirIn, one of the two Coptic sisters sent him by the Egyptian governor as gifts, retaining the other, Mary, for his own harem. As a result, the poet, who until now had been writing lampoons on SafwAn, began writing verses in praise of Aishas purity, slimness, and grace. Aisha also forgave him. Aisha did not like that HassAn should be rebuked in her presence, and she used to say: It was he who wrote this verse also: Verily, my father and my mother are all meant for defending the honour of Muhammad.

After this incident Abu Bakr wanted to withdraw his support from Mistah, his indigent relative. In the language of Aisha, Abu Bakr used to give to Mistah some stipend as a token of kinship with him and for his poverty and he said: By Allah, now I would not spend anything for him. But a special revelation from Allah came to Mistahs rescue. Let not those among you who are endowed with grace and amplitude of means resolve by oath against helping their kinsmen, those in want and those who have left their homes in Gods cause.

Regarding SafwAn, the chief male character in the story, HassAn had lampooned him in a poem. In retaliation, SafwAn gave him a sword wound. HassAns relatives captured him and in spite of Muhammads intervention kept him as a prisoner till HassAns wound was healed. Of course, SafwAn denied the allegation hotly, and though young he died soon after. Hallowed be Allah, by One, in Whose hand is my life, I have never unveiled any woman, he said, according to Aisha. She further says that then he died as a martyr in the cause of Allah. According to another tradition; quoted by Ibn IshAq, she added that people found that SafwAn was impotent.

Though Allah exonerated Aisha in this particular case, He did not refrain from administering an admonition to all the wives of the Prophet: O Women of the Prophet! if any one of you should be guilty of unseemly conduct, your punishment would be doubled and that is easy for Allah. The system of purdah was also made more stringent. And stay quietly in your houses, and make not a dazzling display, like that of the former times of Ignorance, said Allah.

Muhammad also instituted a more careful watch over his household after this event. For example, when he left on the expedition to TabUk, he left AlI behind to keep an eye on his household in his absence. Also, we no longer find Aisha mentioned as accompanying Muhammad on any expedition after this affair. Apparently Umm Salama replaced her as Muhammads companion on subsequent expeditions.

The demand for four witnesses in cases of adultery made it difficult to prove such charges in an Islamic court.

We shall continue with the Book of Repentance. In it appears a long hadIs entitled The Repentance of Kab b. MAlik. This hadIs, the longest in the SahIh Muslim, constitutes a very interesting psychological document. We cannot reproduce it in full here or put it to an adequately searching analysis, but the reader will do well to read it carefully and give it serious thought, for it is an illuminating story with a family likeness to the notorious confessions and self-criticism of Communist countries. Besides the usual breast-beating and protestations of loyalty to the leader, it also indicates to a discerning reader some of the psychological factors that make the members of the ummah or the party fall in line and keep together.

Even in Muhammads time, Islam was not all theology, the appeal of a so-called superior monotheism against an idolatrous and superstitious polytheism, as some scholars and propagandists would have us believe. Monotheism does not have the superiority per se that fanatics often ascribe to it. The monotheism of prophetic Islam is particularly shallow and barbarous, spiritually speaking. But from the beginning, it was combined with other, more secular appeals, negative as well as positive. The Prophet rewarded loyalty and obedience with war spoils, and visited palpable punishments of varying degrees on the lukewarm, the indifferent, and the disloyal. He used the carrot as well as the stick.

Apostasy was severely punished. The sword and its threat were frequent arbiters, but more sophisticated psychological pressures were equally in use. Social cohesion and political and ideological compliance were secured by means of social ostracism, political boycott, and ideological untouchability. The fear of divine hellfire was distant, but the fear of the strongman, the boss, the toughs of the ummah, or party, was ever present. In offending the Prophet, you not only offended Allah-an offense which many could take in stride-but even worse, you offended Umar, Talha, AlI, Zubair, Sad, Abdullah-the Prophets swordsmen and hangmen. You also had to be on guard against the treacherous daggers of his assassins, SAlim b. Umayar, Muhammad ibn Maslama, Muheiasa, Abdullah ibn Oneis and company, Amr ibn Omeya, and so on.

If one invited the Prophets displeasure, besides inviting more concrete punishments, one also invited a pervasive social boycott. This could be a very coercive phenomenon. Ones own relatives and best friends deserted one. And why Because it was the safe thing to do. One had oneself played safe in the past; now others do the same in turn.

Perspicacious readers will be able to detect a close resemblance between the atmosphere described in the following hadIs and the more familiar (but only a little more familiar) atmosphere that obtains under the Communist regimes of our own time. But before we quote from the hadIs, let us provide some background information.

THE TABUK CAMPAIGN

Muhammad planned an expedition for the autumn Of A.D. ; it was his largest and also his last, for he died soon afterward. In planning other campaigns, he used to keep the time and the target of attack to himself in order to effect the maximum surprise; in fact, sometimes he would go north when his intended destination was south. But this campaign was to be of long duration, the enemy was far away (miles to the north), and the weather was dry and hot; so this time he gave advance warning to his followers so that they could prepare and equip themselves adequately, for the expedition was to take them to the very frontiers of Arabia and might embroil them with the garrisons of the Byzantine Empire. Because of its unusually arduous nature, the TabUk campaign was also called the Campaign of Difficulties.

As Muhammad was planning for the biggest campaign of his life, he directed his adherents and allies and the Bedouin tribes to gather in great numbers. He collected tithes from the tribes, which were now reduced to submission, and appealed for donations and gifts from his followers, who were now rich and powerful. They had become governors, generals, contractors, and traders. They gave generously, his own son-in-law, UsmAn, gifting one thousand dinArs, a lordly sum. These funds were used to provide mounts for the poorer soldiers. But even so, many had to be sent away for lack of funds. Though they were sent back, their spirit was considered praiseworthy, and there was even a revelation about them from Allah: Nor is there blame on those who come to thee to be provided with mounts, and when you said, I can find no mounts for you, they turned back their eyes streaming with tears. In the Islamic tradition, these men were subsequently remembered with honor as Weepers.

Muhammad made an appeal to all and sundry in the Muslim world, which now included, at least nominally, the whole Arab world. His appeal was Allahs own appeal. Go ye forth, whether equipped lightly or heavily, and strive and struggle, with your goods and your persons, in the cause of Allah: That is best for you, if ye but knew.

Opposition to the Campaign

Many people were lukewarm to the appeal and unwilling to undertake such an arduous and risky journey and in such hot weather, so they put forward many excuses for not going. Of such people, Allah spoke later on in several Quranic verses: Those who were left behind [in the TabUk expedition] rejoiced in their inaction behind the back of the Apostle of God. They hated to strive and fight with their goods and their persons in the Cause of God: they said, Go not forth in the heat. Muhammad, say to them that the Fire of Hell is fiercer in heat, if only they could understand.

The worst offenders were the Arabs of the desert as well as the Arabs settled in neighborhood of Medina. Both were condemned by Allah in the Quran: The Arabs of the desert are the worst in unbelief and hypocrisy, Allah said of them. And again He warned His Prophet thus: Certain of the Arabs round about you are hypocrites.... They are obstinate in hypocrisy. Thou knowest them not, but We know them. Twice shall we punish them, and in addition shall they be sent to grievous penalty. These Arabs were not exempted from the general conscription and were forced into the march. But there was opposition in Medina itself amongst the ansArs under the very nose of the Prophet, and many Medinans put forward all kinds of excuses. If there had been immediate gain in sight, and journey easy, they would all without doubt have followed thee, Allah tells Muhammad. The Prophet warns these recalcitrants that unless ye go forth, Allah will punish you with a grievous penalty and put others in your place. But Him you would not harm in the least. For Allah has power over all things.

But Muhammad did not leave matters with divine threats. He also took more secular measures. For example, Ibn HishAms biography of Muhammad tells us that when Muhammad learned that certain men opposed to the expedition were meeting at the house of Suwaylim the Jew, he sent Talha with some men to burn the house. This effectively dealt with them. One of the victims, Al-DahhAk, sang: My salams to you, Ill neer do the like again / Im afraid. He whom fire surrounds is burned.

A Large Army Gathered

Eventually a large army gathered and encamped in the outskirts of Medina, although many of its members were still disgruntled. According to some traditions, those who assembled but stayed back were as numerous as those who actually went. Abdullah ibn Ubayy, the leader of the doubters or hypocrites of the Quran, was also there in considerable force. But eventually he did not go, probably for reasons of old age (he died a few months later). The ansArs too were not very numerous. According to some traditions, the expedition was thirty thousand strong, one-third of which was cavalry.

AlI was left behind to maintain order among Muhammads wives and possibly also to keep a watch on Medina. But some people insinuated that he was being left behind because he would have been more of a liability than an asset on such an expedition. AlI was angered and came out with his armor on. Muhammad pacified him by saying: They lie. I left you behind because of what I had left behind, so go back and represent me in my family and yours. Are you not content, AlI, to stand to me as Aaron stood to Moses This satisfied AlI.

Some Christian and Jewish Tribes Submit

When the expedition reached its destination, it found there was not much to do, because the Byzantine army, which supposedly had been assembling on the frontiers, was nowhere in sight. So to occupy his time during the ten days he stayed in TabUk, Muhammad accepted the submission of three Jewish settlements and two Christian princes, which was easily done with such a large show of force. To Yuhanna b. Ruba, the Christian prince of Ayala, he wrote the following: Peace be on you! I praise God for you.... I will not fight against you until I have written thus unto you. Believe, or else pay tribute. And be obedient unto the Lord and his Prophet and the messengers of His Prophet. Honour them and clothe them with excellent vestments.... Specially clothe Zaid with excellent garments.... But if you oppose and displease them, I will not accept from you a single thing, until I have fought against you and taken captive your little ones and slain the elders. For I am the Apostle of the Lord in truth. The prince readily submitted and became a tributary.

Kab Speaks

When Muhammad returned to Medina, he was determined to deal firmly with those who had failed to accompany him. Of the many who had remained behind, three were ansArs who had been loyal followers of Muhammad: MurAra, HilAl, and Kab, the subject of our discussion in this chapter. Kab, who was a poet, expressed his repentance for not joining the TabUk expedition. According to him: I never remained behind Allahs Messenger from any expedition which he undertook except the Battle of TabUk and that of the Battle of Badr. So far as the Battle of Badr is concerned, nobody was blamed for remaining behind as Allahs Messenger and the Muslims did not set out for attack but for waylaying the caravan of the Quraish, but it was Allah Who made them confront their enemies without their intention to do so.

Protesting his loyalty to the Prophet, Kab says: I had the honour to be with Allahs Messenger on the night of Aqaba when we pledged our allegiance to Islam and it was more dear to me than my participation in Battle of Badr. Kab tells us that in undertaking this journey to TabUk, the holy prophet had in his mind the idea of threatening the Christians of Arabia in Syria and those of Rome [i.e., the Byzantine Empire]; he says the expedition was big, more than ten thousand people. He also tells us that when Allahs Messenger intended to set out on an expedition, he kept it as a secret. But this expedition was a different thing. Allahs Messenger set out for this expedition in extremely hot season; the journey was long and the land [which the army had to traverse] was waterless and he had to confront a large army, so he informed the Muslims about the actual situation, so that they should adequately equip themselves for his expedition.

Kab had no excuse for remaining behind, neither age nor health nor lack of means. Never did I possess means enough and my circumstances more favourable than at this occasion.... I had never before this expedition simultaneously in my possession two rides. Though eminently qualified to participate, Kab went on postponing his preparations till one day he found, to his dismay, that the Prophet had departed. I was shocked to find that I did not find anyone like me but the people who were labelled as hypocrites or the people whom Allah granted exemption because of their incapacity, he says.

Now he waited with dread for the return of Muhammad. When this news reached me that Allahs Messenger was on his way back from TabUk I was greatly perturbed. I thought of fabricating false stories and asked myself how I would save myself from the anger of the following day. But later, he decided to speak the truth. Nothing could save me but the telling of truth, he said to himself.

The next day Muhammad arrived, and those who had remained behind began to put forward their excuses and to take an oath before him and they were more than eighty persons. Their excuses as well as their allegiances were accepted. When Kabs turn came, Muhammad asked him what had kept him back. Was it lack of a mount But Kab spoke the truth. By Allah, I never possessed so good means... as I had when I stayed behind. Muhammad dismissed him, saying that he should wait till Allah gives a decision in your case. (In the language of the Quran: There are others held in suspense for the command of God, whether He would punish them, or turn in mercy)

Later, some of Kabs friends came to him in sympathy. They could not compliment him for his inability to put forward an excuse as others did. They also told him that two other pious persons (MurAra b. ar-RabIa AmirI and HilAl b. Ummayya al-QAqifI) have met the same fate as has fallen to you and they have made the same statement as you have made, and the same verdict has been delivered in their case. This comforted him somewhat.

Kabs Ordeal

Then the ordeal began. Allahs Messenger forbade the Muslims to talk with three of us.... The people began to avoid us and their attitude towards us underwent a change and it seemed as if the whole atmosphere had turned hostile against us.... We spent fifty nights in this very state and my two friends confined themselves within their houses and spent most of their time in weeping. Kab himself went to the mosque for prayer to catch the Prophets eye, but he looked at me and when I cast a glance at him he turned away his eyes from me.

Even his close relatives and friends avoided him. He says: When the harsh treatment of the Muslims towards me extended to a considerable time, I walked until I climbed upon the wall of the garden of Abu QutAda, and he was my cousin, and I had the greatest love for him. I greeted him but, by Allah, he did not respond to my greetings. Kab repeatedly adjured him by Allah, and repeatedly protested his love for the Messenger of Allah, but QutAda kept quiet.

While he was enduring this mental torture, Kab received a letter from the King of GhassAn. As I was a scribe I read that letter, Kab says. The letter said: It has been conveyed to us that your friend [Muhammad] is subjecting you to cruelty and Allah has not created you for a place where you are to be degraded and where you cannot find your right honour. This communication could be very incriminating. As I read that letter I said, This also is a calamity, so I burnt it.

When forty days had thus passed, a message came from Muhammad to Kab. Verily, Allahs Messenger has commanded you to remain separate from your wife. Should I divorce her Kab asked the message-bearer. He replied, No, but only remain separate from her and dont have sexual contact with her. As Kab was young, he sent his wife away to her parents house to be on the safe side. The same message was sent to the other two. But HilAls wife got the Prophets permission to remain with her husband, as he was a senile person. But dont go near him, Muhammad told her. By Allah, he has no such instinct in him. By Allah, he spends his time in weeping, she replied.

Kab Pardoned

At last the dark days ended. On the morning of the fiftieth day, an announcer came from the peak of the hill of Sal saying at the top of his voice: Kab b. MAlik, there is glad tiding for you. What other glad tiding was left for him in the world Kab understood at once. I fell down in prostration and came to realize that there was relief for me, he says. Meanwhile, other friends hurried with the glad tidings. A person galloped his horse and came from the tribe of Aslam and his horse reached me more quickly than his voice.

Kab went to Muhammad in gratefulness, and the latter received him with a smiling face. Kab sought his permission to give away his wealth in charity in thankfulness to Allah for the new life that had been bestowed on him. The Prophet advised him to keep some for his own use. Kab obediently followed the advice. I shall keep with me that part of my property which fell to my lot on the occasion of the expedition of Khaibar (the booty won at Khaibar was quite large and considerably enriched Muhammad and his Companions), Kab submitted.

The self-abasement of the three men and their consequent pardon by Allah is celebrated in the Quran thus: Allah turned in mercy also to the Three who were left behind. They felt guilty to such a degree that the earth for all its spaciousness became constrained to them, and so did their souls become straitened within them. And they perceived that there is no fleeing from God and no refuge but to Himself. Then He turned to them, that they might repent. For God is easy to reconcile and Merciful.

Permanent War

The Arabian peninsula had then come under Muhammads sway. His followers heaved a sigh of relief. They wanted to enjoy their new wealth in peace. Some of them even began to sell their arms, saying: The wars of faith are now over. According to Al-WAqidI, the Prophets biographer, when Muhammad heard this, he said: There shall not cease from the midst of my people a party engaged in crusades for the truth, even until Antichrist appear.

The Exoneration of the Prophets Slave-girl

At the end of the Book of Repentance, there is a brief but interesting hadIs. Anas reports: A person was charged with fornication with the slave-girl of Allahs Messenger. Thereupon Allahs Messenger said to AlI: Go and strike off his neck. AlI went to the person and found him in a well cooling his body. AlI said to him: Come out, and as he took hold of his hand and brought him out, he found that his sexual organ had been cut. Hazrat AlI refrained from striking his neck. He came to Allahs Apostle and said: Allahs Messenger, he has not even the sexual organ with him.

This is an interesting hadIs and conceals as much as it reveals. The slave-girl it mentions is none other than Muhammads own Coptic concubine, Mary, the center of great jealousy in the harem; she was never treated with equality by the other wives of Muhammad, particularly Aisha and Hafza, who belonged to the Quraish blue blood. We have already mentioned the incident which caused so much commotion and scandal in the harem. Peace was eventually restored, but in order to avoid further complications, Mary was kept separately in a distant lodging in the upper quarter of Medina, with a male Coptic slave to help her in fetching wood and water. But the wives of Muhammad took their revenge by spreading rumors that the two Egyptians were having illicit relations. Muhammad felt uneasy and jealous and sent AlI to punish him. (Where are the four witnesses) When AlI arrived on the scene with sword in hand, he discovered that the slave was a eunuch. This saved the poor mans life.

HYPOCRITES (MUNAFIQIN)

The thirty-sixth book is on the Hypocrites, Their Characteristics and Command Concerning Them (KitAb SifAt al-MunAfiqIn wa AhkAmihim). It is a small book, containing only twenty-one ahAdIs, but in some ways it is important. The Quran refers to the hypocrites very often (twenty-five times), and there is a whole chapter, or Sura, named after them, called MunAfiqIn. Muhammad repeatedly threatens the hypocrites with blazing hellfire. The Quranic scholars coming after him put them in the hottest region of Hell, HAwiyah, a bottomless pit of scorching fire. Allah has promised the hypocrites, men and women, and the rejecters of Faith, the Fire of Hell; therein shall they dwell.... For them is the curse of Allah and an enduring punishment, as the Quran says.

The name hypocrites does not derive from any moral category but was applied to people who no longer believed in the prophethood of Muhammad in their hearts but were afraid to admit it openly in public. They were doubters, skeptics, men of incomplete faith, men who began to entertain questions about the apostleship of Muhammad as they came to know him somewhat better. But in the peculiar theology of Islam, such doubts were morally the most heinous. Doubting Muhammads prophetic mission was hypocrisy. So those Muslim converts of Medina who became doubters were regarded as hypocrites.

Medinans Downgraded in Their Own City

Many Medinans had offered Muhammad and his followers refuge and protection in their city-some out of conviction, others out of chivalry, and some out of spite for the Meccans. But very soon the refugees became stronger than the citizens. Some of the citizens saw, with pain and alarm but also with increasing helplessness, that they were being reduced to a second-class status in their own hometown. Some of them murmured to each other: See what we have done to ourselves. We have laid open our lands to them and have shared with them all that we possessed. If we had kept our own for ourselves, then by Allah, they would have gone somewhere else. The Medinans gave Muhammad and his followers an inch, and soon they seized a whole yard. It was the proverbial story of the camel and the old woman in a hut.

Now that Muhammad had been in town with them for some days, the Medinans were also able to arrive at a better estimate of him. Some of them thought that he was no better than a religious humbug. But the realization came too late. For now Muhammad was strong and they were weak. Those who no longer believed in him had come to fear him. But the result was the same: paralysis of will and action. The opposition could now be intimidated, and much of it could also be bought, for though they did not believe in Muhammad, many of them believed in war spoils.

Intellectual Opposition

The opposition to Muhammad did not emanate only from munAfiqIn, the disillusioned converts. It also came from those who had never given up their ancestral faith or surrendered their judgment and had not been swept off their feet by the new religious fad. Some of the members of the opposition were gifted. They could put their ideas into verses. A woman poet named AsmA hint MarwAn, belonging to the BanI Aws, appealed to the Medinan tribes of MAlik, Auf, and Khazraj in the name of their old heroes. You obey a stranger who does not belong among you, she sang. Abu Afak, a centenarian poet belonging to the Khazrajite clan, related to Aws ManAt, said in a poem that the different tribes of Medina were good neighbors and loyal allies, Yet there is a rider come among them who divided them. Some of these verses are quoted by Ibn HishAm and WAqidI and reproduced by Maxime Rodinson.

Muhammad was much perturbed. The poets of that time were like the journalists of our age. Muhammad detested them, and lay in wait for an opportunity to deal with them effectively. His victory at Badr in January A.D. brought him the opportunity.

His success against the Quraish gave him a new power in Medina. The equation with respect to both local supporters and local adversaries changed appreciably to his advantage. He seized the opportunity and struck fast. First he dealt with the poets whom he feared the most.

Assassination of Poets

Who will rid me of this pestilential woman he said about AsmA. Omayr ibn AdI, a blind man and a fanatic convert from her own clan, offered to assassinate her, which he did while she was asleep with her child in her arms. Have you slain the daughter of MarwAn Muhammad inquired eagerly when Omayr returned from his mission. When he replied in the affirmative, Muhammad commended him to his Companions. If you desire to see a man that has assisted the Lord and His Prophet, look ye here, he told them.

The same fate overtook Abu Afak the very next month. Who will rid me of this scoundrel Muhammad uttered aloud. And again there was a ready assassin at hand. SAlim ibn Umayr of BanI Amr, the people with whom Abu Afak had cast his lot and lived, stabbed the man one night while he was sleeping.

Most of the local converts, including the two assassins named above, had not fought at Badr. So they still had to prove their loyalty in action to the Prophet and to the new creed. This they did by these perfidious acts.

Hardly had six months elapsed when the blow fell on another influential half-Jewish poet, Kab ibn al-Ashraf. We have already mentioned his case. Muhammad made a special petition to Allah for his elimination. Lord, deliver me from the son of Ashraf... because of his open sedition and verses, he prayed.

Go with the blessings of Allah and assistance from high, he told the departing assassins, and when they returned after fulfilling their task, Muhammad met them at the very gate of the mosque in welcome. One of the conspirators had received a wound by accident. Muhammad treated it in his usual way-he spat on it and it was healed.

A New Fear Descends

According to ancient Arab custom, such willful murders demanded tribal vengeance. But this was not to be thought of under the new circumstances. There was something new in the atmosphere, a new apprehension, a new equation. After AsmAs assassination, the assassin had asked Muhammad if he would have to bear any penalty. Not two goats shall come to blow for her, Muhammad had assured him. This turned out to be only too true. The assassin openly boasted of his act even before the five sons of AsmA, but nothing happened. They were too cowed. The assassin had a powerful patron.

Fear is more potent than a sentimental humanist psychology would like to believe. Fear speaks louder and strikes home quicker than many other modes of communication. The day after Bint MarwAn was killed, the men of BanI Khatma [her husbands tribe] became Muslims because they saw the power of Islam, says Ibn IshAq.

The same author gives us another story to the same effect. The Apostle said: Kill any Jew that falls into your power. Thereupon Muhayyisa b. MasUd, a Muslim convert, leaped upon and killed Ibn Sunayna, a Jewish merchant. The killers brother, Huwayyisa, chided him: You enemy of God, did you kill him when much of the fat on your belly comes from his wealth Muhayyisa answered: Had the one who ordered me to kill him ordered me to kill you, I would have cut your head off. This was the beginning of Huwayyisas acceptance of Islam. He exclaimed, By God, a religion which can bring you to this is marvellous! and he became a Muslim.

The Demand for More Complete Submission

Muhammad took care to give the local converts no unnecessary offense in the beginning. But this period of caution did not last long. Muhammad entered Medina in April A.D., and within two years he was already having his adversaries eliminated with impunity. As his power increased, he began to come out more and more openly against the lukewarm, the doubters among the local converts. Allah began to demand from them a more unquestioning submission to the authority of His Apostle and issued more frequent warnings against them. Allah told Muhammad that the doubters scoffed at him in private while they paid him homage in public and that they were worthless fellows. When the Hypocrites come to thee, they say, we bear witness that thou art indeed the Apostle... but they are indeed liars.... They have made their oaths a screen.... A seal is set on their hearts.... They are as worthless and hollow as pieces of timber propped up. They are enemies; so beware of them.

The Opposition Divided and Demoralized

Muhammads party had a common command, a common goal, common interests, a common ideology and passion, but the opposition was badly divided; it had no ideology but only certain grievances. Furtive in action, it said one thing and did another. Muhammad picked different groups of the opposition and struck at them one by one, now the BanU QaynuqA, now the BanU NazIr, now the BanU Quraizah. They had promised each other mutual help in private but withdrew when the time for this came.

The demoralization was complete. The Quran speaks contemptuously of the Medinans, who were promising their Jewish allies that if ye be driven forth we will go forth with you... and if you be fought against we will help you.... But God bears witness that they are liars. If they be driven forth, these will not go forth with them; and if they be fought against, these will not help them. Muhammad also makes a keen observation about the opposition while fortifying his followers by telling them: Ye indeed are a keener source of fear in their hearts than God.... Thou dost reckon them as one body, but their hearts are separated. It is because they are a people devoid of intelligence.

ABDULLAH IBN UBAYY

There must have been many people opposed to Muhammads growing power, but the traditions have preserved the name of Ibn Ubayy as the epitome of them all.

He was a Medinan chief of the Khazrajite clan of Awf who became an early convert to Islam. He was once the leading citizen of Medina. It is said that just before Muhammad came, his supporters were trying to make him the king of Medina. But after the arrival of Muhammad, a new force entered the scene, and his importance declined fast. But even then, because of his influence, Muhammad was advised by his best friends to treat Ibn Ubayy with circumspection.

Muslim traditions have blackened Ibn Ubayys name, but if patriotism, independence of judgment, and loyalty are qualities, and if to save is better than to kill, he was not an unworthy man. He saved the Jewish tribe of Medina known as QaynuqA from execution. As early as the second year of the Hijra, Muhammad besieged this tribe. When they surrendered, their hands were tied behind their backs and they were taken out for execution. But Ibn Ubayy intervened forcefully. He thrust his hand into the collar of the apostles robe; the apostle was so angry that his face became almost black. But Abdullah insisted and said: No, by God, I will not let you go until you deal kindly with my clients [allies]. Four hundred men without mail and three hundred mailed protected me from all mine enemies; would you cut them down in one morning By God, I am a man who fears that circumstances may change. Ibn Ubayy was still influential in the affairs of Medina, and his appeal was also a threat. Muhammad yielded on condition that the tribe depart within three days, leaving their goods behind to the victor.

This was in February A.D.. Three years later, in March-April A.D., when the same fate overtook another Jewish tribe of Medina known as Quraizah, the Medinan opposition had already lost its influence and Muhammad had a field day. Eight or nine hundred men were led out in groups of five or six with their hands tied behind their backs and were beheaded, and their bodies were thrown into trenches dug in the marketplace of Medina. We have already mentioned the story somewhat more fully.

Dissension Between the Citizens and the Refugees

Only some months after the tragedy of the BanU Quraizah was enacted, dissension had broken out between the citizens and the refugees in which it was proved that the citizens were already the losing party.

On this occasion, Muhammad was returning after looting the BanU Mustaliq, an Arabian tribe inhabiting a region about eight days march from Medina. The booty included two hundred families, two thousand camels, and five thousand sheep and goats. On the way back, a quarrel broke out between a citizen named SinAn and a refugee named JihjA, who was a servant of Umar. JihjA struck SinAn. Tempers were frayed on both sides, and the quarrel soon spread to others. Ibn Ubayy referred to the insolence of the refugees: This is what you have done to yourselves. You have let them occupy your country, and you have divided your property among them.... They are trying to outdo us seeking to outnumber us in our own land! By Allah, I think that between us and these vagabonds of Quraish it is like saying Feed a dog and it will devour you. But when we return to the Medina city, the stronger will drive out the weaker.

The Assassination of Abdullah Proposed

Umar counseled Muhammad to have Ibn Ubayy killed. Command AbbAd ibn Bishr to kill him, he advised. But Muhammad was cautious. He had an image to protect. He did not want people to say that Muhammad kills his own followers. But though he refrained from executing the idea immediately, he gave it serious thought. Hoping to play on the rivalry between the two Medina tribes, Aws and Khazraj, he consulted Usaid b. Huzair, an Awsite chief and a staunch Muslim, about Abdullah, who was a chief of the Khazrajites. But even he advised Muhammad to deal with Abdullah gently and cautiously.

With all the proposals and consultations, the idea of Abdullahs assassination was so much in the air that his own son, a fanatic Muslim, also heard about it. He went to Muhammad and offered to kill his father with his own hands. Muslim traditions and histories tell this story with great pride.

But wiser counsels prevailed. Since Abdullah was an influential citizen, and his assassination would have unnecessarily jeopardized Muhammads own position, he was spared. Later on, when Abdullahs position became weak through his own vacillation and temporizing, and he was isolated from his people and allies, Umar confessed the wisdom of Muhammads decision. Muhammad replied exultantly: If I had killed him on the day you advised me to, other Medinan chiefs would have been furious. But now they themselves would do it if I commanded them. I know the Apostles order is more blessed than mine, Umar submitted, according to Ibn IshAq, who narrates the whole story. The story is repeated by TabarI too.

The last we hear of Ibn Ubayy is in connection with TabUk. By this time, he had already become a back number, and he died two or three months after TabUk. Whatever opposition was still left in Medina evaporated with him.

Now, with this background, let us turn once more to the SahIh Muslim.

Abdullah Incites the Medinans

Zaid b. Arqam reports that while returning from a journey in which they faced many hardships (after sacking Ban! Mustaliq), they heard Abdullah b. Ubayy tell his friends: Do not give what you have in your possession to those who are with Allahs Messenger until they desert him. They also heard him say that on their return to Medina, the honourable would drive out the meaner therefrom. Zaid reported the matter to Muhammad, who questioned Abdullah. The latter, on oath, denied having said any such thing. Muhammad at first accepted this denial at its face value, but a revelation later descended on him attesting that Zaid had told the truth and establishing Abdullah as a liar.

Prayer for Dead Unbelievers Forbidden

The next two ahAdIs tell us that when Abdullah died, the Prophet, at his sons request, gave him his shirt which he would use as a coffin for his father. Muhammad also came to his grave and brought him out from that, placed him on his knee and put his saliva in his mouth. He also prayed for him even against the protest of Umar.

Intimidation

Intimidation of the opposition began as early as the Battle of Uhud, which took place in the third year of the Hijra (January-February A.D.). Zaid b. SAbit reports: Allahs Apostle set out for Uhud. Some of the persons who were with them came back. The Companions of Allahs Apostle were divided in two groups. One group said: We would kill them, and the other one said: No, this should not be done. Then Allah spoke: Why should ye be divided into two parties about the hypocrites So the ranks of the loyal were closed, but the message was successfully conveyed to the future laggards. Thus intimidation had started quite early, and it was one of the methods of securing compliance and participation in Muhammads holy wars. Either you fight for us or we fight you.

An Attempt on the Prophets Life

According to certain traditions, when Muhammad was returning from TabUk, certain of his opponents in Aqaba formed a group with the intention of killing him by throwing him over a cliff. According to Huzaifa, they were twelve men, all veiled and only half-glimpsed. Muhammad knew their identity but told no one except Huzaifa, who was forbidden to divulge the information. The Prophet cursed them all. This tradition is given here in a rather garbled form.

An Outstanding Arab

JAbir gives us an interesting hadIs. One day Muhammad declared: He who climbed this hill, the hill of MurAr, his sins would be obliterated. Many took advantage of this divine amnesty, and there was a ceaseless flow of persons. All were pardoned except one man, the owner of a red camel. People went to him and advised him that he too should go and obtain pardon. But the man replied: By Allah, so far as I am concerned the finding of something lost is dearer to me than seeking of forgiveness for me by your companion [the Holy Prophet], and he remained busy in finding out his lost thing.

The SahIh Muslim does not give us this mans name, but apparently he was a stout and wise soul. Was he a Zen philosopher who lived one day at a time Sufficient unto the day is the work of the day. The hereafter will take care of itself. Other traditions identify him as Harr b. Qays, who refused to take the pledge of the Tree, and was called a hypocrite by the believers.

There is also a hadIs which shows that those who were unacceptable to Muhammad were unacceptable to Allah even in death. A Muslim who transcribed for Muhammad ran away as a rebel and joined the People of the Book. When he died they dug the grave and buried him therein, but they found to their surprise that the earth had thrown him out over the surface. They again dug the grave... but the earth again threw him out.... They again dug... but the earth again threw him out. At last they left him unburied.

Allah both saves and kills for the pleasure of His Prophet. JAbir reports: Allahs Messenger came back from a journey and as he was near Medina, there was such a violent gale that the mountain seemed to be pressed. Allahs Messenger said: This wind has perhaps been made to blow for the death of a hypocrite, and as he reached Medina a notorious hypocrite from amongst the hypocrites had died.

According to other traditions, Muhammad was returning to Medina after his attack on the BanU Mustaliq. The man whose death the storm caused or proclaimed was Ruffaa, a chief of the BanI QainuqA, a Jewish tribe of Medina that was one of the first tribes to suffer at the hands of Muhammad. Ruffaa had been the first to receive Umar and offer him hospitality when the latter came to Medina.

Description of a Hypocrite

The last two ahAdIs of this book describe those who have neither the support of a fanatic faith nor the light of a higher philosophy and who are subject to the doubts and temptations of ordinary men. Ibn Umar, who had already chosen his pastures, reports Muhammad as saying: The similitude of a hypocrite is that of a sheep which roams aimlessly between two flocks. She goes to one at one time and to the other at another time.

The Book of Commentary

The forty-first and last book of the SahIh Muslim is called the Book of Commentary (KitAb al-TafsIr).

The Quran cannot be read like other scriptures, for it is very different from them in temper and subject matter. It is feverish in tone; it threatens and promises; it does not elucidate but merely lays down and prescribes. It does not deal with the heavenly order of the Gnostic traditions (the rita of the Vedas or the MaAt of ancient Egypt), but with the hereafter, merely an exaggerated, sensuous copy of the here.

The Quranic verses are reputed to have come from a mind in trance, but that in itself gives them no true spiritual validity. The Yogas tell us that trance is possible at every level of the mind, but that the trances of a passionate, angry, and deluded mind (i.e., of a mind characterized by kAma, dvesha, and moha) are not to be trusted-behind them often stands a lunatic or a malevolent criminal.

The Quran deals with accidents; Quranic verses often relate to external events, individual men, incidents in the life of the Prophet. The Book of Commentary gives equally external information about some of these verses. It tells us about the time, the place, the circumstances of their revelation, and all such details of little larger spiritual significance. This book would have been very important if it were comprehensive and gave essential information; but in its present form it is sketchy and discusses an important subject in a superficial manner. It contains only fifty traditions.

For example, in the first five ahAdIs of the book we are told when and where was revealed the following Quranic verse: This day I have perfected your religion for you, completed favour upon you, and have chosen for you al-Islam as your religion. It was revealed on the night of Friday and we were in ArafAt with Allahs Messenger, Umar reports. The information throws no particular light on this revelation, which makes such a tall claim, and adds nothing essential to its subject.

The same with another Quranic verse: And if a woman fears ill-treatment from her husband or desertion, it is no sin for them twain if they make terms of peace between themselves. Aisha tells us that it was revealed in case of a woman who had long association with a person [as his wife] and now he intends to divorce her and she says: Do not divorce me, retain me [as wife in your house] and you are permitted to live with another wife. It was in this context that this verse was revealed.

Who were the characters mentioned by Aisha They were the Prophet himself and his wife Sauda. KAtib al-WAqidI also tells us in his TabaqAt that Muhammad wanted to divorce his wife, then in her forties, but she went to him and said: I am not asking you to sleep with me, I yield my turn to Aisha. But I want to be there, on the Day of Resurrection, among your wives. Muhammad agreed. Resurrection Day was far off.

The Last Sura

SaId b. Jubair reports that Sura AnfAl (Spoils of War), the eighth Sura, was revealed on the occasion of the Battle of Badr; that Sura al-Hashr (The Gathering, or Banishment), the fifty-ninth Sura, was revealed in connection with the tribe of BanU NazIr; and that Sura Tauba (Repentance), also known as Sura BarAat (Immunity), was meant to humiliate the non-believers and the hypocrites. In the Quran this appears as the ninth Sura, but chronologically it is one of the last-according to Sir William Muir, the very last. This is understandable. It is entirely fitting that a Sura of such bitterness, condemnation, and intention should be the last inspiration of a life that breathed such pathologic theological hatred toward the nonbelievers who constituted then, and do even now, the majority of men and women in the world.

8

Upper Class Muslims and Luxurious Life

Nobles and courtiers, army commanders and provincial governors, in fact all high officials of the Muslim government formed the upper classes. In civilian upper classes could be counted the Ulama and the Mashaikh, scholars and historians, and some very rich Muslim merchants. A study of the high classes under two major categories - nobles, and Ulama and Mashaikh - would suffice to give a general idea of the life of Muslim upper classes, their composition, their corruption, their licence, their hopes and fears, and their high style of living.

THE NOBLES

The nobles constituted the ruling bureaucracy. In the early years of Muslim rule foreign adventurers and warriors monopolised appointments to high offices. In the beginning the Turks formed the bulk of the ruling elite. Besides, Persians, Abyssinians, Egyptians, Afghans and converted Mongols also continued to obtain high positions. Under the Lodi sultans, Afghan adventurers of various tribes and clans flocked to India like ants and locusts.

Even in the Mughal times (--) the imperial service remained predominantly foreign with Iranis and Turanis forming the core of the cadre. The Turanis hailed from Central Asia where the Turkish language was spoken. Iranis comprised the Persian speaking people and belonged to the region presently extending from Iraq and Iran to Afghanistan.

The Mughal nobles were also known as Mansabdars. The Mansabdars were not only government officers, but also the richest class in the empire. They formed a closed aristocracy; entrance into this class was not usually possible for the common people, whatever their merits. Naturally, therefore, the most important factor which was taken into account when nobles were appointed was heredity. The Khanazads, the scions of royalty and sons and descendants of Mansabdars, had the best claim to such appointments.

The Indian Muslim nobles, who were local converts, also rose to be officers in the upper cadres, but foreigners were always preferred. The fourteenth century Persian chronicler Ziyauddin Barani, who was born in India but traced his ancestry to a Turki Noble, credits the foreigner Turks with all possible virtues and the Indian Muslims with all kinds of imperfections. The invectives he hurls on the converted Sultan Nasiruddin Khusrau Shah (C.E.), are too well known to need repetition. Muhammad Tughlaq always preferred foreign Muslims to Indians for appointment as officers. The rebellion of Ain-ul-mulk Multani during his reign was a symptom of the resentment felt by the India-born nobles against this policy of prejudice. In turn Khan-i-Jahan, a Telingana Brahmin convert, dominated the court of Sultan Firoz Tughlaq. The career of Mahmud Gawan, the minister of the Bahmani Sultan Muhammad III, illustrates both the reasons for which preference was given to foreigners and the jealousy it engendered. Foreign nobles looked down upon Indian Muslim nobles, and considered them as lowborn, although not all foreign Muslims were of high lineage.

Right through the Muslim rule, low origin foreigners used to come as individuals and in groups to seek employment in India. Writing about the foreign element in the Mughal nobility in seventeenth century Bernier says that the Omarahs mostly consist of adventurers from different nations who entice one another to the court; and are generally persons of low descent, some having been originally slaves, and the majority being destitute of education. The Mogol raises them to dignities, or degrades them to obscurity; according to his own pleasure and caprice. W.H. Moreland, however, does not consider all foreign immigrants as of low descent. He says that in Mughal India there were huge prizes to be won and one need not wonder that the service should have attracted to the court the ablest and most enterprising men from a large portion of Western Asia. High and low, foreign and Indian, the Muslim nobles after all belonged to one and the same cadre, and they tried to come closer together. On the one hand, foreign Muslims used to become locals after the lapse of a few generations. Bernier writes that the children of the third and fourth generation (of Uzbegs, Persians, Arabs and Turks) are held in much less respect than the new corners. On the other hand, the low-born Indian Muslim became elitist with rise in economic status. There was a saying: Last year I was a julaha, this year a shaykh; and the next year, if the harvest be good, I shall be a saiyyad. Belonging to Islam was a great cementing force, and, whatever the colour of the skin, all Muslim nobles tried to feel as one, as belonging to the ruling elite, as searching for exotic roots. It was aristocratic on the part of the orthodox Muslim to feel that he was in India, but not of it. He durst not strike his roots deep into the native soil. He must import traditions, language and culture. His civil and criminal law must be derived from the writings of jurists and the decisions of judges in Baghdad and Cairo. The Muslim in India was an intellectual exotic; he considered it infra dig to adapt himself to his environment.

Besides the competition between Indian and foreign Muslim nobles, there was also constant contest between Muslim and Hindu nobles. With the permanent establishment of Muslim rule, the policy of the sultans was generally to keep the Hindus excluded and appoint only Muslims. But the Hindus possessed native intelligence and experience, sons of the soil as they were, and many of the best Hindus had to be employed, especially during the Mughal period. The Hindus in a way were indispensable. To them belonged, according to Badaoni, half the army and half the land. Neither the Hindustanis (Indian Muslims) nor the Moghuls can point to such grand lords as the Hindus have among themselves. Bernier too did not fail to notice this.

These nobles were in attendance on the king in the capital or in camp, and in outstations held civil and military assignments, as governors of provinces or commanders of the army. Indeed they were expected to cultivate versatility, there being no distinction between civil and military appointments and duties. Raja Birbal, after many years as court wit, met his death fighting Yusafzais as commander of troops on the frontier while Abul Fazl, the most eminent literary figure of the time, distinguished himself in military operations in the Deccan.

The nobles were called Umara and were graded as Khans, Maliks, Amirs and Sipehsalars in the Sultanate period, and as Mansabdars under the Mughals. According to Barani a Sarkhail commanded ten horsemen; a Sipehsalar ten Sarkhails; an Amir ten Sipahsalars; a Malik ten Amirs; and a Khan, ten Maliks. According to the author of Masalik-ul-Absar, a Khan commanded more or less, troops, an Amir,, a Malik a thousand, and so on. The term Amir was normally used in a generic sense to denote a high officer. In Akbars time and after, all the great men of the Mughal Empire were graded and appointed to a mansab (rank) in the imperial service. From the lowest rank, that of the commander of ten, upto the rank of an officer was known as Mansabdar. From onwards a noble was known as Amir, or Khan, or Khan-i-Azam. They were all generally spoken of as Umara.

The Umara were highly paid. Their remuneration was paid sometimes in the form of a cash salary, at others by the grant of a revenue assignment or iqta. The iqta was basically a salary collected at source. According to the chroniclers of the Sultanate period every Khan received two lakh tankahs, every Malik from to thousand tankahs, every Amir from to thousand tankahs, and so on. The salaries during the Mughal period were equally high. It has been computed by expert opinion that a commander of could count on at least Rs., a month under Akbar and his successor. He could even improve upon this amount if he practised judicious economy in his military expenditure and had the good fortune of securing a profitable jagir. A commander of could similarly count on receiving Rs. a month (equal to from rupees, to, in), while a commander of would have received the equivalent of Rs. to at the same rate. While therefore the precise figures are uncertain, it appears to be reasonable to conclude that the higher ranks of the Imperial Service were remunerated on a scale far more liberal than that which now prevails in India (C.), or for that matter in any portion of the world.

LUXURIOUS LIFE

Their high salaries and emoluments introduced into the lives of the Umara all the uses and abuses of luxury. They lived with such ostentation that it was not to be seen elsewhere in the world, and the most sumptuous of European courts cannot compare in richness and magnificence with the lustre beheld in Indian courts. Their splendid life-style may be studied in its two aspects - private inside the harem and public outside of it. They lived in magnificent mansions some costing four to six thousand gold tankahs (dinars) and provided with all amenities. By the seventeenth century the Mahals of the nobles had gained in architectural excellence and constructional designs. At Agra, on the banks of the Jumna, many persons have erected buildings of three or four storeys, writes emperor Jahangir Asaf Khans palace had a fair Diwan Khana which was flanked by diverse lodgings for his women neatly contrived with galleries and walks. Asaf Khans palace was exceedingly handsome and costly, but the others were equally elegant. The basic pattern of the mansions of the nobles was the same. One portion of the building was the Diwan Khana or the mens quarters but the greater portion was occupied by their ladies and was called Zenan Khana. In the houses of the nobles the womens apartments are in the centre, and it is generally necessary to traverse two or three large courts and a garden or two before reaching there. Berniers observations about the houses of nobles of Delhi are similar to those of Pelsaert at Agra. They were spacious and along with courtyards, gardens, trees, basins of water, small jets deau in the hall or at the entrance, and handsome subterraneous apartments which are furnished with large fans. While encamping, their tents were made equally magnificient. All the arcades and galleries were covered from top to bottom with brocade, and (even) the pavement with rich carpets.

The nobles ladies were numerous and spendthrift. Pelsaert says that as a rule they have three or four wives All live together surrounded by high walls called the mahal, having tanks and gardens inside. Each wife has separate apartments for herself and her slaves, of whom there may be, or, or, according to her fortune. Each has a monthly allowance for her (expenditure). Jewels and clothes are provided by the husband according to the extent of his affection Their Mahals were adorned with superfluous pomp and ornamental dainties. The ladies made extensive use of gold and silver, for ornaments and jewellery, as well for their utensils and table service. Even their bedsteads were lavishly ornamented with gold and silver. During the earlier period, there is also mention of gold bath-tubs and gold horse-shoes.

For the security and supervision of these hundreds of ladies, dozens and dozens of maids and eunuchs were required. The harem paraphernalia cost tons of money. Furthermore, it was a fashion for the Umara to visit the houses of dancing girls, take them or call them to their own mansions and pay them handsomely. Throughout the medieval times the nobility indulged in the expensive hobbies of women, wine, song and drugs. Chess and chausar they played at home; big game shooting, taming and flying birds, playing chaugan and practicing with swords were their outdoor recreations. Dozens of falconers, pigeon-boys and attendants were employed to keep their birds and horses in trim. The nobles, their ladies, and even their slave-girls dressed in the best of cotton fineries and richest embroidered silks. Their food was rich and full of delicacies. Their boon companions partook of it freely. Most of the nobles were soaked in wine and sunk in debauch but they were also patrons of art and poetry. Since I have made a comprehensive study of the luxurious life of the medieval Muslim nobility in my monograph entitled The Mughal Harem, I shall refrain from repeating here what I have already stated therein in detail except reproducing one paragraph from the book. The large establishment of wives and servants rendered the nobles immobile. No Indian scholars, engineers or travellers went abroad to learn the skills the Europeans were developing in their countries. While people from Europe were frequently coming to Hindustan, no Indian nobleman could go to the West because he could not live without his harem and he could not take with him his cumbersome harem to countries situated so far away. Europe at this time was forging ahead in science and technology through its Industrial Revolution, but the Mughal elites kept themselves insulated from this great stride because of inertia. Consequently, the country was pulled back from marching with progress, a deficiency which has not been able to be made up until now.

Outside their mansions the Umara were extra ostentatious. Since they attained to highest honours at court, in the provinces, and in the armies; and who are, as they call themselves, the Pillars of the Empire, they maintain the splendour of the court, and are never seen out-of-doors but in the most superb apparel; mounted sometimes on an elephant, sometimes on horseback, and not unfrequently in a paleky attended by many of their cavalry, and by a large body of servants on foot - not only to clear the way, but to flap the flies and brush off the dust with tails of peacocks; to carry the spitoon, water to allay the Omrahs thirst.

Over and above the expenses on their large establishment of wives, servants, camels and horses, the nobles were expected to present valuable gifts to the king on birthday anniversaries, Ids, Nauroz and other festivals, according to their pay and status. Some of them, indeed take that opportunity of presenting gifts of extraordinary magnificence, sometimes for the sake of ostentatious display, sometimes to divert the king from instituting an inquiry into their excessive exactions, and sometimes to gain the favour of the king, and by that means obtain an increase of salary. Some present fine pearls, diamonds, emeralds and rubies; others offer vessels of gold set with precious stones; others again give gold coins The king also gave some gift in exchange, but the presents of the nobles were much costlier and often extracted by the king. During a festival of this kind Aurangzeb, having paid a visit to Jafar Khan, the

Wazir made a present to the king of gold coins to the amount of one hundred thousand crowns, some handsome pearls and a ruby about the value of which prevailed great confusion among the principal jewellers, and it might have cost five hundred thousand crowns. Thus the king sometimes took the initiative in contriving to extract costly presents and gathered huge amounts, for says Pelsaert, from the least to the greatest right up to the King himself everyone is infected with insatiable greed. Money spent on bribes and presents often proved profitable investment, for, without presents the nobles could hardly expect timely response to his petition. Not only were gifts presented to the king, means had to be found for making valuable presents, every year, to a Wazir, an eunuch or a lady of the seraglio, or to any other person whose influence at court the nobleman considered indispensable.

BRIBERY AND CORRUPTION

Such high expenses of building spacious mansions, exchanging costly presents, maintaining a large harem of wives and concubines -in short, living in style at home and indulging in pompous display outside, could not be met by the aristocracy from their salaries alone. Therefore, the nobles augmented their income by other means. There were many sources from which extra amounts of money could come to their coffers, like enjoying a large military command, a profitable political appointment and a lucrative revenue assignment, and these were all inter-connected, all providing opportunities of corruption and exploitation.

Every nobleman or Mansabdar was alloted a quota of troops which he was expected to maintain. From the very beginning of Turkish rule the conquered land used to be distributed by the king among army officers, nobles, government officials and even soldiers as gifts, grants and rewards and also in lieu of personal salary, and for paying their soldiers. These grants were not hereditary, and were given as pay for military service. But in course of time the land-holders continued in possession of their land without rendering any military service. On inquiry it was found by Sultan Balban that about, cavalry officers had received villages in the Doab alone by way of pay during the time of Iltutmish, but for the next forty years or more many of the grantees had become old and infirm, or had died. But their sons and even slaves continued to live off the lands as if they were an inheritance. Many of them were clever enough to get the assignments recorded in their own names in the books of the Ariz-i-Mumalik obviously by bribing the officials according to their means by wine, goats, chicken, pigeon, butter and food-stuffs from their villages to the Deputy Muster-Master and his officials.

Sultan Balban tried to improve matters and so did many other rulers but corruption remained entrenched.

The salary of the soldiers and expenditure on their horses usually formed part of the pay of the Umara or Mansabdars who were expected to spend it on them. But this system gave the nobleman an opportunity to retain some money from every mans pay and prepare false returns of the horses he was supposed to provide. Many of the lords who hold the rank of horse, do not keep even in their employ. This practice was universal throughout the medieval period. It rendered the Amirs income very considerable, particularly when he was so fortunate as to have some good jagirs or suitable lands assigned to him. For some of the officers received double, and even more than that, in excess of the estimated value of their grants. There was thus the practice which prevails too much at all times of purchasing governorships against hard cash. Sometimes the king assigned a governorship to the highest bidder. The governor or farmer of revenue so appointed had to compensate himself by mercilessly fleecing the merchants and peasants of the province. In this way many people without the smallest patrimony, some even originally wretched slaves, involved in debt, became great and opulent lords overnight. Bernier even complains that the Great Mogol did not select for his service gentlemen of opulent and ancient families; sons of his citizens, merchants and manufacturers affectionately attached to their sovereign and willing to maintain themselves by means of their own patrimony Instead he is surrounded by parasites raised by the dregs of society. That is how the misery of this ill-fated country is increased. For many an Umara just looted both the government and the people all at once. In this regard certain misconceptions may be removed at the outset. It is generally believed that corruption flourishes in a democracy or a soft state where no one can be punished until proved guilty, and that despotic rulers would not brook it. Another idea repeatedly put forward is that it is poverty and low salaries that breed corruption, and that it is bound to be reduced in proportion to the rise in emoluments and standard of living.

However, on a study of the records of medieval times, when autocracy was the order of the day, we find that corruption was quite well-grounded, and people and the government were unabashedly cheated. Cheating of the people and the government are almost synonymous. In the fourteenth century too, those who cheated the people could not rest at that, and they took every opportunity of defrauding the government whenever an opportunity presented itself. One such opportunity came when Muhammad bin Tughlaq introduced his famous token currency. Another, when he struck upon the novel (now commonly practised) idea of having large-scale farm cultivation. An area of about miles square (krohs) was set aside for intensive farming in which not a patch was to be left uncultivated at any time by changing crops constantly. A hundred shiqdars were appointed to supervise the project. They promised to cultivate thousands of bighas of land and also to reclaim waste land. Each one of them received fifty thousand tankahs in cash as advance (sondhar) from the State. But they turned out to be greedy and dishonest persons. They cheated the government, squandered the money on personal needs and did not care to cultivate the allotted area. In this way the State lost not less then,, tankahs in all. Of the advance not even a hundredth or a thousandth part could be recovered and the avaricious shiqdars embezzled the whole amount. And all this callousness was there about a measure which had been undertaken to ameliorate famine conditions.

A few more instances of corruption from the Sultanate period may be mentioned to appreciate the depth and extensivity of the malady. During the reign of Firoz Shah the profession of soldiers was made hereditary. Also old men were not retired on compassionate ground and efficiency of the army naturally suffered. Over and above this, corruption was galore in the Diwan-i-Arz. Horses of little value were brought to the Diwan and were passed as serviceable, obviously by greasing the palms of the clerks. In this reference a story narrated by Shams Siraj Afif is worth citing. Once the Sultan overheard a soldier complaining to a friend that because he did not have the necessary money to pay as bribe, he had not been able to get a fitness certificate for his horse at the Diwan-i-Arz. The Sultan inquired how much was needed, and the soldier said that if he had a gold tankah he could get a certificate for his horse. The Sultan ordered his purse-bearer to give a tankah to the soldier. The trooper went to the Diwan-i-Arz with the ashrafi and paying it to the clerk concerned got the certificate. He then returned and thanked the Sultan. Encouragement to corruption from the head of the State was a matter of concern. But what else could Afif say but that Firoz Shah was a very kind-hearted and affectionate Sultan!

These cases of bribery, corruption and embezzlement concern government officials of not so high a status among the upper classes. But the highest nobles of the State indulged in them. The story of the deception of Kajar Shah, the Master of Mint, speaks for itself. It is so interesting that its incidents may be given in some detail. Firoz Tughlaq had issued several varieties of new coins and shashgani (or six-jital-piece) was one of them. As the coin went into circulation, it was reported to the Sultan by two courtiers that there was a deficiency of one grain of silver in the shashgani, and they prayed for an investigation. If what they had said was proved to be true, they pleaded, the officials responsible for debasement of the coin must take the consequences. The Sultan immediately directed the Wazir, Khan-i-Jahan Maqbul, to investigate the matter. Khan-i-Jahan was equally keen about the enquiry. Indeed he observed that the coinage of kings was like an unmarried daughter, whom no one would seek after, however beautiful and charming she might be, if any aspersion had, rightly or wrongly, been cast upon her character. So also was the case with the royal coins; if any one honestly or falsely alleged a debasement of the currency, the insinuation would spread, the coinage would earn a bad name, and no one would take it.

The affair was as scandalous as it was unique. To hold an open inquest was ruled out because the bona fides of the government itself were in question. Therefore the Wazir decided on a secret investigation, and sent for Kajar Shah, the Master of Mint, and asked him if his officials had been covetous. Kajar Shah knew that his game was up and he thought it best to make a clean breast of it to the Wazir. Khan-i-Jahan could not displease the Sultan, who had insisted that the intrinsic value of the coin should be tested in his presence. But he also could not allow the government to get into disrepute, and now that he had known the truth, he thought it best to hush up the case. Therefore, he recommended to Kajar Shah to arrange the matter over with the goldsmiths that they so manage their performance before the king that the process of debasement of the shashgani may not be detected. The goldsmiths, charcoal dealers and stove (angusht) managers were all tutored and everything was given a fool-proof finish. Firoz Shah was requested to watch the operation sitting in a private apartment with Khan-i-Jahan Maqbul. Kajar Shah and his accusers were called in. The goldsmiths were also brought in. The charcoal dealers brought the stoves and placed them before the goldsmiths. Several shashgani pieces were placed in the crucible, which the goldsmiths put upon the fire. The Sultan meanwhile entered into a conversation with his minister, and while he was so engaged, the workmen adroitly picked up the required pieces of silver and surreptitiously threw them into the melting pot. After a while the crucible was taken off the fire and the contents were weighed; the shashgani was proved to be of full standard value. Kajar Shah was presented with a robe of honour and other favours. He was seated on an elephant and taken round the city so that people might understand that the shashgani was of full value. The honest accusers were thus proved false and banished.

Another instance. An important nobleman, Shamsuddin Abu Rija, the Auditor General (Mustaufi), had earned wide notoriety as a professional bribe-taker, embezzler and at that a tyrant. Shams Siraj Afif, historian contemporary of Firoz Shah, devotes thirty-five pages to record the crimes of Abu Rija. The three years during which he held the office of the Auditor General, his hand of greed extended to all officers, Zamindars and Amils.

Those who gave him bribes, were permitted to go scot-free; others who did not, were implicated by him on one charge or another and punished. Nobody dared to raise a voice against his criminal breach of trust or his atrocities, because he was a hot favourite of the Sultan. Even before he was made the Mustaufi, he, as the deputy governor of Gujarat, had borrowed thousand tankahs from the Provincial Treasury for his own use, but had not refunded the amount. To hide his improper gains he had built a new mansion in Delhi and had buried underground thousands of gold Ashrafis. At last the Sultan could not keep his eyes closed to Shamsuddins black deeds because a number of nobles, including the Khan-i-Jahan, son of Khan-i-Jahan Maqbul, insisted that he should be brought to book. Shamsuddins mansion was searched and his reserves of gold dug out. He was imprisoned and tortured so severely that he could never ride a horse again. Strangely enough when Firozs son Muhammad ascended the throne, he recalled Shamsuddin Abu Rija and reinstated him with all honours.

But the one man who amassed probably the largest amount of wealth in the Sultanate period, escaped scot-free. This man was Bashir, a slave of Firoz Shah. He had originally come as a part of the dower of Firozs mother. In course of time, and through the favour of Sultan Firoz, he rose into prominence and got the title of Imadul Mulk. His one passion was acquisition of wealth. Related to the sultan as he was, he soon accumulated crores of tankahs. Gunny bags required for storing the coin alone were estimated to cost, tankahs, the price of each bag being four jitals; but Imadul Mulk objected to this extravagant outlay for bags and directed that pits should be dug in the ground and the money placed therein like as corn is stored. He had amassed thirteen crore tankahs but he was greedy about acquiring more.

Just imagine thirteen crore tankahs. The total revenue of a year during Firozs reign was six crore and seventy-five lac tankahs; and one individual slave of the Sultan (Bashir-i-Sultani) had acquired wealth amounting to two years total revenue of the country. Could corruption go further There were many rich Khans and Maliks in the time of Firoz Shah, writes Afif, but no one was so rich as he; indeed there never had been one so rich in any reign or in any kingdom. Still the officers of the Revenue Department could not call him to account; they were indeed afraid of him, for he was a favourite of the Sultan. To please the Sultan, Imadul Mulk once presented him with a crore of tankahs. But twelve crores still remained with him. At his death, the Sultan ordered nine crores to be deposited in the State exchequer on the plea that Bashir is my property (as his slave), and so his property is mine. Three crores were left with Imadul Mulks son Ishaq who also got the title of his father. Afif adds that Ishaq himself was an extremely rich man and did not stand in need of his fathers wealth.

The chronicler philosophises by saying: These nobles accumulated so much wealth by lawful and unlawful means (vajeh na vajeh), and then leaving it undertook the last journey where they were to account for all this wealth. But such ill-gotten gains at least created havoc in this world, because, according to Afif himself, much of the trouble that came about in the time of Sultan Muhammad (son of Firoz) was due to the accumulation of such wealth in the hands of a few nobles.

Thus there was corruption in the army, in civil administration and in the royal mint. Hoarding, black-marketing and bribery were commonly practised. Even the judiciary was not free from corruption, and that too during the reign of a strong and stern monarch like Alauddin. Talking of Qazi Hamiduddin Multani, Ziyauddin Barani cryptically remarks, it would not be proper to write about his qualities in history. He also says that not the godfearing and abstemious but corruptible, greedy and mundane people were appointed as judges. His one complaint was that judges used to stretch the meaning of the Quranic texts to carry out the wishes of the Sultans. The indictment by Maulana Shamsuddin Turk of the judiciary of the day is also worth citing. The Maulana who hailed from Egypt, addressed a letter to Alauddin saying that ill-fated wiseacres of black faces sat in mosques with abominable law books and made money by cheating both the accuser and the accused, and the Qazis did not bring these facts to the notice of the king. It is said that Shamsuddin Turk was opposed to Qazi Hamiduddin, and therefore wrote in such a way, but in Mutla-i-Anwar, Amir Khusrau also observes that the Qazis were ignorant of the principles of law. The appointment of Ibn Battuta, who did not know a word of law, as the Qazi of the capital by Muhammad bin Tughlaq, came to him as the greatest surprise.

Having studied some prominent cases of bribery, corruption and hoarding, of the nobles, and the rich upper class people in the Sultanate times, let us analyse their genesis and their prominent aspects. It is clear that corruption had nothing much to do with poverty or a low standard of living. During Balbans rule the nobility and armymen, who could not or would not perform their duties for which lands had been granted to them, were not poor. But they wanted their privileges to continue; about performing their duties they were not concerned. Fakhruddin, the Kotwal, who pleaded their case with the king was moved as much by compassion as by self-interest. He was himself old and in course of time stood to lose all privileges if the orders of Balban were not amended. The people who minted counterfeit coins found in the token currency of Muhammad bin Tughlaq a challenge to their intelligence and ingenuity, and took advantage of the golden opportunity provided by it to get rich. The officials of the Diwan-i-Arz who took a gold tankah for issuing the fitness certificate to the cavalryman in the days of Firoz were not poor; they were habitual bribe-takers. The shiqdars or officers who embezzled the money advanced to them for cultivation by Muhammad bin Tughlaq again, were not poor. The people who minted debased currency, the wholesalers and retailers who indulged in hoarding and black-marketing, men like Kajar Shah and Bashir-i-Sultani, did not do what they did because they were poor, but because they were greedy and opportunists. The object of the opportunists was to get rich, of the rich to get richer. Their luxurious life, their women and wine and their ambition to amass wealth, kept the torch of corruption burning.

Individual cases of corruption and embezzlement apart, the sure and perennial sources of extra income of the nobles were two-what they could save on their troops and what they could collect in addition to the nominal value of their assignments - and able and unscrupulous men made as much extra wealth as possible from both these. In the words of Shihabuddin Ahmad, The khans, maliks, amirs, and isfah-salars receive the revenues of the places assigned to them by the treasury Generally speaking they bring in much more than their estimated value Some of the officers receive double, and even more than that, in excess of the estimated value of their grants. What this practice meant to the poor peasant would be discussed later. The irony of the matter was that everyone knew about it, including the king himself. The king was even a party to the system for he allotted good lands to his favourites nobles. Even Sher Shah Suri, who is regarded as a friend of the agriculturists, changed his amils (revenue collectors) every year, or second year, and sent new ones, for he said that there is no such income and advantage in other employments as in the government of a district. Therefore I (Sher Shah) send my good old loyal experienced servants to take charge of districts, that the salaries, profits, and advantages, may accrue to them in preference to others; and after two years I change them, and send other servants like to them, that they also may prosper

In the Mughal period the same trends continued. Things might have improved under the able and shrewd Akbar, but only might. He too was part of the system. He too was surrounded by the same sort of people who were ready of speech and expert at intrigue. Corruption in the Mughal times was so widespread - in the army, in civil administration and even in judiciary - that narration of individual cases cannot just be done. Exceptions apart, the more important the Amir, the larger his expenses, and the greater his attempt at grabbing more and more wealth. The biographical notices collected by Blochmann afford instances of the possibilities which Akbars service offered. Hakim Ali, for instance, came from Persia to India poor and destitute, but won Akbars favour, and being his personal servant rose to the rank of. Peshrau Khan again was a slave who was given to Humayun as a present; he rendered service in many different capacities and died a commander of, leaving a fortune of lakhs (equivalent to nearly a crore of rupees at modern values). No one was immune from this temptation. Shaikh Ibrahim Chishti of Jaunpur died at Fatehpur, bidding farwell to mountains of gold, crores in cash taken into the treasury; the rest in the words of Badaoni, fell to the share of his enemies - his sons and representatives. Under Akbars successor things were certainly bad. Jahangir believed in frequent transfers, and the certainty of a speedy change meant increased activity in exploitation Under Shahjahan and Aurangzeb the peasant was systematically fleeced.

The exaction of official perquisites or gratuities was the universal and admitted practice. Official corruption was, however, admitted in society to be immoral, and there were many officers above corruption. But the receiving and even demanding of presents by men in power was the universal rule and publicly acknowledged. Nur Jahans father, when prime minister under Jahangir, was shameless in demanding presents. So also was Jafar Khan, one of the early Wazirs of Aurangzeb. Jai Singh offered a purse of Rs., to the Wazir for inducing the emperor to retain him in the Deccan command. Bhimsen expresses his disgust at having to pay everybody at Court in order to get or retain a petty civil office. The qazis grew enormously rich by taking bribes, the most notorious of them being Abdul Wahab. So also did many sadars. Even the emperor was not exempt from it. Aurangzeb asked an aspirant to a title, Your father gave to Shahjahan one lakh of rupees for adding alif to his title and making him Amir Khan. How much will you pay me for the title I am giving you Qabil Khan in two-and-a-half years of personal attendance on Aurangzeb amassed lakhs of rupees in cash, besides articles of value and a new house for selling to suppliants his good offices. As Jadunath Sarkar says, this pressure was passed from the emperor downwards; each social grade trying to sqeeze out of the class below itself what it had to pay as present to the rank above it, the cultivator of the soil and the trader being the victims in the last resort.

ESCHEAT

In short, the upper classes in the employment of the state were, by and large, ever busy in amassing wealth from all possible sources and enjoying it to their hearts content. But only during their life-time. At the death of a noble, all his property, movable and immovable, was reclaimed by the government. Immediately on the death of the lord, writes Pelsaert, who has enjoyed the kings jagir, be he great or small, without any exception - even before the breath is out of his body - the kings officers are ready on the spot, and make an inventory of the entire estate, recording everything to the value of a single pice, even to the dresses and jewels of the ladies, provided they have not concealed them. Concealing was very difficult. As a rule all the possessions of a noble, and his transactions were managed by his diwan and many other subordinates and accountants. Hence they could not be kept secret. When the noble died all his subordinates were detained, ordered to show all books and papers to the kings officers, and if there was any suspicion about their disclosure, they were tortured till they told the truth. The king takes back the whole estate except in a case where the deceased has done good service in his lifetime, when the women and children are given enough to live on, but no more, while most of the servants were left on the street with a tom coat and a pinched face.

On the face of it, forfeiture of the property of a deceased noble looks unjust, but in reality it was not. Under the escheat system the king saved the corrupt Amir and himself the bother of instituting an enquiry and presenting a charge-sheet. He let the grandee undisturbed to enjoy his ill-gotten wealth as long as he lived, but after his death acquired it in full. In his discretion the king sometimes left part of the wealth as pension to the widow and heirs, but generally the sons of an Amir had to start life anew. It was a bull-dozer law, and applied to both the innocent and the guilty. But there were hardly any innocent grandees. They knew very well about the law, and therefore spent so lavishly while in office, that in addition to their great income, most of them took huge amounts as loan from the State Treasury and the king was justified in recovering the loan from their property.

And after all, as per the convention, the king was the heir of the Umara. The Mughal emperors seem to have followed the Delhi Sultans in making a claim upon their nobles as if they were their slaves. We have seen how a high officer of the title of Imadul Mulk, was declared by Firoz Tughlaq as Bashir is my property (as a slave) and so his property is mine. The Mughal claim to such succession is not elaborated in the Ain-i-Akbari, but is noticed by a number of European travellers from the time of Akbar onwards. It was not declared in so many words but the Mughal nobles in status were not much better off than slaves. The grandees were prohibited from contracting marriage alliances without the emperors permission. The noble was obliged, whatever be his rank, to fall prostrate on the ground in obeisance to his master. Although the price paid in human dignity was terrible, yet he paid it as his position, his promotion, indeed his very existence depended on the pleasure of the king. Manucci, writing about the last years of Aurangzeb says: To get the hazari or pay of one thousand, it is necessary to wait a long time and work hard.

This is one side of the coin. The other is that whether foreign or Indian, the nobles maintained a measure of individual independence. The pleasure of enjoying oneself with vigour and liberty amidst the chances of war and of life; the delights of activity without degrading labour; and the taste of an adventurous career full of uncertainty, inequality and peril, instilled in them a passionate desire of personal independence. There was a degree of brutality and an apathy for the weak and the poor. Nevertheless, at the bottom of this mixture of brutality, materialism and selfishness, lay the love of independence. It drew its strength from the moral nature of man, from a desire to developed ones own personality which the upper class elites loved and cherished in medieval India as is found to be the case in all ages. Their status might have been that of a servant of the ruling power, but they themselves felt as mini-rulers in their own assignments, and carried their swords like whipping sticks. Pelsaert noticed that the houses of the nobles at Agra were hidden away in alleys and corners, and Bernier found that the dwellings of the Umara at Delhi were scattered in every direction. Manucci also observed that in Delhi many nobles are very pleased to have their dwellings far from the royal palace. The reason was that these people enjoyed the pleasures of idleness and womens company away from mutual suspicion and court intrigues, and had it not been for official and court duties, the grandees would never have bothered to leave their houses at all, in order to enjoy uninterrupted intimacy of their female beauties.

The private and public life of the nobles, the system of seraglios, the widespread corruption, the custom of escheat, and so many other conventionalities of the upper classes, all left a legacy which is visible in many spheres of Muslim social life even now. Obviously, these cannot be discussed in any detail in a work of this size. A few observations, however, would indicate areas where such remnants of the legacy of Muslim rule could be found. For instance, because of escheat, writes Pelsaert, everything in the (Mughal) kingdom is uncertain. Wealth, position, love, friendship, confidence, everything hangs by a thread The nobles build (mansions) with so many hundreds of thousands, and yet (because of escheat) keep them in repair only so long as the owners live Once the builder is dead, no one will care for the buildings one cannot contemplate without pity or distress their ruined state. Many old Muslim havelis, which have survived and are still inhabited bear out Pelsaerts statement.

Mughal corruption was of two kinds-polite custom, and outright bribery and embezzlement. In the first, a person did not meet his senior or superior empty-handed; he presented some gift. This practice was not harmful. But the high corruption, bribery embezzlement, widely prevalent under Muslim rule, as averred by contemporary chroniclers and foreign visitors has never left the Indian scene, and the roots of the present day corruption may be traced to earlier times. Similarly, the sophistication associated with the Mughal court etiquette and the luxurious life of the harem is still to be seen in the graceful and refined behaviour of upper class Muslims, especially of their women. In the words of Jadunath Sarkar, the general type of Muhammadan population are more refined and accustomed to a costiler mode of life, while Hindus of the corresponding classes, even when rich, are grosser and less cultured. The lower classes of Hindus, however, are distinctly cleaner and more intellectual than Muslims of the same grade of life. But let us here keep confined to upper classes.

ULAMA AND MASHAIKH

Muslim scholars and Sufi Shaikhs, though not all rich, also belonged to the upper classes because of the respect they enjoyed in society. Most of them were patronised by kings and nobles, many were actually in their employ. Some of them were very well-off.

The Ulama

Ulama (plural of alim or learned) used to be well-versed in the Muslim law. As such they assisted Muslim monarchs in administering their dominions according to the Shariat. That way they also helped the Muslims in organizing their lives according to the Shariat which comprehends not only beliefs and practices, public and personal law, and rules of behaviour but even includes dress and personal appearance. Acquiring knowledge for the sake of earning money was looked down upon; hence tradition classified the Ulama into two categories, Ulama-i-Akhirat (the pious) and Ulama-i-su (the worldly). Knowledge was an extremely valuable ornament in an age when the educated were few and the Ulama were respected for their learning and ability.

Naturally, there was hardly any secular approach to education. Great emphasis was laid on theological education (manqulat). The most important subjects taught were Hadis, Fiqh (jurisprudence) and Tafsir (exegesis). The institutions of higher learning, called madrasas, were essentially schools of theology, with auxiliaries of grammar, literature and logic.

These madrasas were the strongholds of orthodoxy and were subsidised by the state. A high value is placed on Muslim orthodoxy everywhere, because it is claimed that it maintains the identity of the community as against other communities. In actual practice it has served as a force against an integrated living, even coexistence, with other communities.

In a word, the Ulama were an orthodox lot. Those who were denied the life of affluence usually took to teaching (as mutawalli) in some mosque or under the thatched roof of their own mud houses. Some other Ulama or danishmands became pious preachers and scholars. Very often they too had to work under indigent circumstances. Some outstanding scholars were appointed as teachers in madrasas established by the Sultans. It was the ambition of the Ulama to join government service. There were many offices which the establishment could offer to a scholar. In official hierarchy of such appointments the post of the Sadr-i-Jahan came at the top, then followed Qazis (judges), Muftis (interpreters of law) Muhtasibs (censors of public morals), Imams (who led prayers) and Khatibs (reciters of the Quran). The Sadr-i-Jahan was the chief of the judicial department. He served as the Qazi-i-Mumalik (chief judge) and recommended to the king about the appointment of junior Qazis. The Shaikh-ul-Islam was in charge of the ecclesiastical affairs of the empire. All those saints, faqirs and indigent scholars who enjoyed state patronage were looked after by him. Normally, only well-read scholars were appointed as Khatibs and Imams. So also was the case with Muftis and Muhtasibs. Muslim public opinion did not approve of the appointment of less qualified persons to these posts.

The Ulama received salaries pertaining to the offices they held. Most of the Ulama dabbled in politics. They wielded influence with the kings and nobles as interpreters of Muslim law. Their presence was indispensable to a ruler who was generally uneducated. During the protracted struggle between the crown and the nobility which raged throughout the Sultanate period, they aligned themselves with one or the other of political groups. They always remained on the right side of the regime and forgot the community whom they were expected to help in times of economic distress and political oppression. In this way they encouraged political oppression on the one hand and on the other they preached the necessity of obedience and submission by the people even to an oppressor, taking shelter under the Quranic injunction: Obey God and obey the Prophet, and those in authority among you. Naturally, an unholy alliance with them smoothed the path of kings depotism. They themselves did not lag behind in obsequiousness. Their collaboration with and integration into the state apparatus made them subservient to the regime, so much so that when Iltutmish nominated Raziya as his successor, there was not a single theologian in the Delhi Empire who could protest against this nomination on the grounds of Shariat. The way they encouraged Sultans like Ruknuddin Firoz and Muizuddin Kaiqubad not to offer prayers or keep fasts during the month of Ramzan, and live licentious lives, shows how servile they had become and how they were wallowing in the dirty welters of politics. Of course the Ulama were openly critical of one another and, for this they have been criticised by their contemporary writers like Amir Khusrau, Zia Barani, Abdul Haq Muhaddis and Abdul Qadir Badaoni. Kings like Iltutumish and Balban and prince Bughra Khan are also critical of them.

But in one thing they did not fail. They kept the rulers and the ruling class on the path of Islam and virtue by informing them correctly about their duty towards the non-Muslims. Some modern secularist historians blame the Ulama for making Muslim rulers intolerant through their orthodox advice. Such writers fail to realise that it was not safe for the Ulama to cheat the Sultans by giving wrong interpretation of their holy scriptures vis-a-vis the treatment of non-Muslims. I have not come across any instance where the Ulama deliberately gave a distorted version of their scriptures in this context. And why should they have done so They were as much interested in seeing the Muslim state being run according to the Shariat as the Sultans. In short, they always interpreted their scriptures correctly and honestly when it came to the Hindus. So that a foreign visitor like Maulana Shamsuddin Turk, who is very critical of the Qazis of the day, condoned their faults for the reason that because of their right advice their king was prone to treating the Hindus terribly. The lifestyle of the Ulama did not come in the way of serving Islam. Like other Muslims of the higher classes, it was normal for the Ulama to keep harems, live luxuriously and drink wine.

Despite a few faults and a little criticism, therefore, the Ulama as a class were indispensable to the regime. They were advisers of the king and ran the establishment. It was from the Ulama class that the various officers of the government as well as religious institutions were chosen. It was through these people that the regime systematized the religious and social life of the Muslim community just as it organized the extension and administration of Muslim dominions in India through the nobility.

The Mashaikh

Equally influential, if not more, were the Sufi Mashaikh. In the early years of Muslim immigration, and more so with the establishment of Muslim rule in India, many Muslim faqirs, scholars and Sufi Mashaikh arrived in India. They entered Hindustan on their own or came with the invading armies. Later on, the disturbed conditions in Central Asia, consequent upon the Mongol upheaval also encouraged them to leave their homes in search of security. Many came to settle in India where peace and plenty and the protective arm of Muslim rule promised them all they wished.

Sufism may be defined as Islamic mysticism. In its early years in Central and West Asia, it was deeply influenced by Neo-Platonism, the monastic tradition of Buddhism and Christianity and the Vedantist and Yogic philosophy of Hinduism. All these were Islamized by the Sufis in such a way as to make them virtually unidentifiable. Nawbahar was a great Buddhist monastry in Balkh. The name of the city of Bokhara itself is derived from Vihar. Some Khurasan Sufis lived in caves like Buddhists. They were known as Shikafatiyah from the word Shikafat (cave). When Hindu and Buddhist thinkers and saints converted to Islam in Central and West Asia during the eighth to eleventh centuries they carried their thought and philosophy to Sufism. Ibn al-Arabi wrote in his Diwan that idol-worship, Chritian ways and Kaaba were all acceptable to him as he believed in the religion of love.

The Sufism that came to India in the twelfth century with the Muslim Mashaikh did not, by and large, envisage direct communion with God without the intermedium of Islam. Just as the soul and body are one, in Islamic sufism Tariqah and Shariah are so interrelated. Some Sufis believed in the doctrine of Wahadat-ul-Wajud, or the Unity of Being which means There is nothing but God, nothing in existence other than He. This theory, propounded by Shaikh Ibn al-Arabi and akin to Hindu Vedantism, was developed later on in order to harmonise the doctrine of mysticism with the teachings of orthodox Islam.

There were a number of Sufi orders or silsila as they are called. Abul Fazl mentions as many as fourteen. But four orders-Chishti, Suhrawardi, Qadiri and Naqshabandi-became prominent in India. Of these only the first two became more popular, for the latter two were extremely orthodox and legalistic in their strictness. By the thirteenth century, northern India saw the flowering of two Sufi orders, Chishti and Suhrawardi, and we will concern ourselves with the Mashaikh of only these two orders. The founder of the Suhrawardi order was Shaikh Bahauddin Zakariya. He was born near Multan in Sind in H. (- C.E.). He and his disciples played a leading part in the north-west and symbolically asked the Chishtis not to dispute possession (of the region) with them. Shaikh Bahauddin Zakariya (and his successors) mixed freely with the Sultans, took part in political affairs, amassed wealth and accepted government honours.

The Chishtis established themselves at Ajmer in Rajasthan, some parts of the Punjab, Delhi, U.P. and Bihar and further east. They were probably the largest in number and represented what seems to be the most typical in the Sufi way of life. The first great Chishti Shaikh was Khwaja Muinuddin Chishti. He was born in Sijistan in eastern Persia in C.E.. He came to India a little before or after the battle of Taraori or Tarain and settled down at Ajmer. There also he lies buried after his death in. His mausoleum is a great centre of pilgrimage. He is known as

Gharib Nawaz or Friend of the Poor and Nabi-ul-Hind or Prophet of India. Shaikh Saiyyad Muhammad Gesu Daraz (he of the long locks) said that if people were unable to make the pilgrimage to Mecca, a visit once in their lives to the mausoleum of Muinuddin Chishti would convey the same merit.

Shaikh Muinuddin is very famous today. But he was not known as such to his contemporaries. The three contemporary chronicler-Hasan Nizami, Fakhr-i-Mudabbir and Minhaj do not refer to him at all. Early mystic records, the Favaid-ul-Fuad and Khair-ul-Majalis do not give any information about him. Barani makes no reference to him. Isami tells us only this much that Muhammad bin Tughlaq had once visited his grave. In all probability his fame spread from the time of emperor Akbar (- C.E.) who held his memory in great reverence and often paid visit to his dargah in Ajmer. However, the legend and fame of Muinuddin rests, as of all other Shaikhs, on the magic-like miracles (karamah) he is supposed to have performed. It is difficult to say when the stories of the miracles of Sufis be an to be told but once this process had begun, it could not be stopped. It became a criterion by which Sufis were judged, and the common reason why people believed in them. They credited them with supernatural powers and feared and respected them. P.M. Currie quotes Mohammad Habib to say that most of the mystic records and Diwans are forgeries, but regard for public opinion has prevented them (Indian scholars) from making a public declaration that these are forgeries. However, stories of miracles apart, he (Muinuddin Chishti) was Saiyid by descent. He did not depart in any way from Sunna, the Ulama could not fault him, and he performed the hajj.

Shaikh Muinuddin Chishti had a number of disciples two of whom, Shaikh Hamid and Qutbuddin, had earned reverence of great and small. Shaikh Hamiduddin Nagauri lived with his wife as a villager. Shaikh Qutbuddin Bakhtiyar Kaki came to Delhi in the reign of Iltutmish and lived in a khanqah outside the city. He was very fond of sama (devotional music). Once he was so overtaken by wajd (ecstasy) that he collapsed and breathed his last. One of his principal disciples was Shaikh Fariduddin Ganj-i-Shakar popularly called Shaikh Farid.

Shaikh Farid lived in extreme poverty bordering on starvation. He trained a large number of disciples, established many khanqahs and raised the prestige of the Chishti order. The greatest disciple of Shaikh Farid was Hazrat Nizamuddin Auliya. He was born at Badaun. In he settled at Ghayaspur near Delhi where his shrine exists and a railway station is named after him. The Shaikh had a large circle of disciples who hailed from all sections of society, rich and poor, noble and plebian.

In his life of almost a century, Nizamuddin Auliya witnessed the reigns of seven Sultans, but he did not attend the darbar of any one of them. He was popularly known as Mahbub-i-Ilahi (Beloved of God). His popularity was due to his saintly virtues and service to humanity. His disciples included Amir Khusrau, Ziyauddin Barani and the renowned Shaikh Nasiruddin Chiragh-i-Delhi whom he appointed as his successor (Khalifa). Professor Mohammad Habib rightly calls Nasiruddin the last great saint of the Chishti Silsilah to have enjoyed an all India status. This was the best period in India for Sufism in general and the Chishti Silsilah in particular. To this famous line of Sufis belongs Shaikh Salim Chishti, a contemporary of emperor Akbar, for whom the latter built a mausoleum in Fatehpur Sikri.

Many of the Sufi Mashaikh lived in poverty. Shaikh Hamiduddin (d. C.E.) lived in a small mud house in the city of Nagaur in Rajasthan. He eked out his meagre subsistence by cultivating a single bigha of land. His wife spent her time in cooking and spinning like a peasant woman. He was a strict vegetarian. He refused to accept government gift of land and money from the muqta of Nagaur and Sultan of Delhi. Shaikh Muinuddin and Shaikh Qutbuddin Bakhtiyar never owned houses of their own. Shaikh Farid Ganj-i-Shakar built a small kachcha house only when his family had considerably increased For many years during his early life Shaikh Nizamuddin Auliya had to wander from one quarter of the city to another in search of a house Generally starvation conditions prevailed in the houses of the Chishti saints very often these saints did not possess sufficient clothes to cover their bodies.

This is one side of the coin. The other is that Shaikh Muinuddins sons owned land, which may have been granted to them directly or accepted by the Shaikh for their sake. Shaikh Fariduddin was destitute to the end of his days, but gifts were received and distributed at his khanqah. The khanqah of Nizamuddin Auliya, probably after he received money from Sultan Nasiruddin Khusrau, became an institution in which money, food and goods circulated freely. However, the Shaikhs who lived in affluence were deemed to possess no less merit than those who elected to remain destitute.

The Sufi Mashaikh are also reported to have shunned the company of the nobles and nearness to the court. But that too was not always so. On the contrary, the attractions of staying near the throne were compulsive. Sidi Maula was a disciple of Shaikh Farid at Ajodhan. He aspired for name and fame and shifted to Delhi. Once in the capital, Sidi Maula hurled himself headlong in the politics of the court and, after many vicissitudes paid with his life. But Sidi was not alone in this pursuit. As K.A. Nizami has pointed out, Even Chisht the cradle-land of the silsilah looked to Delhi for guidance in spiritual matters. The Mashaikh mostly lived in cities and towns where they were popular with kings and people and enjoyed the respectability of upper class elite. Shaikh Qutbuddin Bakhtiyar Kaki was much admired by the people of Delhi headed by Sultan Iltutmish himself. Muinuddin Chishti was very much liked by the Muslims of Ajmer but he was suspected of dabbling in politics which prompted Prithviraj III to ask Ramdeva to expel him from Ajmer. Shaikh Nizamuddin Auliya used to hold his own darbar which was often more awe-inspiring than even the court of kings. The Shaikh was so popular with the people that Sultan Alauddin Khalji began to entertain suspicions about his influence and authority in Muslim society. With a view to ascertain the real intentions of the Shaikh, and to find out to what extent he was interested in seeking political power, the Sultan sent him a note seeking his advice and guidance on certain political problems. The Shaikh immediately surmised Alauddins motives in sending the letter, and replied that he had nothing to do with politics and so could render no advice on political matters: he kept busy with seeking Gods grace for Muslim monarchs (duagoee). Only after this was the Sultans mind set at rest. But to many he was popularly known as Sultan Nizamuddin and his resting place as Dargah Sultanji Saheb.

Alauddin greatly respected Nizamuddin Auliya for his supernatural powers and knack for correct predictions. But his son Sultan Qutbuddin Mubarak Khalji disliked him because of his political leanings. He even declared a reward of a thousand tankahs for one who would cut off Nizamuddins head. Once when they chanced to meet, the Sultan refused to acknowledge the salutations of the saint and even called Shaikh Ruknuddin from Multan to eclipse Nizamuddins popularity. After Qutbuddins death, Sultan Nasiruddin Khusrau ascended the throne at Delhi, but his authority was challenged by Ghazi Tughlaq. Khusrau Shah, to gain the support of the Shaikhs sent two or three lakhs of tankahs to each of them and five lakh tankahs to Nizamuddin Auliya. When Ghazi Tughlaq ascended the throne as Sultan Ghiyasuddin Tughlaq (C.E.) he asked Nizamuddin to render the account of the amount he had received.

The latter sent a reply, seemingly insolent, that the money belonged to the Bait-ul-mal (Public Treasury) and therefore he had given it to the poor. The Sultan took umbrage at the Shaikhs answer. The relations between the two were sore also because of the Sultans dislike of sama in which Nizamuddin freely indulged. In this scenario, Nizamuddin Auliya began to support Ghiyasuddins son, Muhammad Tughlaq, who aspired for the throne. When Ghiyasuddin Tughlaq went on an expedition to Bengal, Nizamuddin Auliya prophesied that the Sultan would never come back from there. When the news of his return was received in Delhi, a worried Prince Muhammad rushed to Nizamuddin with the tiding at which the Shaikh uttered the famous words, Delhi is still far off (hanuz Delhi dur ast). Nizamuddin Auliya was thus immersed in Delhi court politics, at least towards the end of his life. But he was a Sufi. He had many disciples who were regular visitors to his khanqah. Such an one was Amir Khusrau.

Abul Hasan, popularly known as Amir Khusrau, was the most favoured disciple of Nizamuddin Auliya. He was a historian, a musician, a poet, a litterateur, a Sufi Shaikh, and a full-fledged protege of Delhi Sultans. His first patron was Prince Muhammad, son of Sultan Ghiyasuddin Balban. Thereafter for about forty years he served a continuous succession of monarchs-Muizuddin Kaiqubad, Jalaluddin Khalji, Alauddin Khalji and Mubarak Shah Khalji-and his shrewdness was successful in keeping them all pleased. The Sultan (Kaiqubad) flattered him by calling him the seal of authors and promised to give him a big reward which would free him from all worldly cares ever afterwards. His genius, if not character, helped him spend the whole of his life in spinning yarn (or writing many untruths). Soon after, when Kaiqubad was murdered by Jalaluddin Khalji, he composed a new masnavi, Miftah-ul-Futuh in praise of his new patron. Six years later Jalauddin was murdered by his nephew and son-in-law Alauddin Khalji who marched into Delhi with the late kings head held aloft on the point of a spear and, writes Dr. Wahid Mirza, our poet Khusrau was one of the first to offer his congratulations to the murderer whose hands were still red with the blood of his king, his uncle and his benefactor The poet changed with changing time and turned with shifting wind. No wonder, even Ghiya-suddin Tughlaq, who was hostile to Khusraus pir-o-murshid, Nizamuddin Auliya, receives fulsome praise in Khusraus Tughlaq Nama.

Amir Khusrau was very shrewd. When he found the reign of Qutbuddin Mubarak Khalji nothing to boast about, he wrote Nuh Sipehr, praising all things Indian, including the beauty of Indian women. In Nuh Sipehr he also wrote: They have four books in that language (Sanskrit), which they are constantly in the habit of repeating. Their name is Bed (Vedas). They contain stories of their gods, but little advantage can be derived from their perusal. This betrays the one-track mind of Muslim elite in general. This weakness was shared by almost all Sufi Mashaikh, debunking the belief that Sufi Mashaikh treated Hindus and Muslims on terms of equality or helped bring the two communities nearer to one another. They were keen on maintaining only orthodox Muslim rule and showed a general disregard for others. Since it was believed that Muhammad bin Tughlaq was not orthodox, Shaikh Nasiruddin Chiragh obtained a promise from Firoz Tughlaq before supporting the latters claim to the throne, to the effect that he would rule according to the Shariat. In, when Raja Ganesh (Kans of Muslim chroniclers) obtained the throne of Bengal and sought to establish his authority by keeping the prominent Ulama and Sufis under control, Shaikh Nurul Haqq (Qutbul Alam) wrote to Sultan Ibrahim Sharqi of Jaunpur to come and save the Muslims of Bengal. Sultan Ibrabim responded to the call and Raja Ganesh, finding himself too weak to meet the challenge, came to the Shaikh and begged for his intercession, promising to agree to any conditions. Shaikh Nurul Haqq said he would intercede for him if he accepted Islam. The Raja retired in favour of his son Jadu, who ascended the throne as Sultan Jalaluddin Shah. Shaikh Nurul Haqq induced Sultan Ibrahim, much against his will, to withdraw his armies. Shaikh Abdul Quddus combined spirituality with dogmatism. His letters to Sultan Sikandar Lodi and Babur show that he was as anxious to maintain Muslim rule as any wordly Muslim, that he had no scruples in using the language of a courtier in asking the rulers to establish the Shariah Akbars attempt at secularizing the state had exasperated the divines, and Mulla Shah Ahmad and Shaikh Farid Bukhari exhorted court dignitaries to alter the state of things in the very beginning of Jahangirs reign, otherwise it would be difficult to accomplish anything later on. There are many other such instance. It is understandable if disgruntled nobles and courtiers invited foreigners to rescue Islam, but the Sufi Mashaikh by such actions compromised their image as Indians first and respecters of all people as equals. They were as opposed to national integration as any orthodox Muslim.

Similarly, many modern scholars have shown that some Sufi Mashaikh too resorted to aggressive and violent means in fighting infidelity. Even Shaikh Muinuddin Chishtis picture of tolerance is replaced by a portrait of him as a warrior for Islam. Since I have studied this problem in detail elsewhere, I would not like to repeat the cases of aggressive proselytization of Sufi Mashaikh mentioned therein. However, one shocking instance of forcible conversion not mentioned in my book referred to above, may be given here. Saiyyad Jalaluddin Bukhari Makhdum-i-Jahanian of Sind (d.) fell very seriously ill. Nawahun, the darogha of Uchch, called on him to enquire about his health. As a matter of courtesy and to raise his sinking spirits, Nahawun said: May God restore your health your holiness is the last of the saints as the Prophet Muhammad was the last of the prophets. Sayyid Jalaluddin Bukhari even on death-bed construed it as an expression of faith in Islam and demanded a formal declaration of conversion from him. Nawahun firmly declined to make any such declaration. Thereupon he was charged with apostasy. He fled to the court of Firoz Shah Tughlaq in search of asylum and redress. When Sayyid Jalaluddin Bukhari expired, his younger brother Sadruddin Raju Qattal, rushed to Delhi in order to persuade Firoz Shah to execute Nawahun. Though some scholars of the capital did not agree with the viewpoint of Raju Qattal, the latter prevailed upon Firoz Shah in obtaining his permission for Nawahuns execution as a renegade.

Poor or rich, the Sufi Mashaikh lived as householders. Except Nizamuddin Auliya and Nasiruddin Chiragh, all Sufi Shaikhs married, and had large families. Since the word saint is associated with celibacy in peoples minds of most religions, it would be pertinent to state that marriage is enjoined on every Muslim, and celibacy is frequently condemned by Muhammad. It is related in the Traditions that Muhammad said: When the servant of God marries, he perfects half his religion Consequently in Islam, even the ascetic orders are rather married than single.

Shaikh Muinuddin Chishti took two wives - Ummatullah and Asmatullah, and had three sons and one daughter. He had married in his old age only to realize that his spiritual powers had greatly suffered on that account. Shaikh Qutbuddin Bakhtiyar Kaki Ushi also married twice, late in life. He divorced one of his wives, soon after marriage, as her presence upset his programme of prayers. He had four sons. Shaikh Farid had a number of wives and a large family. Shaikh Nasiruddin Chiragh is reported to have stated that Shaikh Farid had a number of wives (harem bisyar bud). He had at least four wives and eight children. Shaikh Hamiduddin had led a very voluptuous life in his early years, but when he joined the circle of Shaikh Muinuddin Chishti, he adopted the life of a mystic in all sincerity. He had a number of children. Shaikh Qutbuddin Husain Kirmani, uncle of the author of Siyar-ul-Auliya, used to put on the garments of the finest Chinese silks and Kamkhawab and always used to have pan in his mouth. Shaikh Nizamuddin Auliya also relished betel.

All this was normal life and all these were normal pleasures. But Sufi Mashaikh, known by many names like Wali, Shah, Qalandar, Murshid, Marabout, Shaikh, Faqir and Darwesh, indulged in all kinds of pleasures and luxuries. The case of Sidi Maula was exceptional. He had ready at hand brand new tankahs under every coverlet to spend. So many people dined at his khanqah that, if Barani is to be believed, two thousand man of flour (maida), two to three hundred man of sugar and a hundred to two hundred man of vegetables used to be consumed in his kitchen every day. But others were equally non-poor and generous. We know that Shaikh Farid was destitute to the end of his days, but we also know that gifts were received and distributed. It could be said generally of every khanqah that even in the bad days a person was sure to get some sort of a meal and, with luck, a share of money in every khanqah ideals of austerity fought against satisfaction of physical needs, so that there was no dearth of money and parasites because of the well-to-do admirers of the Shaikh.

Sama or devotional music was a common feature of the khanqah. During sama, the Shaikhs and Qalandars placed strong insistence on the practice of Nazar-ilal murd or gazing at good looking boys. One reason why Ghiyasuddin Tughlaq could not see eye to eye with Nizamuddin Auliya was the latters fondness for sama and his ecstatic fits. The Sultan was free from unnatural lust (lawatat) and did not allow handsome beardless boys from coming near him. In the khanqahs were also used drugs of the hashish family, and even drinking was common. Love affairs of sufis were of common occurrence. Ahmad Yadgar mentions the case of a faqir who fell for the newly wed bride of the son of Tatar Khan. He relates another story about the love of a darwesh and a woman. Love between a Hindu girl and a darwesh created flutter and tension.

The Shaikhs used to marry in high families and possessed a clout which sometimes became a problem for Sultans. A sixteenth century Suhrawardi writer says that Shaikh Sadruddin Arif had married a divorced wife of Prince Muhammad, the eldest son of Balban. The circumstances of this marriage are given as follows: The prince divorced his wife, whom he passionately loved, in a fit of fury. When he recovered his normal state of mind, he felt deeply pained for what he had done. Legally he could not take her back into his harem unless she was married to someone else and then divorced by him. A man of genuine piety was searched to restore the broken relationship. Shaikh Arif, the most outstanding saint of the town, promised to marry the princess and divorce her the next day. But, after the marriage, he refused to divorce her on the ground that the princess herself was not prepared to be divorced. This incident led to bitterness between the saint and the prince. The latter even thought of taking action against the Shaikh, but a Mongol invasion cut short the thread of his life. Shaikh Salim Chishti had great influence with emperor Akbar, much more than Sadruddin Arif had in the time of Balban. And both Badaoni and Father Monserrate make unflattering comments about Shaikh Salim. The Sufi Mashaikh lived a full-fledged life, different from saints of other religions. But among Indian Muslims their memory has always been cherished with utmost reverence.

It is said that saint-worship among Muslims is a practice unique to India. Dargahs of Sufis, real or figurative, are found all over the country and Muslims flock to them in. large numbers. It is a legacy of medieval times. One reason for this can be that most Indian Muslims are converted Hindus, who, when their places of worship were converted into (khanqahs and later) dargahs, did not give up visiting them. For instance, at the most holy dargah of Shaikh Muinuddin Chishti, the Sandal

Khana mosque is believed to have been built on the site of a Dev temple. The other is that stories of miracles of saints give a hope and a chance to people to obtain fulfilment of their desires. Hence besides Muslims, a few Hindus also resort to such shrines.

MIDDLE CLASSES AND PROTEST MOVEMENTS

There are very many merchants that are rich: but it is not safe for them that are so, so to appear, lest that they should be used as filld sponges.

Edward Terry

In the medieval period, the luxurious life of the upper classes and the poverty of the exploited peasants and workers attracted the attention of all foreign and Indian writers. These two sections of society were so prominent that the presence of the small, self-respecting, friend-of-the-people middle class was not even noticed by some contemporary writers. Francois Bernier is one of them. Writing in the middle of the seventeenth century, this renowned French visitor to India, found that in Delhi there was no middle state. A man must be of the highest rank or live miserably. Similar is the assertion of Tavernier about Burhanpur and Golkunda.

Why did Bernier and Tavernier make such observations Today most people (except the very poor) consider it a matter of satisfaction or even of pride to belong to the middle class. Ministers, Secretaries, Members of Parliament and high officers of Government, counterparts of medieval ruling class, call themselves not masters but servants of the people. Pride in belonging to high class has been replaced by humility in belonging to the middle class, and administrators and politicians, tradespeople and working men, officers and clerks, are all counted among the middle class. But in the middle Ages ideas of equality, democracy, socialism and Marxism were not there. Consequently, it was not a fashion in medieval India to claim to belong to the middle class. This is probably what Bernier and Tavernier noted and also declared. In medieval India, rulers, nobles and high class people could never think of degrading them- selves by belonging to any class other than the highest. In that age, levelling would have been revolting to the rich and probably embarrassing to the poor. In medieval society the ruling class and the subject people were two well-recognised strata.

But what applied to Mughal India applied also to the Pre-Revolution, Pre-Industrial seventeenth century France. There were there three recognized Estates; the first comprised the Clergy, the second the Nobility, and the third the Commoners. However, side by side with these categories was the yeomanry and the bourgeoisie, the middle state of Bernier. Did a corresponding middle state or middle class exist in India also, and Bernier missed to notice it, or was there no middle class in India at all in the medieval period

The above cited statement of Bernier has been lifted out of context by many scholars, prompting some to deny the existence of a middle class in the pre-British period. Therefore, Bernier has to be quoted at some length to understand why he said so. He gives a detailed description of Delhi and Agra and some other cities of Hindustan in a letter to Monsieur de la Mothe le Vayer dated st July,. In his description of Delhi, he writes about its citizens, its houses, bazars, food, fruit etc., and constantly compares them with those of Paris. In the bazars of the capital city of Delhi, writes he, there are shops where meat is sold roasted and dressed in a variety of ways. But there is no trusting to their dishes, composed, for aught I know, of the flesh of camels, horses, or perhaps oxen which have died of disease. Indeed no food can be considered wholesome which is not dressed at home But it would be unreasonable for me to complain I send my servant to the kings purveyors in the Fort, who are glad to sell wholesome food, which costs them very little, at a high price I am willing to pay. Pigeons were exposed for sale, capons were not, these being wanted for their seraglios good fish may sometimes be bought, particularly two sorts, called sing-ala and rau (Singi and Rohu). The former resembles our pike; the latter our carp The Omrahs alone contrive to force the fishermen out at all times (to sell) by means of the korrah, the long whip always suspended at their door Unquestionably the great are in the enjoyment of everything; but it is by dint of numbers in their service, by dint of the Korrah, and by dint of money. In Delhi there is no middle state. A man must either be of the highest rank or live miserably. My pay is considerable, nor am I sparing of money; yet does it often happen that I have not wherewithal to satisfy the cravings of hunger, the bazars being so ill-supplied, and frequently containing nothing but the refuse of the grandees. Wine, that essential part of every entertainment, can be obtained in none of the shops at Delhi, although it might be made from the native grape, were not the use of that liquor prohibited equally by the Gentile and Mahometan law To say the truth, few persons in these hot climates feel a strong desire for wine

Bernier was only experiencing what Babur had witnessed a century ago. The latter notes in his memoirs that in Hindustan they have no good flesh, no grapes or musk-melons, no good fruits, no ice or cold water, no good food or bread in their bazaars And every artisan there is follows the trade that has come down to him from his forefathers. Bernier did not get food to his liking in the bazar, he could not get good wine, and for both these he himself provides correct explanations. What Bernier saw everyday in the bazars was the arbitrary ways of the nobles and their unfair use of force to get things at low prices. A hungry Bernier felt the pinch of non-availability of good food and heady wine in the open market, what he saw was the Korrah of the Amirs and the wretched condition of the poor hawkers and fisherman. He missed to notice, at that point of time or in that mood at least, the middle or intermediate class, the accomplished artisans, hereditary craftsmen, rich jewellers and influential bankers or sarrafs. Most middle class people carried on with their hereditary crafts, in printing calico, stretching embroidery, or manufacturing jewellery. These worked mostly at home and did not exhibit their artistic products in show-cases in shops. That is why he wrote what he wrote in a limited context and perhaps under the influence of an empty stomach and thirsty throat when he could only see the rich Umara grabbing away the best fish and meat from the poor people with the help of the Korrah. There were no standard hotels serving good food in Delhi and Agra and other large cities where gentlemen like Bernier and Indians of his class could have dined without any doubt about the quality of food. But the Mughal gentry, as he himself noted, preferred to eat at home as the meats in the cooking joints in the bazar were sometimes adulterated. Also eating at home and not in hotels was also a matter of habit. Berniers statement is a case of arriving at a major conclusion on the basis of a minor inconvenience.

For, there has always been a middle class in society in every age, and medieval India was no exception. Among the Muslims the rich people who provided artisans, weavers, embroiderers and jewellers with raw materials to produce goods on order and paid wages, and merchants who dealt in goods, wholesale and retail, surely belonged to the middle class. There is no doubt that besides the two well-known sections of the rich and the poor, there were many who, in terms of wealth and income, could be placed between the two. There is evidence to show that in the contemporary Muslim society of the West Asian countries there were three categories of people - the al-khassa, al-amma (also called al-raiyya) and al-nas. There were the people of great skill, specialists in medicine, architecture and accounting and merchants who had at least a more than average fortune were also al-nas. So middle class or common people, a word so often used by Ibn Battuta in the Indian context, were interchangeable terms. Gustav Grunebaum also says: The Muslim shares to a very high degree sensitivity about rank which is so characteristic of the Middle Ages. Not only is he rank conscious, but he is keenly concerned with expressing social distinctions through a delicate system of etiquette. Questions of precedence are of considerable importance. Mankind was divided into four orders by the Barmakid Wazir Al Fazl bin Yahiya (C. th century A.D.) -. King,. Wazir,. Aristocracy of Wealth,. The middle class was connected with the above class by their culture. The rest of the population counted for nothing.

In medieval times India was well advanced in manufacture, trade and commerce. Indian textiles and other manufactured goods had a market throughout the East and the West. India exported lot of goods and Indian ports served as clearing stations of trade between the East and the West. In industry and manufacture, whether it was of cloth, carpet or leather, or it was metal, ivory or gold, India held the supreme position. There were excellent ship-building and repairing yards (even for European ships) in India. Mahuan, an interpreter attached to the Chinese envoy Chang Ho who visited Bengal in, writes that The rich build ships in which they carry on commerce with foreign nations. Right from the thirteenth-fourteenth centuries, indeed from ancient times, manufacturing centres of all kinds of wares were spread all over the country. Indias position in the field of manufacture, industry and commerce, if not in science and technology, remained important throughout the medieval period.

There were, consequently, big manufacturers and merchants, foreign and Indian, living in the country. According to Yahiya Sarhindi a large number of Khurasani merchants who lived in Delhi possessed some of the best mansions in that prosperous city. Barbosa says that Muslims, settled in Calicut, had large houses and many servants and they lived very luxuriously. About the Muslims at Rander he says, they were well-dressed, had good houses, well-kept and furnished. Della Valle has similar comments to make on the freedom of life in Surat, where there was open exhibition of riches and splendour. Monopolists like Mir Jumla, Virji Vohra and, at a later date, Jagat Seth were renowned for their wealth. And they lived in the elitist fashion.

The exceptional position on the coast is probably to be explained by the privileged status of the Moslem merchants being free to live well while the merchants of the interior (or Hindu merchants) were very far from being free and led the quiet and unostentatious life required by the circumstances of their position. Muslim merchants were to be found at practically every seaport in India. Jews and Armenians and Parsis were few in numbers, but important in commercial life. The horizons of Muslim freedom expanded in a country where every man had a slight tincture of soldiership.

Urbanization helped in development of trade and commerce and the growth of middle class. There was rapid growth of towns and cities in medieval period. In the sixteenth-seventeenth centuries, India had hundreds of cities with a population of more than, and cities like Agra, Lahore and Cambay could boast of more than half a million people each. Their middle class sections comprised traders, goldsmiths, jewellers, bankers (sarrafs), architects, scholars, merchants and many others. Small manufacturers and merchants too possessed gold and silver and its concomitant power. So also was the case with the other sections of middle class Muslims like the learned, such as physicians, mathematicians, architects, historians or chroniclers, and the Ulama. There were the Saheb-i-Qalam va Saheb-i-Saif (masters of the pen and the sword) and people belonging to or descended from distinguished families. Soldiers and warriors - neither the Khans or Maliks nor the common troops - that is, officers of the intermediate grade who, in the words of Abul Fazl, consumed the straw and rubbish of strife and kindled the lamp of rest in this world of disturbances, too belonged to this class. Other government officials like Qazis and Imams of qasbas (as-hab-i-manasib) as well as some sections of lesser note of Saiyyads and Sufis also comprised the middle class.

In contrast to the Muslim bourgeoisie, the life of the Hindu middle classes was different in many ways. They lived under the Muslim theocratic regime and paid the poll tax Jiziyah incumbent upon the non-Muslims. There were three rates of Jiziyah,, and tankahs imposed on three classes or income groups - the high, the middle and the low. This in itself is a proof of the existence of a middle class among the Hindus. If Akbar abolished this tax, Aurangzeb reimposed it and the Hindu middle class paid the Jaziyah at the middle rate, or probably the high, for all through the medieval period they possess almost exclusively the trade and the wealth of the country. Pelsaerts description of the Hindu middle class is apt and elaborate. He writes: First there are the leading merchants and jewellers, and they are most able and expert in their business. Next there are the workmen, for practically all work is done by Hindus, the Moslems practising scarcely any crafts but dyeing and weaving Thirdly there are the clerks and brokers: all the business of the lords palaces and of the Muslim merchants is done by Hindus - book-keeping, buying and selling. They are particularly clever brokers, and are consequently generally employed as such throughout all these countries.

The life of the Hindu middle class was marked by moderation. Ostentatious living was as dangerous in their case as it was desirable in the case of Muslim merchants and courtiers. Nay, the Hindu rich men study to appear indigent, says Bernier, and although 'the profit be ever so great, the man by whom it has been made must still wear the garb of indigence. Terry wrote that there are very many private men in cities and towns, who are merchants or tradesmen that are very rich: but it is not safe for them that are so, so to appear, lest that they should be used as filled sponges. Their traditional caution and the conditions of insecurity created by political conflict and the attitude of the administrators forced them to practice self-effacement. W.H. Moreland rightly observes that they help us to understand the thrifty or even parsimonious scale of living which characterises so many of the commercial classes at the present day. Thus apart from some great monopolists and bankers who belonged to the upper class, the trades-people in general were denied due regard in society and are mentioned by Muslim chroniclers with a contempt which is conveyed in words like Dallal, Bania, Baqqal etc. The treatment meted out to the lower class of traders and retailers by the rulers during the medieval period shares this contempt. The harshness with which Alauddin Khalji treated the traders, wholesalers and retailers, and made their flesh sore, has become proverbial. Pelsaert too says that the condition of shopkeepers was good if they were not made victims of bazar officials. They had gold and silver in their houses but made exhibition of poverty lest they should be squeezed of their wealth at Will. In short, their style of living was unimpressive. This poor style of living was also an important factor in making the middle class of the medieval period invisible to foreign travellers like Bernier.

This unimpressive way of life was due to many other causes besides fear of being exploited and sponged by the rich.

Ibn Battuta, Nicolo Conti, Abdur Razzaq, Athnasius Nikitin and a host of others bear testimony to the poor standard of living of the people even if they belonged to propertied and non-poor classes. As late as the early nineteenth century David Macpherson observed: Born and desiring to pass his life in the same country where his ancestors were born and passed their lives, whose food is rice, whose drink is water or milk, to whom wine or strong liquor is an object of abomination whose warm climate renders clothing, beyond what decency requires, intolerable, and whose light clothing is made by himself and his family from the cotton produced in his own fertile fields, whose customs and religion render utterly inadmissible many articles of enjoyment and comfort can never have any desire to acquire the produce or manufactures of Europe. James Forbes even goes to the extent of declaring that the balance of trade with Europe was in Indias favour because of Indian peoples abstemious habits and simple life. The commodities exported to Europe from India, says he, far exceeded in value those imported from them thence; the natives of India, from the mildness of climate, and fertility of their soil, want but few foreign supplies, gold and silver have been always carried thither by European traders.

In the process the Hindu middle classes helped in capital formation, even though on a limited scale, which the upper classes failed to do. An important contribution of the middle class, especially the Hindu middle class, was capital formation in medieval India. Apart from the accidents of war to which Muslims and Hindus were alike exposed, as witnessed during invasions of the Mongols in the Sultanate period or of Nadir Shah and Abdali in the Mughal times, it seems that the assets of the Hindu capitalist were safer than the wealth of the most powerful Muslim nobleman. The assets of Hindu elites could not be lost as a result of a court intrigue or fall from favour. On the contrary Muslim nobles, even Muslim kings, used to borrow large amounts from Hindu Sahukars who were known to possess wealth. The wealth of the Hindu could pass on from father to son without being divided up. It could not be taken away by the government under escheat. The Muslim officers and merchants believed in good and ostentatious living. The moment they came by some extra money, they raised, their standard of living and set up larger establishments in proportion to their wealth. The Hindu was by nature thrifty. Fear of sponging by the government, kept the possessions of the Hindu capitalist concealed. It was this that made Hindu merchants sahukars, sarrafs and bankers during Muslim rule.

Middle Class Behaviour

In short, the poor style of living of the Hindu middle class of the medieval period made it rather invisible. Besides, it was very small in numbers. Traders, shopkeepers, jewellers, architects, all added up to a very small proportion of the population. With its small numbers, its influence was also limited. But the one chief characteristic of the middle classes was very much present in medieval India. In behaviour, the hall-mark of the middle classes is living with chin up, straight shoulder and chest thrown out, whether the income is less or more and whether it is categorized as lower, middle or upper middle class. The middle class has been found to be the custodian of societys undefined but ever increasing rights. It was so ever, in the medieval period. It was generally the spearhead of any protest movement. It was respected in society, comprised the respectable Citizens in the social milieu. One important identification of the middle classes is its representation of the peoples rights and its readiness to fight for such rights. This distinguishes them from the upper and lower classes.

Muslim middle classes in general and Muslim scholars in particular lived as a privileged community under Muslim government. It was their own government and, by and large, they were at peace with the establishment. But that did not always deter them from protesting injustice. The lower middle classes like artisans, soldiers and the bazar people could remonstrate in a more candid way. Two examples of such protests, one each from the Sultanate and the Mughal periods, would suffice to bring home the point. The Ilbari sultans (of the so-called Slave Dynasty) had ruled from Delhi for almost a hundred years. Therefore when Jalaluddin Khalji ousted the last Ilbari prince, the gentry, commoners and soldiers, rose in a body, poured out of the many gates of Delhi and assembled at the Badaon Gate to march and rescue the abducted boy-king Shamsuddin. Malik Fakhruddin, the Kotwal of Delhi, succeeded in suppressing the tumult, but so apprehensive became the new Khalji king of the peoples resentment that he did not venture to enter the city of Delhi for many months and made Kilughari the seat of his government.

Bigger in nature was the protest lodged by the citizens of Delhi when the vanquished Prince Dara Shukoh was humiliated and later executed by Aurangzeb in. Francois Bernier was present in Chandni Chowk and witnessed the event. He writes that the crowd assembled upon this disgraceful occasion was immense; and everywhere I saw the people weeping and lamenting the fate of Dara. In one of his letters Aurangzeb himself writes: The fate of Dara Shukoh excited the passions of the misguided citizens of Delhi. They wept in sympathy with him and pelted the loyal Malik Jiwan who had brought him to justice with pots full of urine and excreta. Royal troops went into action and according to Khafi Khan, several persons were knocked down and killed and many were wounded If the Kotwal had not come forward with his policemen, not one of Malik Jiwans followers would have escaped with life.

As a king, Muhammad bin Tughlaq was unpopular with the Ulama. Critical of his action, some of them used to write anonymous letters containing complaints and abuses for the Sultan. They would seal the letters writing on the cover By the head of His Majesty none except he should read the letter. These letters they used to throw into the council hall in the course of the night. When he (Md. Tughlaq) tore them open, he found abuses and scandals in the contents. The art of drafting such letters in Persian was the speciality of the Ulama, and the king rightly became suspicious of this group of people. Ibn Battutas account of Muslim bloodshed and the executions of the Ulama under his orders is of a piece with that of Isamis in Futuh-us-Salatin. In short, thinkers, scholars, Ulama and Qazis, sometimes openly, at others discreetly, did not refrain from criticising the sultan and his policies.

There is an equally interesting example of such an independent protest in a seventeenth century work entitled Tarikh-i-Salatin-i-Afghana by Ahmad Yadgar. Writing about the strict rules of the Mughals about the law of escheat, and ruminating over the good old days of the Lodi rule, Ahmad Yadgar says: God be praised for endowing Sultan (Sikandar Lodi) with such a generous spirit (of permitting retention of any buried treasure discovered by someone). In these days (that is, of Mughal emperor Jahangir), if any one was to find even a few tankahs, our rulers would immediately pull down his house to examine every nook and corner for more. If a seventeenth century chronicler could make bold to write in such a way under the very nose of the mighty Mughals, it only shows that the Muslim middle class did sometimes gather courage to ventilate public grievances. But such occassions were rare. As pointed out earlier, the Muslim educated elite, the Ulama and Mashaikh, cooperated with the Muslim regime under which they enjoyed a privileged position.

9

Lower Class Muslims and Unmitigated Exploitation

Lower classes formed the bulk of the population. They were economically poor and socially degraded. They existed to provide food and apparel, services and comforts, to the higher classes, and resided in towns and villages. In urban areas these comprised all kinds of artisans from basket and rope makers to clothprinters, embroiders, carpet makers, silk-weavers, blacksmiths, tin workers, carpenters, oil-men, barbers, jugglers, mountebanks, street singers, brewers, tailors, betel leaf sellers, flower sellers, masons, stone-cutters, bullock-cart drivers, doli-carriers, water-carriers, domestic servants, dhobis and workers in a hundred other skilled and unskilled crafts.

In the villages there lived peasants and shepherds, besides a few artisans of the vocations enumerated above, although of inferior skill. The quality of work of the urban artisans and craftsmen used to be good. Let us take one example, that of stone-cutters and builders of edifices. Timur or Tamerlane, who invaded Hindustan in, was highly impressed with Indian craftsmen and builders and on his return home from India he took with him architects, artists and skilled mechanics to build in his mud-walled Samarqand, edifices like the Qutb Minar and the (old) Jama Masjid of Delhi constructed by Firoz Shah Tughlaq. Babur too was pleased with the performance of Indian workmen and described how thousands of stone-cutters and masons worked on his buildings in Agra, Sikri, Biana, Dholpur, Gwalior and Koil. In the same way there are numberless artisans of every sort in Hindustan. Despite this they were an exploited lot, and so were all others, tillers of the soil in the villages and workmen in towns.

It is true that in the medieval times the concept of welfare state was not widely prevalent, although it was not entirely unknown, and many kings and nobles are known to have tried to promote the general wellbeing of the people. On a study of contemporary source materials, it appears that the condition of the people of India up to the fifteenth century was not deplorable. This is borne out by the evidence provided by Indian writers and foreign travellers from the eleventh to the fifteenth century. But thereafter there is hardly any foreign visitor to India in sixteenth-seventeenth century in particular, who was not struck by the extremely miserable existence of the lower class people. Such a situation prevailed in all parts of the country, north and south, east and west. We may attempt a study of the economic and social condition of these lower classes under two categories: peasants and agriculturists, and artisans and labourers, for better comprehension about their exploitation by the upper classes as well as the government of the day.

PEASANTS AND AGRICULTURISTS

The condition of the peasantry in India, up to the fourteenth century, was not bad. Contemporary Indian writers and foreign travellers do not generally talk about poverty; on the contrary they give an impression of the wellbeing of the tillers of the soil. Alberuni (eleventh century) has said many things about the Hindus, but nowhere does he say that the people were living in suffering or want. Minhaj Siraj, Ibn Battuta, Shihabuddin Abbas Ahmad, the author of Masalik-ul-Absar, Al-Qalqashindi, the author of Subh-ul-Asha, Amir Khusrau and Shams Siraj Afif (thirteenth-fourteenth centuries), even talk of the prosperity of the people. Even Barani is impressed with their wealth and conveys this impression when he feels delighted at the action of contemporary Muslim rulers against rich landlords and cultivators. The decline of the political power of the Sultanate in the fifteenth century, saw a general recovery of people's strength and prosperity in good measure.

But by the sixteenth and seventeenth centuries conditions are quite different. They change to such an extent that almost all foreign and many Indian writers are struck by the crushing poverty of the Indian peasant and do not fail to write about it. Athanasius Nikitin, Varthema, Barbosa, Paes, Nuniz, Linschoten, Salbank, Hawkins, Jourdain, Sir Thomas Roe, Terry and a host of others, all talk of the grinding poverty of the Indian people. It will serve no purpose to cite from each one of them, but one or two quotations may be given as specimens to convey the general trend of their impressions. Pelsaert, a Dutch visitor during Jahangirs reign, observes: The common people (live in) poverty so great and miserable that the life of the people can be depicted or accurately described only as the home of stark want and the dwelling place of bitter woe their houses are built of mud with thatched roofs. Furniture there is little or none, except some earthenware pots to hold water and for cooking Salbank, writing of people between Agra and Lahore of about the same period, says that the plebian sort is so poor that the greatest part of them go naked. These two quotations would suffice to show how miserable the common people in the middle of the seventeenth century were. These and many others that follow lead one to the inescapable conclusion that the condition of the peasantry in India during the sixteenth and seventeenth centuries had considerably deteriorated.

It is pertinent to ask how the peasant during this period was reduced to such straits. India of the medieval times was mainly agricultural, and histories and legends of the times do not tire of singing in praise of the wealth and glory of the Great Mughals. Then how did the peasant become so miserably poor Were there any ideas and actions of rulers which led to the impoverishment of the agriculturists Also, were there any ideas of the peasants themselves which taught them to reconcile themselves to their lot and did not prompt them to fight against their economic disablement Contemporary chronicles do betray the existence of such ideas. That these have not yet been analysed by historians, does not mean that these ideas were not there. An attempt is being made here to discover such ideas and assess their effects. To find the roots of the miserable condition of the agriculturists in the seventeenth century, one has naturally to look back to earlier times and, indeed, at the very nature of the Muslim conquest of India beginning with the thirteenth century. In the history of Muslim conquest, a unique phenomenon was witnessed in India. Contrary to what happened in Central Asia, Persia or Afghanistan, India could not be completely conquered, nor could its people be converted to the Islamic faith. On the other hand, a ceaseless resistance to the Muslim rule in the thirteenth, fourteenth and fifteenth centuries is clearly borne out by the records of the times. If Muslim chroniclers gloat over unqualified victories for their Turkish kings, there are a large number of inscriptions of Hindu kings who too lay exaggerated claim to military successes. One thing which is clear beyond doubt is that throughout the Sultanate period (and also the Mughal period), there was stiff resistance to Muslim rule, and in one region or the other of the country, the authority of the Sultanate was being openly challenged.

Naturally, the Muslim kings gave much thought to finding some means to suppress the recalcitrant elements. Besides other things, one idea that struck Alauddin Khalji was that it was wealth which was the source of rebellion and disaffection. It encouraged defiance and provided means of revolt. He and his counsellors deliberated that if somehow people could be impoverished, no one would even have time to pronounce the word rebellion. How was this to be done The Ulama would not have found it difficult to suggest a remedy. It is laid down in the Hidaya that when an infidel country is conquered, the Imam can divide it among the Muslims. He can also leave it in the hands of the original inhabitants, exacting from them a capitation tax, and imposing a tribute on their lands. If the infidels are to lose their lands, their entire moveable property should also be taken away from them. In case they are to continue with cultivating the land, they should be allowed to retain such a portion of their moveable property as may enable them to perform their business. In India the conquered land was divided among Muslim officers, soldiers and Ulama in lieu of pay or as reward. Some land was kept under Khalisa or directly under the control of the regime. But in all cases the tiller of the soil remained the original Hindu cultivator. As an infidel he was to be taxed heavily, although a minimum of his moveable property like oxen, cows and buffaloes (nisab) was to be left with him. The principle of the Shariah was to leave with him only as much as would have helped him carry on with his cultivation, but at the same time to keep him poor and subservient.

BARE SUBSISTENCE

According to W.H. Moreland the question really at issue was how to break the power of the rural leaders, the chiefs and the headmen of parganas and villages Sultan Alauddin therefore undertook a series of measures to crush them by striking at their major source of power-wealth. But in the process, leaders and followers, rich and poor, all were affected. The king started by raising the land tax (Kharaj) to fifty percent. Under rulers like Iltutmish and Balban, it does not seem to have been above one-third of the produce. Furthermore, under Alauddins system all the land occupied by the rich and the poor was brought under assessment at the uniform rate of fifty per cent. This measure automatically reduced the chiefs practically to the position of peasants. The king also levied house-tax and grazing tax. According to the contemporary chronicler Ziyauddin Barani, all milk-producing animals like cows and goats were taxed. According to Farishtah, animals up to two pairs of oxen, a pair of buffaloes and some cows and goats were exempted. This concession was based on the principle of nisab, namely, of leaving some minimum capital to enable one to carry on with ones work. But it was hardly any relief, for there were taxes like kari, (derived from Hindi word Kar), charai and Jiziyah. The sultans of Delhi collected Jiziyah at the rate of forty, twenty and ten tankahs from the rich, the middleclass and the poor respectively.

In short, a substantial portion of the produce was taken away by the government as taxes and the people were left with the bare minimum for sustenance. For the Sultan had directed that only so much should be left to his subjects (raiyyat) as would maintain them from year to year without admitting of their storing up or having articles in excess. Sultan Alauddins rigorous measures were taken note of by contemporary writers both in India and abroad. In India contemporary writers like Barani, Isami and Amir Khusrau were inclined to believe him to be a persecutor of the Hindus. Foreigners also gathered the same impression. Maulana Shamsuddin Turk, a divine from Egypt, was happy to learn that Alauddin had made the wretchedness and misery of the Hindus so great and had reduced them to such a despicable condition that the Hindu women and children went out begging at the doors of the Musalmans. The same impression is conveyed in the writings of Isami and Wassaf. While summing up the achievements of Alauddin Khalji, the contemporary chronicler Barani mentions, with due emphasis, that by the last decade of his reign the submission and obedience of the Hindus had become an established fact. Such a submission on the part of the Hindus has neither been seen before nor will be witnessed hereafter. In brief, not only the Hindu Zamindars, who had been accustomed to a life of comfort and dignity, were reduced to a deplorable position, but the Hindus in general were impoverished to such an extent that there was no sign of gold or silver left in their houses, and the wives of Khuts and Muqaddams used to seek sundry jobs in the houses of the Musalmans, work there and receive wages. The poor peasants (balahars) suffered the most. The fundamentalist Maulana Ziyauddin Barani feels jubilant at the suppression of the Hindus, and writes at length about the utter helplessness to which the peasantry had been reduced because the Sultan had left to them bare sustenance and had taken away everything else in kharaj (land revenue) and other taxes.

But there was much greater oppression implicit in this measure. It was difficult to collect in full so many and such heavy taxes. One of the standing evils in the revenue collection consisted in defective realization which usually left large balances, and unrealised balances used to become inevitable. Besides, lower revenue officials were corrupt and extortionate. To overcome these problems, Sultan Alauddin created a new ministry called the Diwan-i-Mustakhraj. The Mustakhraj was entrusted with the work of inquiring into the revenue arrears, and realizing them. We shall discuss about the tyranny of this department a little later; suffice it here to say that in Alauddins time, besides being oppressed by such a grinding tax-structure, the peasant was compelled to sell every maund of his surplus grain at government controlled rates for replenishing royal grain stores which the Sultan had ordered to be built in order to sustain his Market Control.

After Alauddins death (C.E.) most of his measures seem to have fallen into disuse, but the peasants got no relief, because Ghiyasuddin Tughlaq who came to the throne four years later (C.E.) continued the atrocious practice of Alauddin. He also ordered that there should be left only so much to the Hindus that neither, on the one hand, they should become arrogant on account of their wealth, nor, on the other, desert their lands in despair. In the time of Muhammad bin Tughlaq even this latter fear turned out to be true. The Sultans enhancement of taxation went even beyond the lower limits of bare subsistence. For the people left their fields and fled. This enraged the Sultan and he hunted them down like wild beasts.

Still conditions did not become unbearable all at once. Natures bounty to some extent compensated for the cruelty of the king. If the regime was extortionist, heavy rains sometimes helped in bumper production. Babur noted that Indias crops are all rain grown. Farming in north India depended upon the monsoon rains coming from the Bay of Bengal. Artificial irrigation was there on a very limited scale, for irrigation is not at all a necessity in cultivating crops and orchards. Autumn crops (Kharif season) grow by the downpour of the rains themselves; and strange it is that spring crops (Rabi season) grow even when no rain falls. Young trees are watered during two or three years after which they need no more (watering) as the ground gets soaked with rain in the monsoon season. Ibn Battuta gives a detailed description of the crops grown in India and adds: The grains that have been described are Kharif grains. They are harvested days after sowing. Thereafter Rabi grains like wheat, barley and massoor are sown. These are sown in the very same field in which Rabi grains (are harvested).

The soil of this country is very fertile and is of excellent quality. Rice is sown three times in the year. Production of rice is the largest in the country. Sesame and sugar-cane are also sown with Kharif. Shams Siraj Afif writes that when, during the monsoon season, there were spells of heavy rains, Sultan Firoz Tughlaq appointed officers to examine the banks of all the water courses and report how far the inundations had extended. If he was informed that large tracts had been made fertile by the spread of waters, he was overwhelmed with joy. But if any village went to ruin (on account of floods), he treated its officials with great severity.

But the basic policy of impoverishing the people, resulted in crippling of agricultural economy. By the Mughal period the condition of the peasantry became miserable; if there was any progress it was in the enhancement of taxation. According to W.H. Moreland, who has made a special study of the agrarian system of Mughal India, the basic object of the Mughal administration was to obtain the revenue on an ever-ascending scale. The share that could be taken out of the peasant's produce without destroying his chances of survival was probably a matter of common knowledge in each locality. In Akbars time, in Kashmir, the state demand was one-third, but in reality it came to two-thirds. The Jagirdars in Thatta (Sindh) did not take more than half. In Gujarat, according to Geleynsen who wrote in, the peasant was made to part with three-quarters of his harvest. Similar is the testimony of De Laet, Fryer and Van Twist. During Akbars reign, says Abul Fazl, evil hearted officers because of sheer greed, used to proceed to villages and mahals and sack them. Conditions became intolerable by the time of Shahjahan when, according to Manucci, peasants were compelled to sell their women and children to meet the revenue demand. Manrique writes that the peasants were carried off to various markets and fairs, (to be sold) with their poor unhappy wives behind them carrying their small children all crying and lamenting Bernier too affirms that the unfortunate peasants who were incapable of discharging the demands of their rapacious lords, were bereft of their children, who were carried away as slaves. Here was also confirmation, if not actually the beginning, of the practice of bonded labour in India. In these circumstances the peasant had little interest in cultivating the land. Bernier observes that as the ground is seldom tilled otherwise than by compulsion the whole country is badly cultivated, and a great part rendered unproductive The peasant cannot avoid asking himself this question: Why should I toil for a tyrant who may come tomorrow and lay his rapacious hands upon all I possess and value without leaving me the means (even) to drag my own miserable existence - The Timariots (Timurids), Governors and Revenue contractors, on their part reason in this manner: Why should the neglected state of this land create uneasiness in our minds, and why should we expend our own money and time to render it fruitful We may be deprived of it in a single moment Let us draw from the soil all the money we can, though the peasant should starve or abscond The situation made the tax-gatherer callous and exploitative on the one hand and the peasant fatalistic and disinterested on the other. The result, in Berniers own words, was that most towns in Hindustan are made up of earth, mud, and other wretched material; that there is no city or town (that) does not bear evident marks of approaching decay. Wherever Muslim despots ruled, ruin followed, so that, writes he, similar is the present condition of Mesopotamia, Anatolia, Palestine, the once wonderful plain of Antioch, and so many other regions anciently well cultivated, fertile and populous, but now desolate Egypt also exhibits a sad picture

To revert to the Mughal empire. An important order in the reign of Aurangzeb describes the Jagirdars as demanding in theory only half but in practice actually more than the total yield. Describing the conditions of the latter part of the seventeenth century Mughal empire, Dr. Tara Chand writes: The desire of the State was to extract the economic rent, so that nothing but bare subsistence. remained for the peasant. Aurangzebs instructions were that there shall be left for everyone who cultivates his land as much as he requires for his own support till the next crop be reaped and that of his family and for seed. This much shall be left to him, what remains is land tax, and shall go to the public treasury.

Conditions could not always have been that bad. There were steps taken from time to time to help cultivation and ameliorate the condition of the agriculturists. Shamsuddin Iltutmish constructed a large tank called Hauz-i-Shamsi. Traces of Alauddin Khaljis Hauz-i-Khas and Firoz Tughlaqs irrigation canals still exist. Similar steps taken in Mughal times are also known. But such steps in aid of the development were taken because these could offer better means of increasing the revenue. Some steps which looked like helping the agriculturists, sometimes resulted in their perpetual penury. For example, a very common administrative measure of the medieval times was to advance loans to peasants to help them tide over their difficulties. But the important ideal entertained by rulers can be best summarized in the words of Sher Shahs instructions to his Amils: Be lenient at the time of assessment, but show no mercy at the time of collection. This was, on the face of it, a good principle. But even Sher Shah Suri, renowned for his concern for the wellbeing of cultivators, was much more keen about the benefits to be drawn by his Afghan clansmen from the lands they administered. He sent his good old loyal experienced servants to districts which yielded good profits and advantages and after two years or so transfered them and sent other servants like them that they may also prosper. It was of course the peasant who paid for this prosperity.

COLLECTION OF ARREARS

We have earlier referred to the problem of collection of arrears. When agriculture was almost entirely dependent on rainfall and land tax was uniformally high, it was not possible for the peasants to pay their revenue regularly and keep their accounts ever straight with the government. The revenue used to fall into arrears. From the study of contemporary sources it is almost certain that there were hardly any remissions - even against conversion to Islam. Muslim rulers were very keen on proselytization. Sultan Firoz Tughlaq rescinded Jiziyah for those who became Muhammadan. Sometimes he also instructed his revenue collectors to accept conversions in lieu of Kharaj. Rajas and Zamindars who could not deposit land revenue or tribute in time had to convert to Islam. Bengal and

Gujarat provide specific instances which go to show that such rules prevailed throughout the Muslim-ruled regions. But remissions of Kharaj were not allowed. On the other hand arrears went on accumulating and the kings tried to collect them with the utmost rigour. In the Sultanate period there was a full-fledged department by the name of the Diwan-i-Mustakharaj. The work of this department was to inquire into the arrears lying in the names of collectors (Amils and Karkuns) and force them to realize the balances in full. Such was the strictness in the Sultanate period. Under the Mughals arrears were collected with equal harshness. The system then existing shows that the peasants were probably never relieved of the burden of arrears. In practice it could hardly have been possible always to collect the entire amounts and the balance was generally put forward to be collected along with the demand of the next year. A bad year, therefore, might leave an intolerable burden for the peasants in the shape of such arrears. These had a natural tendency to grow It also seems to have been a common practice to demand the arrears, owed by peasants who had fled or died, from their neighbour. And peasants who could not pay revenue or arrears frequently became predial slaves.

In short, between the thirteenth century when armies had to march to collect the revenue, and the seventeenth century when peasants were running away from the land because of the extortions of the state, no satisfactory principle of assessment or collection except extortion could be discovered. The situation became definitely worse in the eighteenth and nineteenth centuries as attested to by contemporary historians Jean Law and Ghulam Hussain. It is this general and continued stringency that was the legacy of the Mughal empire and the Indian Muslim states which continued under the British Raj.

Another idea of the rulers of medieval India was to keep the prices of commodities of everyday necessity low. This idea too emanated in the time of Alauddin Khalji. It was either his own brain-child or that of his courtiers and Ulama. His passion for incessant conquests and constant invasions of Mongols had rendered maintenance of a large army unavoidable. Even if he had recruited the large number of soldiers on a moderate salary, the entire treasure of the state would have been exhausted in five or six years. Alauddin, therefore, decided to cut down the salary of soldiers; but to prevent their falling victim to economic distress, he also decided to reduce the prices of commodities of daily use.

To the contemporary chronicler these prices were quite low and fluctuation, not even of a dang (small copper coin), was ever allowed whether in seasons of drought or of plenty. Indeed the low and fixed prices in the market were considered to be one of the wonders of the age. But when a husbandman paid half of his hard earned produce in land tax, some portion of the remaining half in other sundry duties, and then was compelled to sell his grain at cheap rates to the governments, it does not speak well of the general condition of the peasantry in those days. They could never have been happy in selling their grain cheap in the open market nor to the government itself at fixed rates without making profit. Profit is the greatest incentive to production, but it was completely checked by Alauddins market regulations and the peasants seem to have lived a life of monotony and low standard.

Without caring to understand that low prices cripple production and impoverish the producer, many sultans after Alauddin Khalji took pride in competing with him in keeping prices low. But their actions led not only to the impoverishment of the peasantry but also of shopkeepers and businessmen. Shams Siraj Afif feels jubilant at describing and listing the low prices during the reign of Firoz Tughlaq, claiming that while Alauddin had to make strenuous efforts to bring down the prices, in the time of Firoz Tughlaq they remained low without resorting to any coercion.

Like Alauddin, Sikandar Lodi also used to keep a constant watch on the price-level in the market. Abdullah, the author of Tarikh-i-Daudi, says that during the reign of Ibrahim Lodi the prices of commodities were cheaper than in the reign of any other Sultan except in Alauddins last days, and adds that whereas in Alauddins time the cheapness of prices was maintained through compulsion, force and dire punishments, in Ibrahims reign prices remained low naturally.

So Alauddin Khalji had pioneered the idea of maintaining prices of necessaries at cheap rates. It was followed by his successors up to the beginning of the sixteenth century, without perhaps caring for its implications on the condition of the peasantry. Historians of Sher Shah affirm that he was indebted to Alauddin in laying down his agrarian policy and Akbar adopted many measures of Sher Shah. During the Mughal period prices by and large went up, although as late as in the reign of Aurangzeb, sometimes the prices reported were regarded as exceptionally cheap. But since the land revenue accounted for by far the larger portion of the peasants surplus produce, it is obvious that this increase must have wiped out any possible advantage that the peasantry might have obtained through a rise in the prices.

Besides these handicaps, the peasant suffered because there were no clear ideas about a regular commissariat service to maintain supply-line for the army during a campaign. There is evidence that camp-markets were sometimes established for the convenience of soldiers. There are also situations on record when the soldiers were encouraged to loot the peasants to obtain grain. Sher Shah took appropriate measures to see that agriculturists were not harassed by an army on march, but Babur noted that on the news of the arrival of an army the peasants used to leave their land, flee for life and establish themselves elsewhere. Encouragement to soldiers to loot was inherent in khums tax, through which the state obtained as its share one-fifth of the booty collected by the troops, while four-fifth was left with the soldiers.

And above all, one fact is clear in the chronicles of medieval India - any measures against the higher classes ultimately affected the peasants, because any loss to the former was surreptitiously transferred to the peasants. For, as Sir Thomas Roe wrote, the people of Hindustan lived as fishes do in the sea - the great ones eat up the little. For first the farmer robs the peasant, the gentlemen robs the farmer, the greater robs the lesser and the King robs all. Bernier corroborates the conclusion when he writes: In eastern countries, the weak and the injured are without any refuge whatever; and the only law that decides all controversies is the cane and the caprice of a governor.

Of all the ideas, motivations and actions mentioned above leading to the impoverishment of the peasantry, the one of leaving nothing but bare subsistence, was the most atrocious. Writing about the times of Aurangzeb, Dr. Tara Chand rightly observes that the policy (of leaving) bare subsistence was suicidal for it killed the goose that laid the golden eggs. It left no incentive for increasing the production or improving the methods of cultivation. Consequently, there was a progressive deterioration in the living standards of the peasantry as decades and centuries passed. As said earlier, Alberuni, Barani, Ibn Battuta and Shams Siraj Afif talk about the prosperity of the people right up to the fourteenth century. R.H. Major in his translation of the works of Nicolo Conti, Athnasius Nikitin, Santo Stefano etc., only refers to the poverty of the Indian peasant in the fifteenth century. But Babur in the sixteenth century witnessed extreme poverty; he repeatedly talks about langoti as the only apparel and khichri as the only food. Witnesses for the seventeenth century are unanimous in observing extreme poverty of the peasantry.

RESISTANCE OF THE PEASANTRY

The idea of leaving only the bare minimum to the peasant and collecting the rest of his hard-earned produce in land revenue and other taxes, remained the basic policy of the rulers during the medieval times. Some chroniclers were aware of its evil effects. Shams Siraj Afif, writing in the days of Firoz Shah Tughlaq says that Unwise regulations had been made in former reigns, and the raiyyats and subjects were oppressed in the payment of revenue. Several writers told the author of this work that it was the practice to leave the raiyyat one cow and take away all the rest. Such a policy proved counter-productive. It not only harmed the agriculturists but also the Muslim regime, for, in place of minimising opposition, it actually encouraged resistance. In the unequal struggle between the poor peasantry and the mighty government carried on over a long period of time the tillers of the soil ultimately lost. But not without stiff resistance. Hindu Zamindars as the leaders and the peasants as their followers, both fought against the unjust demands of the king. Under Alauddin himself the Khuts and Muqaddams (Zamindars) avoided to pay taxes, did not care for the summons of the Diwan-i-Wazarat or Revenue Department, ignored to call at his office and paid no heed to the revenue officials. And the peasants, finding continuance of cultivation uneconomic and the treatment of the regime unbearable, left the fields and fled into the jungle from where they organized resistances. In this confrontation Zamindars played the role of leaders and the peasants joined under their banner.

Ibn Battuta describes this scenario. The Muslims dominate the infidels, writes he, but the later fortify themselves in mountains, in rocky, uneven and rugged places as well as in bamboo groves (or jungles) which serve them as ramparts. Hence they cannot be subdued except by powerful armies. The story of the resistance of the Hindus to Muslim dominance and injustice is repeated by many contemporary writers. Ziyauddin Barani says that if the Hindus do not find a mighty sovereign at their head nor behold crowds of horse and foot with drawn swords and arrows threatening their lives, they fail in their allegiance, refuse payment of revenue and incite a hundred tumults and revolts. Similar is the testimony of Amir Khusrau, Ibn Battuta, Vidyapati and the Muslim chroniclers of the fifteenth century. In the fifteenth century, when the Sultanate of Delhi had grown weak, the tillers of the soil evaded, more than ever, payment of land tax, and revenue could be collected only through army sorties in regular yearly or half-yearly expeditions. Such resistance continued throughout, for the Indian peasant had his own survival strategies. These comprised mainly of two options - to fight with determination as far as possible, but, if resistance proved of no avail, to flee and settle down elsewhere. Medieval Indian society, both urban and agrarian, was to some extent an armed society. In cities and towns the elite carried swords like walking sticks. In villages few men were without at least a spear or bow and arrows, and they were skilled in the use of these arms. In, Peter Mundy actually saw in the present day Kanpur district, labourers with their guns, swords and bucklers lying by them while they ploughed the ground. Similarly, Manucci described how in Akbars days the villagers of the Mathura region defended themselves against Mughal revenue-collecting officers: The women stood behind their husbands with spears and arrows, when the husband had shot off his matchlock, his wife handed him the lance, while she reloaded the matchlock. The countryside was studded with little forts, some surrounded by nothing more than mud walls, but which nevertheless provided centres of the general tradition of rebellion and agrarian unrest. Armed peasants provided contingents to Baheliyas, Bhadauriyas, Bachgotis, Mandahars and Tomars in the earlier period, to Jats, Marathas and Sikhs in the later.

But as the people put up a continual resistance, the Muslim government suppressed them ruthlessly. In this exercise the Mughal emperors were no better than the pre-Mughal sultans. We have often referred to the atrocities of the Delhi sultans and their provincial governors. Abul Fazl, Bernier and Manucci provide detailed accounts of the exertion of the Mughals. Its summing up by Jahangir is the most telling. In his Tarikh-i-Salim Shahi he writes:

I am compelled to observe, with whatever regret, that notwithstanding the frequent and sanguinary executions which have been dealt among the people of Hindustan, the number of the turbulent and disaffected never seems to diminish; for what with the examples made during the reign of my father, and subsequently of my own, there is scarcely a province in the empire in which, either in battle or by the sword of the executioner, five or six hundred thousand human beings have not, at various periods, fallen victims to this fatal disposition to discontent and turbulence. Ever and anon, in one quarter or another, will some accursed miscreant spring up to unfurl the standard of rebellion; so that in Hindustan never has there existed a period of complete repose.

In such a society, observes Kolf, the millions of armed men, cultivators and otherwise, were its (governments) rivals rather than its subjects. This attitude was the consequence of the Mughal governments policy of repression. As an example, the exploits of one of Jahangirs commanders, Abdullah Khan Uzbeg Firoz Jung, can provide an idea of the excessive cruelty perpetrated by the government. Peter Mundy, who travelled from Agra to Patna in saw, during his four days journey, minars (pillars) on which a total of about heads were fixed with mortar. On his way back four months later, he noticed that meanwhile another minars with between and heads had been added and that the erection of new ones had not yet stopped. Abdullah Khans force of, horse and, foot destroyed, in the Kalpi-Kanauj area, all towns, took all their goods, their wives and children as slaves and beheaded and immortered the chiefest of their men. Why, even Akbars name stands besmeared with wanton killings. In his siege of Chittor (October) the regular garrison of Rajputs was vigorously helped by, armed peasants who had shown great zeal and activity. This infuriated the emperor to massacre, of them.

In short, the Indian peasant was clear in his mind about meeting the onslaughts of nature and man. Attached to his land as he was, he resisted the oppression of the rulers as far as his resources, strength and stamina permitted. If conditions went beyond his control, he left his land and established himself in some other place. Indeed, migration or flight was the peasants first answer to famine or mans oppression. Baburs description of this process may be quoted in his own words: In Hindustan, says he, hamlets and villages, towns indeed, are depopulated and set up in a moment. If the people of a large town, one inhabited for years even, flee from it, they do it in such a way that not a sign or trace of them remains in a day or a day and a half. On the other hand, if they fix their eyes on a place in which to settle, they make a tank or dig a well; they need not build houses or set up walls, khas-grass abounds, wood is unlimited, huts are made and straightaway there is a village or a town.

Similar is the testimony of Col. Wilks about South India. On the approach of a hostile army, the inhabitants of India bury underground their most cumbrous effects, and issue from their beloved homes and take the direction sometimes of a strong fortress, but more generally of the most unfrequented hills and woods. According to Amir Khusrau, wherever the army marched, every inhabited spot was desolated When the army arrived there (Warangal, Deccan), the Hindu inhabitants concealed themselves in hills and jungles. This process of flight seems to have continued throughout the Mughal period, both in the North and the South. Writing of the days of Shahjahan, Bernier says that many of the peasantry, driven to despair by so execrable a tyranny, abandon the country and sometimes fly to the territories of a Raja because they find less oppression and are allowed a greater degree of comfort.

To flee was a good idea, when it is realized that this was perhaps the only way to escape from the cruel revenue demand and rapacious officials. Some angry rulers like Balban and Muhammad bin Tughlaq hunted down these escapists in the jungles, others clamped them in jails, but, by and large, the peasants did survive in the process. For, it was not only cultivators alone who fled into the forests, but often even vanquished Rajas and zealous Zamindars. There they and people at large organized themselves to defend against the onslaughts of the regime. For it was not only because cultivation was uneconomic and peasants left the fields; it was also a question of saving Hindu religion and Hindu culture. Under Muslim rule the two principal Muslim practices of iconoclasm and proselytization were carried on unabated. During the Arab invasion of Sind and the expeditions of Mahmud of Ghazni, defeated rulers, garrisons of captured forts, and civilian population were often forced to accept Islam. The terror-tactics of such invaders was the same everywhere and their atrocities are understandable. But even when Muslim rule had been established in India, it was a matter of policy with Muslim rulers to capture and convert or disperse and destroy the male population and carry into slavery their women and children. Minhaj Siraj writes that Sultan Balbans taking of captives, and his capture of the dependents of the great Ranas cannot be recounted. In Katehar he ordered a general massacre of the male population above eight years of age and carried away women and children. Muhammad Tughlaq, Firoz Tughlaq, Sikandar Lodi, Sikandar Butshikan of Kashmir, Mahmud

Beghara of Gujarat and emperor Aurangzeb were more enthusiastic, some others were lukewarm, but it was the religious duty of a Muslim monarch to capture people and convert them to Islam.

In these circumstances the defeated Rajas and helpless agriculturists all sought refuge in the forests. Forests in medieval India abounded. Ibn Battuta says that very thick forests existed right from Bengal to Allahabad. In his time rhinoceroses (gender) were to be found in the very centre of the Sultanate, in the jungles near Allahabad. There were jungles throughout the country. Even the environs of Delhi abounded in forests so that during the time of Balban, harassed Mewatis retaliated by issuing forth from the jungles in the immediate vicinity of the south-west of Delhi, attack the city and keep the king on tenter-hooks. When Timur invaded Hindustan at the end of the fourteenth century, he had learnt about this resistance and was quite scared of it. In his Malfuzat he notes that there were many strong defences in India like the large rivers, the elephants etc. The second defence, writes he, consists of woods and forests and trees, which interweaving stem with stem and branch with branch, render it very difficult to penetrate the country. The third defence is the soldiery, and landlords and princes, and Rajas of that country, who inhabit fastnesses in those forests, and live there like wild beasts.

Growth of dense forests was a cause and effect of heavy rains. Forests precipitated rainfall and rains helped in the growth of forests. Therefore, like forests, rains also helped the freedom loving wild-beasts living in the jungles in maintains their independence and culture. It is truly said that in India it does not rain, it pours. The rainfall in the north and the northeastern India - Uttar Pradesh, Bihar and Bengal, including eastern Bengal (now Bangla Desh) and parts of Assam (the Hindustan of medieval times) - is in the following order: The average annual rainfall in U.P., Bihar and Bengal is to cms. (to inches), in eastern Bengal and Assam it is to cms. and in some parts above cms. (to and above inches). In all probability a similar average obtained in the medieval period also. Medieval chroniclers do not speak in quantitative terms: in their language rivulets used to turn into rivers and rivers into seas during the rainy season. The situation is best depicted by the sixteenth century conqueror Zahiruddin Muhammad Babur himself in his memoirs Tuzuk-i-Baburi or Babur Nama. He writes about Hindustan: Sometimes it rains,, or times a day, torrents pour down all at once and rivers flow where no water had been. Such intensity of rainfall had rendered precarious the grip of Turkish rulers in many parts. For example, the government at Delhi could not always maintain its hold on Bengal effectively. There were very few roads and hardly any bridges over rivers in those days, and the almost primitive medieval communication system used to break down during the rainy season. Local governors of the eastern region - Bihar and Bengal - did not fail to take advantage of this situation and used to declare independence. Governor Tughril Beg of Bengal depended on the climate and waterlogged soil of the province to wear out the Delhi forces, for three years. Bengal almost remained independent till the middle of the sixteenth century.

In short, heavy rains and thick forests affected the mobility of the governments army, leaving the refugees safe in their jungle hide-outs and repulse any intrusion. Ibn Battuta describes how people used to fight behind barricades of bushes and bamboo trees. They collect rain water and tend their animals and fields, and remain so strongly entrenched that but for a strong army they cannot be suppressed. Babur confirms this: Under the monsoon rains the banks of some of its rivers and torrents are worn into deep channels, difficult and troublesome to pass through anywhere. In many parts of the plains (because of rains) thorny jungle grows, behind the good defence of which the people become stubbornly rebellious and pay no taxes. It was because of this that Muslim conquest could not penetrate the Indian countryside nor Muslim rule affect it. If there was any fear of attack, the villagers just fled and re-established themselves elsewhere, or returned after the storm was over.

SC, ST AND OBC

Those who took to the jungle, stayed there, eating wild fruits, tree-roots, and the coarsest grain if and when available, but surely preserving their freedom. But with the passing of time, a peasant became a tribal and from tribal a beast. William Finch, writing at Agra about C.E., describes how Jahangir and his nobles treated them - during Shikar. A favourite form of sport in Mughal India was the Kamargha, which consisted in enclosing a tract of country by a line of guards, and then gradually contracting the enclosure until a large quantity of game was encircled in a space of convenient size. Whatever is taken in this enclosure (Kamargha or human circle), writes Finch, is called the kings shikar or game, whether men or beasts The beasts taken, if mans meat, are sold if men they remain the Kings slaves, which he sends yearly to Kabul to barter for horses and dogs: these being poor, miserable, thievish people, that live in woods and deserts, little differing from beasts. W.H. Moreland adds: Other writer (also) tell it besides Finch. Even Babur, always a keen observer, had not failed to notice that peasants in India were often reduced to the position of tribals. In our countries, writes he in his Memoirs, dwellers in the wilds (i.e. nomads) get tribal names; here (i.e. Hindustan) the settled people of the cultivated lands and villages get tribal names.

In short, the avalanche of Turco- Mughal invaders, and the policy of their Government turned many settled agriculturists into tribals of the jungles. Many defeated Rajas and harassed Zamindars also repaired to forest and remote fortresses for security. They had been defeated in war and due to the policy of making them nest-o-nabud (destroy root and branch), had been reduced to the position of Scheduled Castes / Tribes / Backward Classes. For example, many Parihars and Parmars, once upon a time belonging to the proud Rajput castes, are now included in lower castes. So are the Rajputs counted in Backward Classes in South India. Two examples, one from the early years of Muslim rule and the other from its closing years, would suffice to illustrate the point. In the early years of Muslim conquest, Jats had helped Muhammad bin Qasim in Sind; later on they turned against him. Khokhars had helped Muhammad Ghauri but turned hostile to him and ultimately killed him. This made the Turkish Sultanate ill-disposed towards them, and in course of time many of these Jats and Khokhars were pushed into belonging to low castes of to-day. For the later times is the example of the Satnamis. This sect was an offshoot of the Raidasis. Their stronghold in the seventeenth century was Narnaul, situated about kms. south-west of Delhi. The contemporary chronicler Khafi Khan credits them with a good character. They followed the professions of agriculture and trade on a small scale. They dressed simply, like faqirs. They shaved their heads and so were called mundiyas also. They came into conflict with imperial forces. It began as a minor trouble, but developed into a war of Hindu liberation from the persecution of Aurangzeb. Soon some five thousand Satnamis were in arms. They routed the faujdar of Narnaul, plundered the town, demolished its mosques, and established their own administration. At last Aurangzeb crushed them by sending, troops (March,) and facing a most obstinate battle in which two thousand Satnamis fell on the field and many more were slain during the pursuit. Those who escaped spread out into small units so that today there are about million Satnami Harijans found in Madhya Pradesh, Maharashtra, Bihar and Uttar Pradesh.

Thus were swelled the numbers of what are today called Scheduled Castes, Scheduled Tribes and Other Backward Classes (SC / ST / OBC). The eleventh century savant Alberuni who came to India in the train of Mahmud of Ghazni, speaks of eight castes / sections of Antajya (untouchable), or workers in low professions in Hindustan such as fuller, shoemaker, juggler, fisherman, hunter of wild animals and birds. They are occupied with dirty work, like the cleaning of the villages and other services. In his time their number was obviously not large. Today the SC / ST alone comprise percent of the population or about million, according to census.

Add to this the Other Backward Classes and they all count to more than fifty percent. This staggeringly high figure has been reached because of historical forces operating in the medieval times primarily. Muslim rule spread all over the country. Resistance to it too remained widespread. Jungles abounded through out the vast land from Gujarat to Bengal and Kashmir to Kanyakumari, and flight into them was the safest safeguard for the weak and vulnerable. That is how SC / ST people are found in every state in large numbers. During the medieval period, in the years and centuries of oppression, they lived almost like wild beasts in improvised huts in forest villages, segregated and isolated, suffering and struggling. But by settling in forest villages, they were enabled to preserve their freedom, their religion and their culture. Their martial arts, preserved in their Akharas, are even now practised in different forms in many states. Such a phenomenon was not witnessed in West Asian countries. There, in the vast open deserts, the people could not save themselves from forced conversions against advancing Muslim armies. There were no forests into which they could flee, hide themselves and organize resistance. Hence they all became Muslim.

In the Indian forest villages these primitive Hindus continued to maintain themselves by engaging in agriculture and simple cottage industries. They also kept contact with the outside world for, since they had remained Hindu, they were freely employed by Rajas and Zamindars. They provided firewood and served as boatmen and watchmen. The Hindu elite engaged them for guard duty in their houses, and as palki-bearers when they travelled. Travelling in the hot climate of India was mostly done at night, and these people provided guard to bullock carts and other conveyances carrying passengers and goods. There are descriptions of how these people ran in front and rear of the carts with lighted torches or lanterns in one hand and a lathi in the other. They also fought for those Hindu leaders who organized resistance from remote villages and jungle hide-outs. The exaspertated and starving peasantry sometimes took to highway robbery as the only means of living. Raiding bands were also locally formed. Their main occupation, however, remained menial work, including scavenging and leather tanning. But with all that, their spirit of resistance had made them good fighters. Fighting kept their health replenished, compensating for the non-availability of good food in the jungles. Their fighting spirit made the British think of them as thugs, robbers and bandits.

But the British as well as other Europeans also embarked upon anthropological and sociological study of these poor forest people. In trying to find a name for these groups, the British census officials labelled them, in successive censuses, as Aboriginals, Animists and as Adherents of Tribal Religions.

These days a lot of noise is being made about helping the SC / ST and OBCs by reserving their quotas in government jobs. It is argued that these people have been oppressed by high caste Hindus in the past and they should now be helped and compensated by them. But that is only an assumption. It is they who have helped save the Hindu religion by shunning all comforts and taking to the life of the jungle. That is why they have remained Hindu. If they had been harassed and oppressed by high-caste Hindus, they could have easily chosen to opt for Muslim creed ever so keen on effecting proselytization. But they preferred to hide in the forests rather than do so. There is another question. Was that the time for the Upper Caste Hindus, fighting tenaciously to save their land, religion and culture, to oppress the lower strata of Hindus whose help they desperately needed in their struggle The mindset of upper-caste / backward-caste conflict syndrome needs reviewing as it is neither based on historical evidence nor supported by compulsions of the situation. The present day isolated conflicts may be a rural politician / plebian problem of no great antiquity.

Another relic of the remote past is the objection to the entry of men of lower class people into temples. In Islam slaves were not permitted to bestow alms or visit places of pilgrimages. In India, according to Megasthenes, there were no slaves. But slavery (dasta) probably did exist in one form or the other. Were the dasas also debarred from entering temples and the practice has continued; or, was it that every caste and section had its own shrines and did not enter those of others The picture is very blurred and origins of this practice are difficult to locate.

Above all, there is the question: Would the SC / ST by themselves accept to change their way of life and accept the assistance Perhaps yes, perhaps no. An example may help understand the position. In June Maharana Pratap of Chittor had to face Akbars armies in the famous battle of Haldighati. Rana Pratap fought with exemplary courage and of his soldiers only a little more than half could leave the field alive. In the darkness of the evening, the wounded Rana left the field on his favourite horse Chetak. A little later, in October, Akbar himself marched in person in pursuit of the Rana, but the latter remained untraced and unsubdued. Later on he recovered all Mewar except Mandalgarh and Chittor. His nearest associates, the Bhil and Lohia tribals, had taken a vow that until their motherland was not freed, they would not eat in metal plates, but only on leaves; they would not sleep on bedsteads, but only on the ground; and they would renounce all comforts. The bravest among them even left Chittor, to return to it only when Mewar had regained independence. That day was not destined to come in their life-time. It was not to come for decades, for generations, for centuries. During these hundreds of years they lived as tribals and nomads, moving from city to city. On India regaining independence, Prime Minister Jawaharlal Nehru, who knew about these peoples poignant history, decided to rehabilitate them in Chittor. In March an impressive function was arranged there and Pandit Nehru led the descendants of these valiant warriors back to their homes in independent Chittor in independent India. But most of them did not care to return. They live as nomads even today. The SC / ST and OBCs too may find their way of life too dear to relinquish for the modern urban civilised ways. Many welfare officers working in their areas actually find it to be so.

SLAVES

The forest-village-dwellers, whether escapees or resisters, suffered untold privations. Still they had the satisfaction of being able to preserve their freedom, their religion and their culture. But all victims of aggression were not so lucky. Many vulnerable groups and individuals could not extricate themselves from the clutches of the invaders and tyranny of the rulers; they used to be captured, enslaved and even sold, not only in India but also outside the country. It was not only Jahangir, a comparatively kind hearted emperor, who used to capture poor people during his hunting expeditions and send them to

Kabul in exchange for dogs and horses, all Muslim invaders and rulers collected slaves and exploited them as they pleased.

When Muhammad bin Qasim invaded Sind, he took captives wherever he went and sent many prisoners, especially women prisoners, to his homeland. Parimal Devi and Suraj Devi, the two daughters of Raja Dahir, who were sent to Hajjaj to adorn the harem of the Caliph, were part of a large bunch of maidens remitted as one-fifth share of the state (Khums) from the booty of war (Ghanaim).

The Chachnama gives the details. After the capture of the fort of Rawar, Muhammad bin Qasim halted there for three day, during which time he masscered, men. Their followers and dependents, as well as their women and children were taken prisoner. When the (total) number of prisoners was calculated, it was found to amount to thirty thousand persons (Kalichbeg has sixty thousand), amongst whom thirty were the daughters of the chiefs.

They were sent to Hajjaj. The head of Dahir and the fifth part of prisoners were forwarded in charge of the Black Slave Kaab, son of Mubarak Rasti. In Sind itself female slaves captured after every campaign of the marching army, were married to Arab soldiers who settled down in colonies established in places like ManSura, Kuzdar, Mahfuza and Multan. The standing instructions of Hajjaj to Muhammad bin Qasim were to give no quarter to infidels, but to cut their throats, and take the women and children as captives. In the final stages of the conquest of Sind, when the plunder and the prisoners of war were brought before Qasim one-fifth of all the prisoners were chosen and set aside; they were counted as amounting to twenty thousand in number (they belonged to high families) and veils were put on their faces, and the rest were given to the soldiers. Obviously, a few lakhs of women were enslaved and distributed among the elite and the soldiers.

In the words of the Andre Wink, From the seventh century onwards, and with a peak during Muhammad al-Qasims campaigns in -, a considerable number of Jats [and also others] was captured as prisoners of war and deported to Iraq and elsewhere as slaves. Some Jat freemen became famous in the Islamic world, as for instance Abu Hanifa, the founder of the Hanafite school of law.

So, from the days of Muhammad bin Qasim in the eighth century to those of Ahmad Shah Abdali in the eighteenth, enslavement, distribution and sale of captives was systematically practised by Muslim invaders. A few instances are necessary to have a clear idea of the monstrous practice of taking captives. When Mahmud Ghaznavi attacked Waihind (near Peshawar) in -, he took, persons of both sexes as captive. This figure of Abu Nasr Muhammad Utbi, the secretary and chronicler of Mahmud, is so mind-boggling that Elliot reduces it to. The point to note is that taking of slaves was a matter of routine in every expedition. Only when the numbers were exceptionally large did they receive the notice of the chroniclers. So that in Mahmuds attack on Ninduna in the Salt Range, Utbi says that slaves were so plentiful that they became very cheap; and men of respectability in their native land (India) were degraded by becoming slaves of common shopkeepers (of Ghazni). His statement finds confirmation in Nizamuddin Ahmads Tabqat-i-Akbari which states that Mahmud obtained great spoils and a large number of slaves. Next year from Thanesar, according to Farishtah, the Muhammadan army brought to Ghaznin, captives so that the capital appeared like an Indian city, for every soldier of the army had several slaves and slave girls. Thereafter slaves were taken in Baran, Mahaban, Mathura, Kanauj, Asni etc. so that when Mahmud returned to Ghazni in, the booty was found to consist (besides huge wealth) of, captives according to Nizamuddin. But Utbi is more detailed. He says that the number of prisoners may be conceived from the fact, that each was sold for from two to ten dirhams. These were afterwards taken to Ghazna, and the merchants came from different cities to purchase them, so that the countries of Mawaraun-Nahr, Iraq and Khurasan were filled with them. The Tarikh-i-Alfi adds that the fifth share due to the Saiyyads was, slaves, therefore the total number of captives comes to,.

This was the practice throughout the medieval period. Furthermore, it was also a matter of policy with the Muslim rulers and their army commanders to capture and convert, destroy or sell the male population, and carry into slavery women and children. Ibn-ul-Asir says that Qutbuddin Aibak made war against the provinces of Hind He killed many, and returned home with prisoners and booty. In Banaras, according to the same authority, Muhammad Ghauris slaughter of the Hindus was immense. None was spared except women and children." No wonder that slaves began to fill the households of every Turk from the very beginning of Muslim rule in India. Fakhr-i-Mudabbir informs us that as a result of the Muslim achievements under Muhammad Ghauri and Qutbuddin Aibak, even a poor householder (or soldier) who did not possess a single slave before became the owner of numerous slaves of all description (jauq jauq ghulam har jins)

In Sultan Iltutmish attacked Gwalior, and captured a large number of slave. Minhaj Siraj Jurjani writes that Sultan Balbans taking captives, and his capture of the dependents of the great Ranas cannot be recounted. Talking of his war in Avadh against Trailokyavarman of the Chandela dynasty (Dalaki wa Malaki of Minhaj), the chronicler says that all the infidel wives, sons and dependents and children fell into the hands of the victors. In, in his campaign against Ranthambhor also Balban appears to have captured many prisoners. In, in an attack on Haryana (the Shiwalik Hills), many women and children were enslaved. Twice Balban led expeditions against Kampil, Patiali, and Bhojpur, and in the process captured a large number of women and children. In Katehar he ordered a general massacre of the male population of above eight years of age and carried away the women and children.

The process of enslavement during war went on under the Khaljis and the Tughlaqs. Of Alauddin Khaljis, slaves some were mere boys, and surely mainly captured during war. Firoz Tughlaq had issued an order that whichever places were sacked, in them the captives should be sorted out and the best ones should be forwarded to the court. His acquisition of slaves was accomplished through various ways - capture in war, in lieu of revenue and as present from nobles. Soon he was enabled to collect, slaves. Ziyauddin Baranis description of the Slave

Market in Delhi, (such markets were there in other places also), during the reign of Alauddin Khalji, shows that fresh batches of captives were constantly replenishing them. The practice of selling slaves was well established and widely known. Amir Khusrau in the fourteenth century writes that the Turks, whenever they please, can seize, buy, or sell any Hindu. He is corroborated by Vidyapati in the next century. The latter writes that the Muslim army commanders take into custody all the women of the enemys city, and wherever they happened to pass, in that very place the ladies of the Rajas house began to be sold in the market. Alauddin Khalji fixed the prices of such slaves in the market, as he did for all other items of common use like wheat and rice, horse and cattle. The sale price of boys was fixed from to tankahs; the ill-favoured could be obtained for or. The slave boys were classified according to their looks and working capacity. The standard price of a working girl was fixed from to tankahs, that of a good looking girl from to, and a beauty of high family even from thousand to thousand tankahs. Under Muhammad bin Tughlaq, as per the information of Shihabuddin al Umri, a domestic maid in Delhi could be had for tankahs and one deemed fit to be a concubine sold for about tankahs. In other cities, says he, prices are still lower.

Muhammad bin Tughlaq became notorious for enslaving captives, and his reputation in this regard spread far and wide so that Umri writes about him thus: The Sultan never ceases to show the greatest zeal in making war upon the infidels Everyday thousands of slaves are sold at very low price, so great is the number of prisoners. Ibn Battutas eye-witness account of the Sultans arranging marriages of enslaved girls with Muslims on a large scale on the two Ids confirms the statement of Al Umri. First of all, writes he, daughters of Kafir (Hindu) Rajas captured during the course of the year, come, sing and dance. Thereafter they are bestowed upon Amirs and important foreigners. After this the daughters of other Kafirs dance and sing the Sultan gives them to his brothers, relatives sons of Maliks etc. On the sixth day male and female slaves are married. It was a general practice for Hindu girls of good families to learn the art of dancing. It was a sort of religious rite. They used to dance during weddings, festivals and Pujas at home and in temples. This art was turned ravenous under their Muslim captors or buyers.

In short, female slaves were captured or obtained in droves throughout the year. Such was their influx that Ibn Battuta appears having got bored of them when he wrote: At (one) time there arrived in Delhi some female infidel captives, ten of whom the Wazir sent to me. I gave one of them to the man who had brought them to me, but he was not satisfied. My companion took three young girls, and I do not know what happened to the rest. Thousands (chandin hazar) of non-Muslim women (aurat va masturat) were captured during the yearly campaigns of Firoz Tughlaq and under him the Id celebrations were held on lines similar to those of his predecessor. Their sale outside, especially during the Hajj season, brought profits to the state and Muslim merchants. Their possession within, inflated the harems of Muslim kings and nobles beyond belief.

Some feeble attempts were sometimes made by some kings to put a stop to this inhuman practice. The Mughal emperor Akbar, for example, abolished the custom of enslaving helpless women and children in times of war. Jahangir ordered that a government collector or Jagirdar should not without permission intermarry with the people of the pargana in which he might be for abduction and forced marriages were common enough. But there was never an abjuration of the policy of enslavement as mainly it was not the Mughal emperors but the Mughal nobility who must have taken the lions share of the states enslavement, deportation and sale. To make the long and painful story short, it may just be mentioned that after the Third Battle of Panipat, the plunder of the (Maratha) camp was prodigious, and women and children who survived were driven off as slaves - twenty-two thousand (women), of the highest rank in the land, says the Siyar-ul-Mutakhkhirin.

The above study points to some hard facts about enslavement of Hindus under Muslim rule. It is not pertinent here to make a detailed study of the Muslim slave system which was an institution as peculiar as it was unique. Examples of men like Iltutmish and Balban are cited to show how well the slaves fared in the Islamic state and society, how well they were brought up and how easily they could rise to the highest positions in life. Iltutmish received nourishment like a son in the house of his master. Firoz Tughlaq and his nobles too treated their slaves in a similar fashion. But it is the captured and enslaved victims who felt the pinch of slavery. Here only their sufferings may be briefly recapitulated under three separate sections-the fate of men, of women and of children. Of the men captives, the Muslim regime did not have much use. Male prisoners were usually put to the sword, especially the old, the overbearing and those bearing arms, as had happened during Muhammad bin Qasims invasion, Ghauris attack on Banaras, Balbans expedition to Katehar, Timurs campaign in Hindustan or Akbars massacre at Chittor.

Of the captured men, those who could fetch good price were sold in India and outside. A lucrative trade in Indian slaves flourished in the West Asian countries. Many chroniclers aver that an important export item of commerce abroad comprised of Indian slaves who were exchanged for horses. If the trade in slaves was as brisk as the horse-trade, then many thousands of people must have been deported from India each year. For example, over the years from the eleventh to the early years of the nineteenth century, three quarters of the population of Bukhara was of mainly Indian slave extraction. The Hindu-Kush (Hindu-killer) mountain ranges are so called because thousands of Indian captives yoked together used to die while negotiating them. Ibn Battuta himself saw Indian slaves being taken out of the country.

Many of the slaves who were not sold by their captors, served as domestic servants, as artisans in the royal Karkhanas and as Paiks in the army. The Paiks cleared the jungles and prepared roads for the army on march. They were also sometimes used as human shields in battle. But others, especially professional soldiers captured in war and willing to serve the Muslim army, joined the permanent cadre of the infantry, and were known for their loyalty. Alauddin Khalji, Mubarak Khalji, and Firoz Tughlaq were saved by Paiks when attempts were made on their lives.

Child captives were preferred to grown up men. It may be recollected that in his campaigns in Katehar, Balban massacred mercilessly, sparing only boys of eight or nine. The age factor is material. As these boys grew in years, they gradually forgot their parents and even their native places and developed loyalty only to the king. They could thus be reared as Janessaries were brought up in the Ottoman Empire. The price-schedule of Sultan Alauddin Khalji is evidence of the importance attached to boy-slaves. In his time, while the price of a handsome slave was twenty to tankahs and that of a slave-servant ten to tankahs, the price of a child slave (ghulam bachchgan naukari) was fixed at to tankahs. Therefore during a campaign it was aimed at capturing lots of children. But no Hindus wished their children to become slaves, and in the face of an impending defeat Hindu mothers used to burn their little children in the fire of Jauhar rather than let them fall into the hands of the enemy to lead the life of perpetual bondage and sometimes meet a most detestable death.

The women captives in Muslim hands were treated as objects of sex or for making money through sale. Al Umri writes that in spite of low prices of slaves,, tankahs and even more, are paid for young Indian girls. I inquired the reason and was told that these young girls are remarkable for their beauty, and the grace of their manners.

This was the position from the very beginning. It has been mentioned before that Muhammad bin Qasim sent to Hajjaj some thirty thousand captives many among whom were daughters of chiefs of Sind. Hajjaj forwarded the prisoners to Caliph Walid I. The latter sold some of those daughters of the chiefs, and some he granted as rewards. When he saw the daughter of Rai Dahirs sister, he was much struck with her beauty and charms and wished to keep her for himself. But as his nephew Abdullah bin Abbas desired to take her, Walid bestowed her on him saying that it is better that you should take her to be the mother of your children. Centuries later, in the time of Jahangir, Abdullah Khan Firoz Jung expressed similar views when he declared that I made prisoners of five lacs of men and women and sold them. They all became

Muhammadans. From their progeny there will be crores by the day of judgement. The motive of having progeny from captured women and thereby increasing Muslim population was at the back of all marriages, abductions and enslavements throughout the medieval period.

One recognised way of escape from sex exploitation in the medieval period was Jauhar or group-self-immolation. Jauhar also was naturally resorted to because the motives and actions of the victors were never in doubt. For example, before Qasim could attack the Fort of Rawar many of the royal ladies themselves voluntarily immolated themselves. The description of the holocaust in the Chachnama is like this: Bai, the sister of Dahir, assembled all her women and said God forbid that we should own our liberty to these outcast cow-eaters. Our honour would be lost there is nowhere any hope of escape; let us collect wood, cotton and oil and bum ourselves. If any wish to save herself she may. So they went into a house, set it on fire and burnt themselves. It is those of the lesser mettle who used to save themselves and used to be captured. The repeated Jauhars at one place, Chittor, during the attacks of Alauddin Khalji, Bahadur Shah of Gujarat and Emperor Akbar have become memorable for the spirit shown by the Rajputnis. Captured and enslaved women often had to lead a life of misery and dishonour as happened with Deval Devi, daughter of Raja Karan Baghela of Gujarat.

As the legacy of this scenario, Indian girls are still being sold to West Asian nationals as wives, concubines and slave girls. For example, all the leading Indian newspapers like The Indian Express, The Hindustan Times and The Times of India of August, flashed the news of a sixty year old toothless Arab national Yahiya H.M. Al Sagish marrying a - year old Ameena of Hyderabad after paying her father Rs., and attempting to take her out of the country. Al Sagish has been taken into police custody and the case is in the law-court now. Mr. I.U. Khan has pointed out that no offence could be made out against his client as he had acted in accordance with the Shariat laws. He said that since this case related to the Muslim personal law which permitted marriage with girls who had attained Puberty (described as over years of age), Al Sagish could not be tried under the Indian Penal Code (IPC). Besides Ameenas parents had not complained. (Times of India, August).

But this is not an isolated case. I was in Hyderabad for about four years, -. There I learnt that such marriages are common. There are regular agents and touts who arrange them. Poor parents of girls are handsomely paid by foreign Muslims for such arrangements. Every time that I happened to go to the Hyderabad Airlines office or the Airport (which was about at least once a month), I found bunches of old bridegrooms in Arab attire accompanied by young girls, often little girl brides. A rough estimate indicated that as many as such marriages were solemnised during the past one decade in Hyderabad alone. (Indian Express Magazine, August). In short, the sex slave-trade is still flourishing not only in Hyderabad but in many other cities of India after the medieval tradition.

ARTISANS AND LABOURERS

After a brief survey of the misery and exploitation of the peasants, backward classes and slaves, let us look at the condition of artisans and labourers. In the medieval period, as sometimes even now, the work and vocation of agriculturists approximated, bordered, converged and telescoped into many other subsidiary professions. A peasant, when he was free from his field, in terms of time and seasons, or was compelled to leave his village, generally worked as basket-maker, weaver or water-carrier in his village or in the town nearby temporarily or after migrating to it. With the passage of time some of these agriculturalists became efficient and skilled craftsmen while the majority remained engaged in unskilled jobs. In urban setting their life-style may have improved a little - only a little in the medieval age-but they all remained an exploited lot. There was hardly any contemporary foreign visitor to India who was not struck by the extremely miserable existence of the lower class people. Such a situation obtained in all parts of the country, north and south, east and west.

Athnasius Nikitin, who travelled in the Deccan between and says that the land is overstocked with people: but those in the country are very miserable Durate Barbosa was horrified by the poverty existing on the Malabar coast and says that some of the lower classes in the region were so poor that they lived on roots and wild fruits and covered themselves with leaves. His near contemporary Varthema and the later visitor Linschoten wrote in a similar strain. Writing around the year, Della Valle gives glimpses of life in Surat by pointing out that the people were numerous, wages were low, and slaves cost practically nothing to keep. Similar is the testimony of Pyrard. The Portuguese writer Paes (wrote in) and Nuniz, confirm the assertion that the mass of the people were living in the greatest poverty and distress. In the seventeenth century John De Laet summarised the information he had collected from English, Dutch and Portuguese sources regarding the Mughal empire as a whole. The condition of the common people in these regions (south and west) is, says he, exceedingly miserable; wages are low; workmen get only one regular meal a day, the houses are wretched and practically unfurnished, and people have not got sufficient covering to keep warm in winter.

This about the south and west. About the east and north, Bengal and the region between Agra and Lahore, Joseph Salbank writing of the thickly populated country between Agra and Lahore observes that while the nobles are said to be very wealthy the plebian sort, is so poor that the greatest part of them go naked. In this regard, and for the urban scene in particular the testimony of Pelsaert and Bernier is of immense value. They lived and wrote mainly about Agra and Delhi respectively. Pelsaert laments the utter subjection and poverty of the common people-poverty so great and miserable that the life of the people can be depicted or accurately described only as the home of stark want and the dwelling place of bitter woe. He continues: There are three classes of people who are indeed nominally free, but whose status differs very little from voluntary slavery-workmen, peons or servants and shopkeepers. For the workmen there are two scourges, the first of which is low wages. Goldsmiths, painters (of cloth or chintz), embroiderers, carpet makers, cotton or silk weavers, black-smiths, copper-smiths, tailors, masons, builders, stone-cutters, a hundred crafts in all-any of these working from morning to night can earn only or tackas (tankahs), that is or strivers in wages. The second (scourge) is (the oppression of) the Governor, the nobles, the Diwan, the Kotwal, the Bakshi, and other royal officers. If any of these wants a workman, the man is not asked if he is willing to come, but is seized in the house or in the street, well beaten if he should dare to raise any objection, and in the evening paid half his wages, or nothing at all. From these facts the nature of their food can be easily inferred For their monotonous daily food they have nothing but a little khichri in the day time, they munch a little parched pulse or other grain, which they say suffices for their lean stomachs Their houses are built of mud with thatched roofs. Furniture there is little or none, except some earthenware pots to hold water and for cooking Their bedclothes are scanty, merely a sheet or perhaps two this is sufficient in the hot weather, but the bitter cold nights are miserable indeed, and they try to keep warm over little cowdung fires the smoke from these fires all over the city is so great that the eyes run, and the throat seems to be choked. In the capital shifted from Agra to Delhi, but the story of exploitation remained the same. Bernier writes that grandees pay for a work of art considerably under its value, and according to their own caprice. When an Omrah or Mansabdar requires the services of an artisan, he sends to the bazar for him, employing force, if necessary, to make the poor man work; and after the task is finished, the unfeeling lord pays, not according to the value-of the labour, but agreeably to his own standard of fair remuneration; the artisan having reason to congratulate himself if the Korrah has not been given in part payment.

The artisans and craftsmen in the permanent service of the monarch and the principal Omarahs were a little better off than the casual wage earners. They tended to preserve the arts for they were paid more and regularly. Akbar sanctioned the following daily wages for workers and artisans- dams (copper coins, / of Rupia) for ordinary labourers, to dams for superior labourers, to dams for carpenters and to dams for builders. According to Moreland carpenters and builders got, in Akbars days, equivalent to about one rupee per day on the average, and they were rather better off than the modern workmen of the United Provinces, if not Punjab in the early years of the twentieth century. But there are many buts. It is not certain if the workmen got full sanctioned rates. Then for the slightest mistake they were heavily fined. If a horse lost condition, the fines came down to the water carriers and sweepers employed in the stable. When an elephant died through neglect, the attendants (some of whom drew less than three rupees a month) had to pay the price of the animal. During the process of investigation and imposition of punishment some money had to be paid to middlemen and Mughal officers. Naturally, such artisans and workers can never become rich, and he feels it no trifling matter if he have the means of satisfying the cravings of hunger and of covering his body with the coarsest raiment.

Peons or servants are exceedingly numerous in this country, writes Pelsaert, for every one-be he mounted soldier, merchant or kings official-keeps as many as his position and circumstances permit. Outside the house, they serve for display, running continually before their masters horse; inside, they do the work of the house, each knowing his duty, like the bailwan, the farrash, the masalchi, the mahawat etc. Edward Terry, Pelsaert and many others note that men stood in the market places to be hired and many of them were paid very low wages or even paid in kind, for most of the great lords reckon days to the month, and pay from to rupees for that period: while wages are often left several months in arrears, and then paid in worn-out clothes or other things. Such fleecing was naturally responded to by cunning and very few of them serve their master honestly; they steal whatever they can; if they buy only a pice-worth of food, they will take their share or dasturi (commission).

Transporters and coolies were no better off. On land, elephants, camels, horse, bullocks and donkeys were the main means of conveyance of kings, nobles, landlords and big merchants. Agricultural products were transported from fields to the markets in the cities in bullock carts. Grain was also carried and sold by roving merchants (banjaras) on mules in places which were not easily accessible. Big merchants with their merchandise generally moved only in large convoys using chariots, horses, bullock carts, mules, camels, and even buffaloes, depending on the terrain. The government officials with treasures also travelled in convoys and under proper escorts.

Transport between rural and urban areas, between cities and within the city was provided by coolies, horses, bullock carts and dola or doli. In the days of Firoz Tughlaq, hire for a bullock cart was to jitals, and jitals for a horse. A dola which was carried by kahars cost half a tankah. The dola or palanquin was the common conveyance of ladies of high rank. But this sophisticated means of transport was also being brought into more and more use by the old and infirm and the ease loving elite. When Qutbuddin Mubarak Khalji felt miserable without the company of his favourite Khusrau Khan, he sent orders to the latter to return from the Deccan as quickly as possible (about C.E.), and Khusrau Khan was taken in a palanquin post haste from Devagiri to Delhi. And Sikandar Lodis boast, if I order one of my slaves to be seated in a palanquin, the entire body of nobility would carry him on their shoulders at my bidding, clearly indicates that besides ladies, the use of palanquin had also become a fashion with men of means. In the fifteenth century Ekka and Tonga had also come into vogue, but for long journeys the horse was the common conveyance. A footmans services could be requisitioned for tankahs a month, and a man could travel from Delhi to Agra spending only one Bahloli, which sufficed for him, his horse and his small escort / retinue during the journey. A large number of people were engaged on this work, and they plied a brisk trade. In the Mughal times comparatively better roads added some sort of sophistication to land travel.

Those employed by the Government on the work of transport and communication were not ill paid. Ibn Battutas description of the same pertains to governments communication system which facilitated smooth running of administration. According to Barani and Ibn Battua there were two types of news-carriers: the mounted runners (Aulaq) and the foot runners (Dhava). The administration of the Sultanate, Sur and Mughal governments was greatly facilitated by an efficient postal service which connected different parts of the empire. According to Pelsaert, postmen carrying their masters letters could cover to Kos a day, but that was also because they ate opium regularly.

To sum up, Professor Mohammad Habib in his review of G.N. Sharmas Social Life in Medieval Rajasthan has this to say about artisans and workers and their wages in northern India of the Mughal times: The industries of Rajasthan were well-developed, (but) further progress was made impossible owing to the low social position assigned to the worker, forced labour or begar and administrative oppression of all types. The cultivator had to be satisfied with a meagre reward for the hard work of himself and his family. The inventories of thefts committed show that a well-to-do peasant had two dhotis and two turbans for himself, four saris costing about Rs. - for his wife and some ten utensils costing Rs.. The wages recorded tell the same sad tale. The account papers (- A.D.) of the construction of the palaces of Jaipur and Kotah show that skilled labourers got annas to and a supervising architect Rs. / per day. The wages of un-skilled labourers as mentioned in the Kotah records of A.D. vary from one anna to two annas. Payment was sometimes made in grain- Chataks daily for skilled workers and to Chataks for women workers. The Bikaner Bahis throw some light on wages-a chaukidar Rs. per month, grooms, sweepers and gardeners Rs. to Rs. per month. From the point of view of wages the prospects of government officials were not very encouraging. The pay of officers of position, according to the Bikaner Bahi (V.S.) varied from Rs. to Rs. per month. An accountants pay according to the Kotah records was Rs. per year. An ordinary clerk could be engaged for Rs. per year, while a senior clerks pay was about Rs. a year. A Kotwal was generally paid Rs. to a month. Such low wages would only be possible with the low price of grain. According to Dr. Sharma maunds of wheat could be purchased for Rs. to ; the same quantity of millet for Rs. to and of barley for Rs. to.

The low scale of both grain prices and wages proves only one thing-the thorough exploitation of the peasants and the workers. But this was an Indian-and not a Rajasthani-misfortune. Tavernier, for example, could on his journey from

Surat to Agra get guards at Rs. per month each. aThe states and the governing classes tried to appropriate the whole surplus value of labour. Still the condition of the workers and peasants was probably better in Rajasthan than in, the Mughal empire. The situation in the Mughal empire is summed up by W.H. Moreland like this: In several instances the lowest grades of servants were entitled to less than two rupees monthly (dams for a sweeper, for a camel-driver, for a wrestler, and so on), while the bulk of the menials and of the ordinary foot-soldiers began at less than three rupees. The minimum for subsistence at the court is probably marked by the lowest grade of slaves, who were allowed one dam daily, equivalent to three-quarters of a rupee monthly in the currency of the time artisans were, as a rule badly off, and they can scarcely have been able to pay high wages to their journeymen The facts available regarding the wages paid by travellers and merchants come almost entirely from the south and west of India. Terry insists on the excellence of the servants obtained for five shillings, or say two rupees a month, and he adds that they would send half this sum home; probably this statement relates to servants hired in Surat, but in any case it refers to this part of the country, as Terry went no farther north than Mandu. Valle, writing of Surat about ten years later put the rate at not more than three rupees, while De Laets informants gave him from three to four rupees, which could be supplemented in some cases by commission charged on purchases. A messenger between Surat and Masulipatam was in allowed seven or eight mahmudies (say something between three and four rupees) for the journey These instances appear to justify the conclusion that early in the seventeenth century foreigners could secure capable servants for somewhere about three rupees a month. What this represents in real wages is uncertain (But) The rates struck Europeans as extraordinarily low, and taken with those which prevailed in the northern capital they enable us to understand the great development of domestic employment which characterised the life of India at this period. The important point to note is that servants, messengers and escorts were in great demand. Any journey seems to have been inconceivable without a certain number of them. William Hawkins, who was in India in Jahangirs reign, found that almost a man cannot stir out of doors throughout all his dominions without great forces, for they are all become rebels. Tavemier said that, in about, to travel with honour in India, one hired to armed men, some with bows and arrows and others with muskets. They cost Rs. a month. The profession must have been well organised and yet the wages were miserably low.

The economic position of artisans was no better. Bernier writing to Colbert, said: No artisan can be expected to give his mind to his calling in the midst of a people who are either wretchedly poor, or who, if rich, assume an appearance of poverty, and who regard not the beauty and excellence but the cheapness of an article; a people whose grandeess pay for a work of art considerably under its value and according to their own caprice For it should not be inferred that the workman is held in esteem, or arrives at a stage of independence. Nothing but sheer necessity or blows from a cudgel keeps him employed; he never can become rich, and he feels it no trifling matter if he have the means of satisfying the cravings of hunger and of covering his body with the coarsest garment. If money be gained it does not in any measure go into his pocket, but only serves to increase the wealth of the merchant. Berniers description is corroborated by what Thevenot was told about the same period of the state of the arts in Delhi.

The story of the exploitation of the poor, both rural and urban, is unending. And the guiding principle of this pernicious practice was to leave the people with bare subsistence. No foreign traveller fails to notice it with disapproval if not actual disgust. It would appear that the lords and the upper classes in Turco-Mughal India derived a cynical pleasure in oppressing the poor.

The result was as expected. Artisans, workers and labourers became lazy. Scarcely any one made an effort to climb the ladder to better prospects, so that for a job which one man would do in Holland, here passes through four mens hands before it is finished. Such exploitation in the Mughal period provided droves of khidmatgars to British officers and men when they established and ran their Raj in this country.

POOREST OF THE POOR

Before closing, a word may be said about the exploitation of the poorest of the poor, the beggars and the handicapped. Muslim law decrees mutilation as punishment for certain crimes and a large number of healthy people were blinded, mutilated and made physically handicapped under Muslim rule. The punishments of sultans like Balban and Muhammad bin Tughlaq were terribly severe. Alauddin Khalji had ordered that if any shopkeeper sold any article short-weight, a quantity of flesh equal to the deficiency in weight was to be cut off from his haunches. Firoz Tughlaq lists some of the punishments for common offences, which were prevalent before his time. These comprised of cutting of hands and feet, noses and ears, putting out eyes, pulverizing the bones with mallets, burning parts of the body, nailing the hands and feet, hamstringing etc., etc. As seen earlier, many cultivators and labourers were also reduced to the position of beggars from the Sultanate through Mughal times because of high rate and severity of collection of Kharaj.

All such unfortunate people could only resort to begging for a living. They were sometimes given doles and meals by kind-hearted people: free feeding (langar) was common for the poor beggars. But sometimes even such helpless people were exploited by the rich who extracted their pound of flesh even from them. An Amir by the name of Saiyyad-ul-Hijab was very close to Sultan Firoz Shah Tughlaq. He used to help all and sundry, but for a consideration. It is narrated, says Shams Siraj Afif, that one day a helpless faqir (beggar) approached him for assisting him get some help from the Sultan. The nobleman gave him necessary guidance for achieving his purpose. The faqir did as advised, and the Sultan ordered that the suppliant be given one tankah per day from the Zakat fund. But the help rendered was not gratuitous. The said Amir, continues Afif, after rendering help to the needy used to extract something by way of shukrana. No further comment is necessary.

Index

Bibliography

Amery, Reeves : *The Anatomy of Peace,* Oxford, New York, 2001.

Arnold, Sir Thomas : *The Caliphate,* MacMillan, London, 1965.

Dawud, Rahbar : *God of Justice*, Mac & Jac Pub., Leiden, 1960.

Gins Berg, M. : *Evolution and Progress,* William Heinemann Ltd., London, 1982.

Haq, M. Anwarul : *The Faith Movement of Mawlana Muhammad Ilyas,* Country Pub., London, 1972.

Husaini, Waqar : *Islamic Thought,* Goodword Books Pvt. Ltd., New Delhi, 1999.

Imamuddin, S. M. : *Arab Muslim Administration,* Kitab Bhavan, New Delhi, 1984.

Kalerji : *From War to Peace,* Oxford, New York, 1991.

Landau, R. : *The Philosophy of the Ibn Arabi,* Century Pub., London, 1959.

Muir, William : *Early Caliphate,* Oxford, New York, 1970.

Narayan : *Pan Islamism,* MacMillan, New York, 1953.

Qureshi, A. Iqbal : *Islam and the Theory of Interest,* Kitab Bhavan, New Delhi, 1994.

Stanton : *Teaching of the Quran,* Discovery Publishing House, New Delhi, 1989.

Titus, M. : *Indian Islam,* Milford, New Delhi, 1979.

Watt, W.M. : *Islamic Surveys,* Edinburgh University Press, Edinburgh, 1999.

Wolfson, H.A. : *The Philosophy of the Kalam*, Oxford, London, 1976.

Zahid, Malik : *Subjects of Quran,* Kitab Bhavan, New Delhi, 1998.

□□□